C000175096

HOLLYWOOD HEAT

HOLLYWOOD HEAT

UNTOLD STORIES OF 1950S HOLLYWOOD

STEVE ROWLAND

Book Guild Publishing
Sussex, England

This book is dedicated in loving memory of Ruth and Roy, without whose undying belief and constant encouragement none of this would have been possible.

These pages contain memoirs of my years spent in Hollywood from 1954 to 1963, reflecting the language and style of that time.

First published in Great Britain in 2008 by
THE BOOK GUILD LTD
Pavilion View
19 New Road
Brighton, BN1 1UF

Design by Simon Goggin

Printed and bound in Thailand under the supervision of MRM Graphics Ltd, Winslow, Bucks

A catalogue record for this book is available from The British Library.

ISBN 978 1 84624 127 7

Contents

Foreword

By Richard Niles

Around the middle of the twentieth century a profound change occurred in America that affected world culture. In a way, people finally let go of the Victorian values of the 1800s. Though this started as early as the 1920s with the excesses of the 'jazz age', it wasn't until after World War II that the general public began to change their basic beliefs. Though we usually think of the 1960s (flower power, sex, drugs and rock'n'roll) when we chronicle this revolution of spirit, it could not have happened without the transitional period of the 1950s that are far more rarely remembered. In both cases, the venue was the scene of the Gold Rush, the end of the rainbow, the fertile soil of California.

Ever since Cecil B. DeMille and Jesse Lasky accidentally made Hollywood the centre of the film industry in 1913, public imagination all over the world had been inspired by the home of the movies. The laid-back lotus eaters who lived in this quiet town lazing in the perpetual sunshine of Southern California influenced fashions and morals from Houston to Hong Kong. During World War II governments had seen the effectiveness of using Hollywood for propaganda. The 'mean streets' of Los Angeles were made famous in books, by Raymond Chandler and Nathaniel West. The music industry began to move from New York to LA. By the 1950s Hollywood could be said to have become the pop culture capital of the world.

Today, when the 1950s are discussed or depicted in drama, 'grease is the word' as the period is stylized into a cartoon pastiche of slicked back pompadour hairdos, electric pink skirts with puffy petticoats, cut-down customized cars, doo-wop groups in sharkskin suits, dreamy girls in pointy bras, Doris Day and pre-gay Rock Hudson, Wally and Beaver, Ozzie and Harriet, and Eisenhower and McCarthy. In fact, important developments were taking place that would alter our collective consciousness forever.

Although already marginally exposed to 'black' music through jazz, white American popular music was now being cross-pollinated with black rhythm and blues styles. Much of this integration was effected by white entrepreneurs like Jerry Leiber and Mike Stoller, Hollywood producers and writers of hits for both black acts like the Coasters and white acts like Elvis Presley. When the 1950s began, segregation was the norm. By 1960 the voices of dissent were loud and clear.

In film, a new voice was being heard, influenced by the European 'art house' and the Stanislavski Method that still influences actors today. Even mainstream films began to be seen as more than just spectacle or entertainment. Real life situations began to be depicted: prejudice, rape, prostitution, drug addiction and inter-racial sex.

We are rarely given a chance to get inside the skin of someone who actually was at the epicentre of the 1950s cultural earthquake, to hear what they were thinking at the time, to see and consider events as they did. Steve Rowland gives us that opportunity, and for anyone interested in how our past informs our future, browsing through these pages will be a fascinating ride.

Growing up in luxurious Beverly Hills, the years 1950 to 1960 marked a young man's coming of age, from 11 to 21. His father, Roy Rowland, had been one of Hollywood's most respected directors since the late 1930s. His mother Ruth was a writer and Louis B. Mayer was her uncle. This put the teenage Steve in a kind of maelstrom of magnificence, where stars witnessed at close hand quickly lost their shine. Wanting to be part of the world his parents created for him, he became an actor, a columnist and a singer. He cruised the Sunset Strip like Candide in leather jacket and jeans (as worn by James Dean) in search of some elusive, unholy Hollywood grail that contained fame, fortune and fun. Like the rest of the world, Steve looked to Hollywood for his values. And despite repeated betrayals, like the rest of us, he held on to the dream even when it became a nightmare.

Despite a career that never quite mirrored his Hollywood dreams, Steve was forever surrounded by hot and cold running women. Was this because he was the son of a famous showbiz family? Possibly. Was it because he had the kind of photogenic face that made him ideal fodder for the fan magazines? As we look at the mass of photographic evidence in this book, that is undeniable. But perhaps the main reason was the self-deprecating charm that Steve shows on every page. Always ready for fun at any hour of the day or night, always a perfect gentleman even when he was acting like the devil, what self-respecting starlet could resist this guy?

His star-studded lifestyle inspired his five monthly columns in various fan magazines, 'The View from Rowland's Head' being the most famous. Excerpts from these columns appear in these pages exactly as they were originally printed. In addition, his monthly record reviews tied in with his weekly radio broadcast on Hollywood station KGIL that included music, reviews and live interviews.

The thing that strikes us as we read the excerpts from 'The View from Rowland's Head' is the overpowering innocence of the times. Hard to believe in our era of total ethical bankruptcy, that here was a time when people called each other Miss and Mister until they knew each other well; a time when only prostitutes slept with a man on the first date; a time when you could go to a club and not come out with your ears ringing; when smoking was considered harmless; when drug use was extremely rare, even among actors and musicians; when 'parking and petting' was the big dating objective and parents expected their daughters to be virgins when they married.

Steve's fan magazine columns similarly speak in the innocent street vernacular of the time. In a style which is a cool cocktail of beatnik slang with Sunset Strip hip, Steve puts you right there — in the car with Elvis — nervously negotiating a date with a starlet — sincerely digging the music at the most happening clubs in town.

We also get to hang out with Steve's pals like Jimmy Dean, Bob Wagner and Tony Curtis, and go on dates with babes Natalie Wood, Kathleen Case and Carmen Phillips. We feel with him the terrible pressure to be considered 'hip', to be accepted as part of 'the scene'. And despite the necessity to be 'cool' at all times, Steve bravely and honestly exposes all his insecurities.

He was muscularly good-looking, intelligent with a great sense of humour, talented and the son of an important director. This gave him entrée to a dazzling social life. The fact that he qualified for the Olympics as a springboard diver confirms his prowess as an athlete. But he also had some handicaps that made him feel slightly out of the 'in crowd': he was 'vertically challenged' at five foot eight, at a time when leading men and 'hunks' had to be over six feet tall (like sheep-in-hunk's-clothing Rock Hudson). Having a famous father had negative effects, as some said he only got parts because of nepotism (which Hollywood could be said to have invented). Though known for his abilities as a singer, actor and writer, he lacked the success of a big hit record or a leading part in a successful movie. Talent in New York is appreciated as an end in itself, but in LA you're only as good as your last success (and the car you drive). And if you don't have the big hits, you experience the 'Hollywood Shuffle'. This term originally referred to the 'dance' showbiz people do to avoid talking to you as you approach them on the street (if you don't have the hits).

Despite this, Steve Rowland survived the ups and downs of an amazing career. In 1950s Hollywood, he went on to act in 35 TV shows like *Bonanza, Wanted Dead or Alive* and a two-year role in *The Legend of Wyatt Earp*. His film appearances include co-starring roles in *The Battle of the Bulge* with Henry Fonda, *Gun Glory* with Stewart Granger, *Crime in the Streets* with John Cassavetes and Sal Mineo, and the original *Thin Red Line* with Kier Dullea and Jack Warden. This book will give you intriguing private glimpses of all of them.

Steve will take you racing cars with James Dean, riding dirt bikes with Steve McQueen, chasing girls with Elvis Presley and getting drunk with Robert Mitchum. You'll see photos of a few of the sultry starlets who appeared at LA's hotspots and film premieres hanging on Steve's arm. Other friends included the cream of 1950s Hollywood elite including Debbie Reynolds, Jane Powell, Edd 'Kookie' Burns, Tony Curtis and his wife Janet Leigh.

During the making of five films in Spain, Steve enjoyed Spanish chart success with the popular recording group, Los Flaps. The lure of the exciting British music scene brought him to London where he produced thirteen top five hits for Dave Dee Dozy Beaky Mick & Titch. Among those worldwide hits were 'Hold Tight', 'Zabadak', 'Bend It' and 'The Legend of Xanadu' (a million selling British number one).

He also discovered Peter Frampton and the Herd, and with 'Way of Life' had a number two British hit with his own group the Family Dogg (named after his obsessive love of animals). He produced hits for other 1960s icons including P.J. Proby and the Pretty Things. In the 1970s he won a gold album and ASCAP award for producing Jerry Lee Lewis (the London Sessions). When I met him in 1976, he was creative manager/A&R for Hansa/Ariola, where he discovered and signed The Cure and The Thompson Twins, and handled Boney M and Japan.

As his musical arranger, I had a lot of fun making records with Steve for the disco scene, including the million selling 'I Lost My Heart To a Starship Trooper' with Sarah Brightman and Hot Gossip. We became friends because we were both from Hollywood, with parents in the film industry — my stepfather Jesse Lasky Jr knew Roy and Ruth in 'the old days'. Steve's production style has always been to make records as if he was making a Hollywood movie — action packed. Never a dull moment on the record or in the studio, which was always filled with opportunistic, underdressed, oversexed girls and barking dogs. (Actually, it was Steve who was barking.)

In 1985 he produced *The Lost Opera* with Kimera and the L.S.O which remained in the top five of the French charts for 20 weeks selling 1.5 million albums. In 1986 he discovered, demoed and developed Mel & Kim, and signed them to Supreme Records.

Steve ran his own dance label Dr Beat and wrote, produced and collated music for the TWI TV series *Hi Five,* broadcast in 38 countries. At the end of 1993 Steve became a director of Pavilion Studios, forming a production company working with a number of young DJs, producers, artistes and programmers. During this time he auditioned and tried to sign the then-unknown Spice Girl, Geri Halliwell.

Now you've been introduced, sit back and enjoy the 1950s with my crazy friend Steve, who is still racing, dating, laughing and barking after all these years.

Richard Niles is a composer, producer, arranger, journalist and BBC broadcaster living in London.

How It All Began

Growing up in Hollywood certainly had its rewards. I had opportunities coming out of my ass. However, for what I was to encounter along the way, I sure as hell wasn't always prepared.

It was a bruised and swollen September sky that hid the sun and strangled the Saturday afternoon with unbearable humidity. A low and menacing rumble of thunder like a theatrical fanfare gave the announcement of my three o'clock entrance into the world. Believe me, I came out fighting. If one believes in reincarnation, then this time around I was definitely gonna jump into the action and score some heavy points.

The weather on that steamy afternoon should have thrown down all the clues needed for anyone who had psychic power. Trouble was a comin' disguised in smiling green eyes and a curly clump of wavy light brown hair. At the time however, no one made a song and dance out of it. To the passing parade it was just another ordinary Hollywood afternoon.

Some people said that I wasn't born at all, but that a passing crow shitted me on a stump and the sun hatched me. However, that's a matter of opinion and not open for discussion.

To make it through this life, you've got to have a certain amount of luck riding on your shoulders. I've always said that you make your own luck. I remember reading somewhere that luck is really opportunity meeting preparation. That's reality and you can take it to the bank.

Here's an important rule for Hollywood survival. Luck can be a funny thing. Many times it'll kick you up the backside. When it does you'd better possess a good sense of humour and check that you're covered with a thick veneer of rhinoceros skin. That'll protect you from the bullets of rejection.

I was born into a famous motion picture family. My destiny was mapped out before my ass hit the grass. Believe me, everyone in Hollywood has a lawn mower. When I picked myself up, brushed myself off, and looked around, I discovered that Mom and Dad were struggling with a short supply of money and were desperately trying to keep their heads above water. That's never an enviable situation. My mother wasn't used to it. My father had seen it all before as a kid facing the world on the mean streets of Hell's Kitchen, New York.

My dad spent his impressionable early youth growing up amongst rows of teeming tenements that blocked the sun and helped create a crime-infested neighbourhood war zone. Hell's Kitchen in the early 1900s was a junkyard community of despair, where everyone lived on the poverty line and did what they could to survive. Those early years shaped and toughened my father's character.

Through many painful years of struggle in a low life existence and realizing that they were trapped in futility, my father's family began plotting their great escape. Finally the day arrived. Pulling up stakes, they headed west toward unknown territory — the alluring pastures of Southern California. After shuffling about, searching for solace, they finally established their homestead in Edendale, a small Los Angeles suburb, known today as Glendale. It was here that my father lived his teenage life, along with his brother Roger, and his two sisters, Alice and Cydell. By the time my father saw in his sixteenth year he had already formed a game plan.

My mother's maiden name was Ruth Cummings. The seed from which she spiralled was planted in St. Johns, New Brunswick, a small town situated in the Maritime Provinces on Canada's East Coast. The weather there has a lot to answer for. Luck, however, was about to enter my mother's life when she, along with her mother Ida, her two brothers, Jack and Leonard and her younger sister Mitzi, packed up and moved to Southern California.

Jack Cummings, my mother's big brother, would soon become a top gun Hollywood film producer. He had an attitude to accompany his self-importance. Ida Mayer Cummings, my grandmother, was the sister of Louis B. Mayer. Everybody and his dog must have heard of him.

Right: Roy Rowland, film director. A man to be respected.

L.B. Mayer started his worldwide empire selling slot machines.

His fascination for the entertainment business, eventually led him to making silent movies then feature films. When he moved his operation west, Hollywood was a natural setting, as it was a small, sleepy town, surrounded by orange groves.

The Southern California temperature suited L.B. completely, but the business atmosphere was an entirely different matter. He was shocked by the easy going attitudes of all the men and women working in the film industry. He found it impossible to understand their indifference to making money. Louis B. Mayer would change all that.

In the making of his first Hollywood film *In Old Kentucky*, starring Anita Stewart and Rudy Cameron, Mickey Neilan the director would disappear for days, thus holding up the expensive process of film-making. He was wasting a ton of money, which cost the company a small fortune. This drove L.B. absolutely nut city. He immediately put the straightener on that, and applied new rules. His savage backlash as he cleared out the dead wood put fear in the hearts of every Jack and Jill in the film business.

Making movies gave Uncle L.B. the chance to proclaim the name of Louis B. Mayer to the world. His personal fame enabled him to act as a godly figure to men, and a father figure to women, handing out favours as and when it suited him — like your ordinary, everyday benevolent despot.

As L.B. Mayer made his 'mark' on Hollywood, he was being marked himself. His enemies far outnumbered his friends and they would continue to multiply.

Mayer was into movie making like shit off a shovel. He rented a house on fashionable Franklin Avenue, which crosses Highland Avenue in the heart of Hollywood. From there he began his ruthless march toward building his empire. By the time my parents accidentally collided on the sands of Santa Monica beach, Louis B. Mayer's dynasty had become world famous. It was to be known as Metro-Goldwyn-Mayer Studios.

Accidents usually happen when one person isn't looking, and the other isn't particularly paying attention. Roy Rowland wasn't looking or paying attention. Ruth Cummings was doing both. It was love at first sight — from Ruth's point of view, that is.

It was a picture-card-perfect midsummer's day. The sun, along with a cloudless blue sky, smiled down on Santa Monica beach, wrapping the area in a contented embrace. It was Sunday afternoon. A young girl in a red bathing suit had been checking out the two cool looking dudes that were sitting together close to the water, about twenty five yards away. The guys weren't concerned with girly action. They were shooting the breeze and collecting the sun's rays, oblivious to the surrounding activity. One of the guys, a dark haired Adonis, stood out with dazzling magnetism. Every girl within fifty yards only had eyes for him. He, however, appeared to be unaware of the commotion that his presence was causing amongst the female social gathering.

Ruth Cummings was one of the young girls, concussed by the power of the man's handsome features. Lying on a striped beach towel, a straw hat protecting her fragile skin from the baking sun, she was getting her mojo working.

Ruth's twenty-two-year-old eyes locked focus — hypnotized with a flood of hero worship. 'Who's that?' she said, nodding her head and indicating the Valentino look-alike.

'Who are you talking about?' came the startled reply as Mitzi, Ruth's younger sister, quickly turned over on to her tummy to get a better look.

'Mitzi, who is that? He's gorgeous,' Ruth squealed in choked excitement to her pretty, younger sister.

'Oh that's Roy — Roy Rowland. He knows a friend of mine. I've seen them together a few times,' came Mitzi's blasé reply.

'God he's so good-looking,' Ruth whispered, desperately trying to align her thoughts. 'You've got to introduce me to him,' she pleaded. 'Come on, please. You've got to.'

'Listen,' snapped Mitzi, 'every girl on the beach wants to know him and he couldn't care less. He has girls coming up to him all the time. Forget it. You've got no chance.'

'Oh yeah,' said Ruth. 'I want to tell you something. I'm going to marry him. Put that in your milk and drink it.'

'Oh really! Is that so!' said Mitzi, laughing out loud and a bit shocked at Ruth's positive statement. 'That'll be the day.'

'Oh yeah,' said Ruth. 'Watch me!'

Those were the last words that Mitzi heard, as Ruth jumped up, flipping sand over her bemused sister. With heat clouding her eyes and her body in motion, she was off, striding in the direction of Roy Rowland.

Ruth's slender legs casually drifted to a stop, just past where the two young guys were sitting engrossed in conversation. Ruth carefully put her plan into action. Just as she was passing the target area she allowed the sunglasses that had been perched precariously on the brim of her sun hat, to fall at the feet of her intended prey. Her mojo began to work.

Roy and his friend were riding on a full vocal current when Ruth's words broke the flow. 'Hi' she said, as she bent down seductively to retrieve her glasses from the sand. 'I haven't seen you two down here before. Do you come around here often?' She almost choked with the obviousness of her line. She stared straight into the ocean blue-steel of Roy's eyes as she flirtatiously baited her hook. A momentary wave of dizziness clouded her vision. The thunder in her heart was deafening. Roy sat speechless staring at Ruth's angelic face. He'd been caught unprepared by her alluring smile. All escape routes were locked down. Passing traffic was diverted. The sign read: woman at work!

Ruth Cummings was a positive thinker and a go-getter. 'Be an inner winner,' she would always say. 'Don't think about defeat. Only picture success.' The woman took no prisoners. Roy was definitely trapped and tied up with a rope of positive thinking. Ruth's magic mojo had done the job. Roy Rowland was spellbound.

My grandmother however, didn't share the same enthusiasm about her daughter's new love interest. She had other ideas for Ruth. Roy Rowland wasn't included. 'From all the eligible guys in Hollywood, you have to pick a struggling assistant prop man from Universal Studios. What's L.B. gonna think?' said Ida.

'I don't give a good goddamn what he thinks.' Ruth was never short on independence or voicing her thoughts, and she sure as hell didn't care what L.B. thought. 'I'm going to marry Roy Rowland,' she said with determination.

'Well, he is a charming fellow and extremely good looking, I must admit. I can see why you feel the way you do, but he hasn't got a future.' Genuine concern shaded Ida's Mayer's expression. To her, Roy Rowland did not appear to posses that killer instinct that one needs for success in the tangles of the Hollywood jungle.

'Roy has got a future, and I believe in him. I love him and no one's going to change my mind.' Ruth angrily slammed her mother's front door. The thundering vibration echoed her defiant exit.

Three months later, Ruth Cummings and Roy Rowland eloped and married in secret. Even L.B. Mayer, with all his power and influence over the minions of Hollywood, couldn't stop them. His anger at their clandestine elopement rumbled throughout

Hollywood for months. He was not going to forget it.

It wasn't long however, before Ida and all the immediate family subjects had fallen under the irresistible spell of the Roy Rowland charm offensive. Ida had grown so fond of him that she insisted he and Ruth have a 'proper' wedding. To her way of thinking, that would make everything 'legit' in the eyes of the Hollywood community, not forgetting L.B. of course.

After their second marriage-go-round, my parents bought a small house on the now famous Rodeo Drive in Beverly Hills. The street number was 526 North, one block above the Santa Monica Boulevard streetcar tracks. At that time Rodeo Drive was divided down the middle by a dusty bridle path, which snaked along Sunset Boulevard nosing down tree-lined Rodeo Drive, reigning to a sudden stop at Park Way. The lure of shopping lay 200 yards further on across Santa Monica Boulevard. Many a horse and rider raced for glory along that bridle path in the frivolous 1920s. Later bicycles took the centre stage, as beautiful girls in tight sweaters with ambitious eyes pedalled seductively along the same route, always on the alert for any opportunity they might encounter. Today, all that remains is a narrow grass-filled street divider and volumes of romantic memories.

During those early years, the family residences were divided in two — those who had and those who had not. Jack Cummings and L.B. Mayer were high scorers and lived in mansions above Sunset Boulevard. Ruth and Roy Rowland were out there battling the elements.

My father started working at Universal Studios in his late teens, labouring long, hard, unsociable hours. His dream always was to become a motion picture film director. Determined to obtain success and to fully understand the difficulties of the film industry, he served his apprenticeship and paid his dues working as a prop man, gaffer, assistant cameraman, lighting man and second assistant director. The day that he became a first assistant director was seen as a major step toward realizing his dream.

Because of Roy's good looks and immense charm, his well-

Left: Trapped in a family portrait at 12 years old.

meaning friends tried to persuade him to become an actor. They saw him as the perfect leading man. Flattered though my father was by their encouragement, he was initially shy and therefore wanted no part of gaining focus in the celebrity spotlight. Unlike me, always in everyone's face, my father preferred working behind the camera, thus avoiding the sour taste of phoney adulation.

After several years of hard graft an opportunity landed at my father's feet. Jack Cummings, now an important producer at MGM Studios, decided to introduce my father to an executive friend. That introduction at the time seemed innocent. However, it put Roy on the pathway to realization.

Roy's respectful manner always got him through the door. This time was no exception. He was rewarded with a job offer, helping to run MGM Studios' prop department. Though it may have seemed as if he was starting all over, his working at MGM was a great coup and it wasn't long before he was clawing his way up the ladder with the exciting prospect of directing a feature film.

Then opportunity met preparation. Roy was given the chance to become an assistant director on one of the famous Tarzan films, starring Johnny Weissmuller. He was more than prepared. He grabbed the opportunity, and turned it into success. Lady Luck was waiting just around the corner. The Tarzan film had only been finished a short while when Roy met and became fast friends with Robert Benchley. The two of them really hit it off and became practically inseparable.

Because of their friendship and Roy's professional attitude, he was given a shot at directing one of MGM's famous Robert Benchley short films. The result was a huge financial success. Robert insisted that Roy continue directing the entire series of Benchley shorts and made sure that the word was loudly shouted in the studio's ear.

Short features always played with the main film on release. As a 'two reeler', they usually ran a maximum of twenty minutes. They were shown, along with a current news reel as a warm-up

Left: The Rowland family homestead on Rodeo Drive.

for the full-length feature that followed.

The series won the hearts of an enthusiastic public. The overall appreciation of these superb comedies, along with the harmonious relationship between Roy Rowland and Robert Benchley, created a successful and award-winning package.

Roy Rowland was now the hot new kid on the block and loving it. He and Bob Benchley really put meaning to the word 'party'. They became infamous on the Hollywood turf. The stories of their activities became legendary. They're remembered today with reverence.

Roy Rowland's talent was beginning to be recognized. His chance to direct a feature film surely wasn't far off. Roy's success however, didn't really cut the ice with L.B. Mayer. There's no proof, but the popular theory always lingered that L.B. still carried resentment over Roy and Ruth.

Their Houdini escape to the altar without ever discussing or asking for the L.B. Mayer stamp of approval, was considered an insult. L.B. was the type of guy that wanted everybody under his thumb. When he was ignored there'd be trouble. To him it was personal.

There were many young directors working in the shorts

Above: Dressed to thrill. Ruth and Roy Rowland, with Steve and Kathy Case, attend a gala event.

department at MGM. All were hustling for the chance to direct a feature film. L.B. was the decider. It was he alone who doled out the opportunities.

My father had been working in the shorts department longer than most, constantly hoping for the chance to direct a feature film. Everybody but Roy Rowland appeared to be getting into the frame. The reason seemed obvious. L.B. was gonna dangle the opportunity in front of Roy's face but make him wait for the connection.

My mother poured a constant stream of encouragement over my father. 'Keep thinking positive. You'll get your break. It'll come, just keep your eye on the ball. Don't worry about L.B.'

L.B. Mayer resented my mother's determination and loyalty towards my father, and her furious show of independence. In spite of this, my parents ignored the bullshit and never allowed themselves to become embroiled in the idle gossip, and acute jealousies that were forever poisoning family relationships.

Everything circled around Louis B. Mayer. All the members of his immediate family fought to please him, jockeying for social position with sycophantic enthusiasm.

My uncle, Jack Cummings, was one of those people. He constantly kept his tongue inserted in the nether regions of the Louis B. Mayer posterior. It wasn't a surprise when Jack got the opportunity to become a producer. From that moment on he never looked back and proved to be a talented operator. His tongue however, continued to remain brown.

Seven Brides for Seven Brothers, *Teahouse of the August Moon*, *Kiss Me Kate*, are just a few of his enormously successful films. The stars that he worked with were numerous — Elvis Presley, Marlon Brando, Howard Keel, Kathryn Grayson, Jane Powell, Debbie Reynolds, Esther Williams, etc. These names alone could create a Who's Who of legendary Hollywood film personalities.

In spite of Louis B Mayer's cynical tactics, my father's talent and determination broke free and was eventually recognized throughout the industry. Considered one of Hollywood's most sensitive directors and with a stream of successful motion pictures enchanting the public's taste, Roy Rowland was in orbit.

Our Vines Have Tender Grapes, *Hit the Deck*, *Meet Me in Las Vegas*, *Two Weeks with Love* and *The Seven Hills of Rome* are a few shining examples of his universally celebrated films.

Edward G. Robinson, Robert Taylor, Barbara Stanwyck, Mario Lanza, Janet Leigh, Frank Sinatra, James Cagney, Cyd Charisse, Mickey Rooney, Stewart Granger, Debbie Reynolds, Van Johnson, Victor Mature, Rhonda Fleming are a partial menu of star names that embraced his talent throughout his career. Always a professional and clothed with a strong suit of understanding, he had the ability to create impact on the screen. My father's name stands out amongst a glowing list of credits — Roy Rowland, Film Director. A man to be respected.

As well as being a talented scriptwriter at MGM Studios, my mother, Ruth Rowland, was also an accomplished journalist. She was on first name footing with most of Hollywood's top stars and was constantly being invited to the many big film-land parties and events. She was a favoured member of the Hollywood in-crowd. Ava Gardner, Van Johnson, Debbie Reynolds, Edward G. Robinson, Janet Leigh and Jane Powell are just a few of the names that constantly filled her social calendar. My mother was a woman in demand.

An Early Education

To my ears my voice had the deep sexual tones of Clark Gable. In truth, the pitch was high and nasal, making me sound like Porky Pig with a bad sinus condition. Armed with these attributes, I boldly stepped forth into new adventure.

It was July of my fourteenth summer when sexual frustration first made an entrance with all the Hollywood bells and whistles blazing. I had just graduated from the eighth grade at Hawthorne Grammar School, a pristine structure nestling quietly on Rexford Drive, a few blocks south of Sunset Boulevard in the very heart of Beverly Hills. The calm exterior belied its interior turmoil.

The building's turn of the century, mock Spanish architecture was in complete contrast to the spoiled, pampered Beverly Hills brats who screamed through the halls and filled the classrooms, from kindergarten to the eighth grade. I definitely was one of them and had always fitted right in. Now, with graduation over, I was at last free to move on to new territory.

Vacation time had arrived and with over inflated enthusiasm, I bounded into it with short hair, a summer tan, and pretty boy looks that read twelve years old not fourteen. I wouldn't hit fifteen until September 3rd. Overconfident and overflowing with exciting thoughts of entering high school in the autumn I was out to stake my claim — to put some notches on my gun. Girls had invaded my brain. They were all I could think about.

In my mind, I was a six foot two, super cool young dude. In reality, I was just nudging five foot five and looking barely old enough to buy ice cream and chocolate cigarettes.

To my ears my voice had the deep sexual tones of Clark Gable. In truth, the pitch was high and nasal, making me sound like Porky Pig with a bad sinus condition. Armed with these attributes, I boldly stepped forth into new adventure.

I always did my hanging out at the Beverly Hills Hotel swimming pool, coming on like a real life, comic book hero. I thought I was pretty hip, seeing as I had just won the junior diving championship of Beverly Hills. It made my day when all

the young girls would gather around the poolside to watch my heroics off the three-metre springboard. In reality I was actually an annoying show-off.

Like I said, I truly believed that I was a world-class diver. I loved the sport. Therefore I always made sure to make great use of my talent every time a new young female fell upon the scene.

My favourite trick for attracting attention would be to march proudly to the end of the diving board and bounce up and down as high as I could without losing my balance. This always generated a loud racket, causing everybody to cast looks in my direction — most of these were disapproving.

Billie-Jean White was an Osage Indian girl from Texarkana on the border of Texas and Arkansas. Her mother worked as a chambermaid at the exclusive Beverly Hills Hotel on Sunset Boulevard, the same hotel where I'd been causing juvenile disruption. When I first caught sight of fabulous Billie, she rattled my foundation with the shock of a California earthquake. I wasn't ready for someone like her, especially as I hadn't yet discovered the pleasures of original sin.

It was during one of those crowd-pleasing routines that my eyes first fell upon dazzling Billie-Jean who appeared to be watching me from the shallow end of the pool. My startled orbs locked on her as I became engulfed in her huge, sensual black-eyed smile that came beaming back at me. The impact almost stopped my breathing.

Billie-Jean was a drop-dead gorgeous, glowing package of pure sexual fire. She spun my brain like the wheel of fortune. I wasn't worried about landing on bankrupt 'cause I was going to launch my charm offensive and win her heart's desire as my star prize.

I threw a fourteen-year-old grin back in Billie's direction and immediately began bouncing higher on the diving board, creating even more of a racket. At the same time I tried my best to play the cool, confident hero. Suddenly, I lost my balance and fell flailing, into a frenzied, spastic descent toward the water. 'Splat'. I hit like a 100-pound pancake, flat out on the surface, showering everyone

Left: Fourteen years old and about to lose all innocence.

innocently relaxing in the sun around the pool. Slightly dazed and ducking the hostile looks and sardonic chuckles that were rocketing in my direction, I eased myself up out of the pool and hurried toward Billie's distant shape like a nerd on a mission.

The tops of my legs and stomach were bright red — and stinging from my impact on the water. Ignoring the pain, I frantically began searching for the glorious, dark haired girl. Where was she? She had disappeared.

With as much cool as I could muster, I raised myself to my full height and casually sauntered around the pool, searching in the direction of where I'd last seen her standing.

I could always suggest a meeting with my father, who by now was a very important film director at MGM Studios. That should grab her interest. She had to be a model or an actress or something. A few little words like, 'Hey baby, you're beautiful. I'd like to try to get you a screen test at MGM — you've got it all.' That line could work wonders.

The talent department at MGM Studios in Culver City was regularly auditioning for new faces to put under contract so it wouldn't actually be a lie. Girls always found the prospect of meeting my father at the studio and visiting the film set completely irresistible. From a very young age I realized that I held a trump card. It had always worked with my impressionable friends.

As I rounded the pool and hurriedly pushed my way through a small cluster of suntanned folk — there she was. Her white sundress barely grasped her shoulders, as it caressed her luscious body. Wow! She looked sensational with her honey brown skin, dark eyes and thick black hair cascading down almost to the centre of her back. My brain was concussed — I'd fallen in lust.

A baby hit man was suddenly born and about to strike for the very first time.

'Hi,' I croaked, dropping my voice as low as possible.

'Hello,' she answered shyly. 'Hey — you're a great diver.'

'Thanks,' I said, with a humble tone in my voice. I was already drowning in her huge black eyes. My brain was in neutral. My mouth was in overdrive.

'I'll dive some more for you if you like,' I said anxiously.

'OK' she answered, smiling. 'Do another like that last one. There are a couple of people over there who have just dried off.' She had a sense of humour that was killing. My motor was racing.

I spent the rest of the day showing off, trying like mad to impress her. My heart was on an adrenalin rush. I was dizzy with afternoon delight. At that moment I would have made a pact with the devil for the chance to fire those white bullets of joy from the pink pistol in my pocket.

I can honestly say that after that day I became one hell of a diver. I began trying new combinations that up until then, I had been too terrified even to think of attempting. In fact, Billie-Jean gets the full credit for my becoming a high school diving champion and later qualifying for the 1956 Olympic tryouts.

After that magical day, Billie-Jean and I started going out together. At first it was only a couple of Saturday nights at the movies with milk shake treats afterwards at Stan's Drive-Inn on Wilshire Boulevard. This was the in-crowd's favourite pleaser. Fast food, custom cars and solid action. Billie-Jean and I became regulars, always finding a spot amongst the circle of assembled hot rods and high dollar machinery, where high school jocks draped in Levis and letterman sweaters strutted their cheer-leader girl friends from car to car. Many had hostile eyes, seeing us as unworthy interlopers in what they considered their hallowed terrain. However, togetherness with Billie-Jean gave me sanctuary.

Above: The view from the Palisades. The Pacific Coast Highway stretches out below.

We hit the ground running into a continual round of breathless days and evenings. The pool of my inexperience was overflowing. I was in love. My every thought was of capturing gorgeous, sensual Billie. Fantasies consumed me. The more I tried to play it cool, the more my body sizzled. I was a prisoner of my overheated imagination.

I would borrow my parents' Chrysler Highlander and together Billie-Jean and I would go for long, rapturous rides down Sunset Boulevard to the Pacific Coast Highway. Then turning right, we'd cruise past the Malibu Beach colony and head west toward Trancas Beach where we'd park and play until the sun disappeared into the ocean.

With one arm around Billie-Jean and her head nestled against my shoulder, I felt 'more powerful than a locomotive' and I knew that I could 'leap tall buildings in a single bound'.

In California at that time, you were allowed a junior driver's licence at the age of fourteen as long as the person riding with you held a full driver's licence. Billie-Jean was sixteen years old and had a license to thrill. I was almost fifteen with a constant hard-on and an over-worked right hand.

We investigated every secluded spot imaginable. With the car radio sounding out the latest tunes, I was in my element, as I emotively tried to sing along with Johnnie Ray and Eddie Fisher hoping that my slender musical talent would help me imprison Billie-Jean's heart. Her smile said it all. I felt that we'd really connected. We liked the same things and harboured the same fears and frustrations. Laughter was our constant companion. Young love was alive and throbbing.

Every desire-filled moment I was plotting and planning as to how I was going to score with Billie-Jean. When and where were the most important factors? However, for the time being, I had to be content with in-car entertainment. Teenage, erotic thoughts had set up permanent residence in my trousers, erecting skyscrapers, but kissing and groping was the only game in town. My frustration level was fast reaching overload.

It had taken several weeks of springboard diving and romantic, afternoon excursions before my hands finally made a serious attempt to capture Billie's curves. Then came an after shock. Ka-pow! My memory screams, as if it happened yesterday.

The moment arrived suddenly on a sweltering, hot California afternoon, as we sat making out in the car, while overlooking the Pacific Ocean. The scene is etched in my mind forever, programmed on constant replay. I can still hear the irritation in Billie-Jean's voice as she angrily shot me down in flames. 'Hands off, Columbus — you've discovered enough.' I had become a little overeager with my advancing fingers.

In the daytime I was a prisoner of our passion. At night I drowned in my own liquid dreams.

During those weeks with Billie-Jean, I relied on my equalizer. Little gems like, 'You know — my father is starting production on a new film — I'm sure that I could get him to see you for a part, or a screen test or something.'

'Oh really — that would be great' came the answer, each and every time. However, Billie never pushed it. She always remained blasé, as if her only interest was in me. A career move did not appear to be on her agenda. Her attitude stoked my fire even hotter. Still I wanted to keep her interest boiling. I felt this was my edge, so I kept the promise dangling. I assumed that I was in control. I had it all cleverly worked out. I was determined to score.

Then our relationship really warmed up. Could it be my diving, my singing, my sense of humour, my summer tan, my cool posture behind the wheel of my parents' chariot, or was it that slight possibility — a chance for her to get a screen test? No way. Billie-Jean wasn't like that.

Then one afternoon she changed from a kitten into a tiger. 'Can we go some place to be alone — really alone?' she purred, as her hand gently stroked my cheek. 'I don't mean in the car either, Steve.' Something told me that she was serious, and that I'd better not blow it. Anxiety grabbed me in a wrestler's sweaty grip. Where could we go? – Shit! My button was pushed. Caution was in the wind. I only hoped that she hadn't noticed the increase in my heart rate or the small drops of perspiration that had sneaked out on to my forehead. I had to remain Captain Cool. I headed for my parents' home on Rodeo Drive — post haste.

On the way, two thoughts occupied my mind. I hoped that

I hadn't read her wrong, and most important, I prayed that we would have the house to ourselves. Something told me that the curtain of reality was about to descend on my innocence.

As I eased open the back door and stepped into the kitchen, I heard a sound that froze me on the spot. 'Is that you Steve?' came my mother's cheerful voice from the upstairs hallway, her happy tone resounding through the walls like thunder. In what seemed like a microsecond she entered the kitchen and confronted us. 'I wasn't expecting you home so soon.'

'Hi Mom — uh — this is Billie-Jean.' I reluctantly introduced them, desperately hoping to divert any suspicion that my mother may have gathered as to my intentions. One false move and I'd have had it. 'How come you're here?' I asked, hoping my frustration wasn't showing.

'Oh, I'm working on a deadline for one of the magazines,' she replied. 'If you need anything — I'm in the den. OK?'

'Great,' I sighed, desperately grasping for my fast fading confidence. I had to keep Billie-Jean from penetrating my 'man of the world' disguise. At the same time, I had to act the innocent with my mother. This was not always an easy task.

Her prominence certainly helped give credence to the fantasy world that I was beginning to inhabit. Reality hadn't yet blown up in my face.

'Listen — if you two want anything to eat or drink — just help yourselves. You know where everything is, Steve. I've got to get back to work. What are you two going to do?'

'Oh we're just going to listen to some records.' My reply was swift and stilted.

'Alright — but please don't have the sound up too loud because I'm working. OK?'

'Don't worry, Mom, I'll keep it down. You won't hear a thing.' Anticipation of what I hoped was about to occur almost blew my cover, as I swiftly closed and locked my bedroom door.

My heart was hammering through my chest, as I showed Billie-Jean the box of records in the corner next to my bed. She seemed impressed with the collection. I quickly grabbed my favourite hum of the day and dropped it on the player, turning the volume down low as my mother had asked. At the same time, I fell back on the bed pulling Billie-Jean with me. The sounds of 'Heart and Soul' by the Four Aces whose four-part harmony serenaded my intention. 'Heart and Soul I fell in love with you. Lost control-' I prayed that I didn't have it turned up too loud.

My eyes were fixed on Billie-Jean's firm breasts bursting out of her low-cut yellow, summer dress. Instantly we locked against each other in loving combat. A Leaning Tower of Pisa was instantly erected in my Levis, as her hard nipples pushed against my white teeshirt. The scent of her skin burned my nostrils, as my hands started working overtime — tearing at her skimpy garment. 'Careful' she said, as she seductively began undoing the buttons at the front of her dress, at the same time pushing me down on the bed. 'Don't be in such a hurry.'

'Steve, listen,' she whispered. 'I've been waiting all this time. Don't spoil it, make it last. We haven't got a lot of time. I'm leaving for Texas tomorrow night — but it'll only be for a couple of weeks,' she quickly added, suddenly realizing that she'd made a slip of the lip.

'What?' A jagged flash of nausea squirmed through my system. I had no idea. I thought that we were destined to be together forever. Her words stained my vulnerability.

I had questions, but I was too deep in the honey to think about it. My torpedo was about to be launched. The moment was gathering momentum. I suddenly heard myself groaning with delight, as she gently kissed my face and neck. Then, brushing her lips down my arm, she began to gently suck the tips of my fingers. Slowly she started downward, expertly lifting my teeshirt. 'Take your Loafers off,' she whispered with mounting fervour, as she effortlessly moved her body astride me. 'Let me help you with your socks.' Her suntanned legs snaked against me, as she deftly hooked my white sock tops with her toes.

In a complete frenzy, I pushed her back and started tearing off my clothes. Panic flashed in for a second, as I was about to enter unknown territory. I shoved all fear from my mind and stumbled forward. Then, as if by magic, her dress vanished to the regions of the floor. I remember noticing the perfect togetherness of her yellow dress, lying against the deep blue of my bedroom carpet, as my eyes became dazzled with the impact of her naked beauty. My senses fell away. With the gentle touch of a butterfly's kiss, she traced my mouth with her now moistened lips. Instantly the room seemed awash with perfume, as if invaded by a presence of angels. All my Christmases and birthdays had come at once. I was smothering in her thick, black, tumbling hair, as she passionately explored my mouth with her tongue. For a split second, I thought I heard my mother, listening outside my bedroom door, but any panic was quickly blocked by the vision of Billie-Jean's cinnamon coloured perfect breasts, jutting inches from my face. Her fingers eagerly worked at the buttons of my Levis. Could she have done this before, I wondered? I let the thought slip from my mind. By now I was beyond any reasoning, I couldn't wait. I was in a rage of desire. Shazam! I was Captain Marvel about to save the world.

Her soft skin melted against my anxious body as she deftly eased me on top of her. Soft hands formed around the curve of my ass and gently guided me towards a genital encounter. Slowly she arched upwards, then gripping me tighter, she pressed against me with her eyes closed. Gentle moans of ecstasy began escaping from her parted lips. I let out a silent scream and tried desperately to retain my cool as she deftly took hold and guided me toward heavenly nirvana.

Then suddenly, like a guided missile off course, I exploded in shame before I reached my destination, covering her silken fur in a splash of liquid passion. My head sank into the pillow. I was completely humiliated. 'Steve, don't worry — it's alright,' Billie-Jean said. 'Just make love to me again — do it now — do it now. You've got to,' she rasped, as she desperately tried to re-inflate my humbled weapon.

If only the bed could have opened up like a trap door. I would have fallen into the darkness and hidden from the reality of that moment. My head was spinning with embarrassment. I was out of breath, and out of fuel. Her pleas for total recall only increased my deflation.

'Please Steve — make love to me — please — you've got to. If you're gonna talk like a man, please act like one.'

The irritation and frustration in her voice battered my ears. My brain was on ignition, but as hard as I pushed the button, my engine wouldn't start. I had a flat battery and I was a long way from lift off.

Suddenly Billie-Jean was up and dressing. Fiercely gathering the rest of her clothes she fired a hostile glance directly at me. 'Hey what's wrong?' I asked anxiously.

'You may as well take me back to the hotel, Steve,' she answered stiffly.

'What do you mean – take you back to the hotel? We've got plenty of time. Why do you have to go back now?' I was shocked by her sudden change of mood.

'Listen, Steve, if you can't get it together, I know plenty of others who can,' she answered coldly, heading toward the door. She fumbled with the lock, thus allowing me vital seconds to regain reality and try to stop her.

'But Billie please — I love you — I really do,' I pleaded in desperation. 'You can't just go like this. Please hang on.'

'Listen, this may have been exciting for you' she snapped, the tone in her 16 year-old voice suddenly mature, 'but I haven't got time for hand holding.'

'Billie, please listen. We've had great times together. We have, haven't we? Please stay — just a little longer.' I was now in total confusion and fighting back tears with all my strength.

'No. I'm not going to stay, Steve. You're not what I thought

Right: Cooling it by the pool.

you were — and anyway you've lied to me as well. You're just full of bullshit!'

'What do you mean?' I gasped, my voice rising even higher. By now I was standing naked at the door, desperately trying to block her exit.

'You've never taken me to the studio or introduced me to your father like you promised. If you really love me like you say — you'd help me. You'd ask your father to give me a screen test. The least you could have done was to introduce me. But no, all you do is talk about it — and you sure as hell didn't come through this afternoon either.'

My long-playing mouth had kicked me in the ass. I was almost 15 years old and already hitting burn-out. All talk — no do.

Dejectedly, I drove Billie-Jean back to the hotel in silence. I felt deeply humiliated and totally flattened. Acute depression began sneaking in with heavy boots and I was running on empty.

As I turned the Chrysler into the hotel parking lot, Billie suddenly put an arm around my shoulder. 'Listen Steve, I'm sorry. I don't mean to hurt you. I really don't, but right now I need my space. We've had some fun, but I don't want to get serious. I'm not even sure what love is. You're nice, Steve, and I do like you a lot.' She kissed me softly on the cheek. 'Don't worry — we'll keep in touch and I'll call you tomorrow before I leave and we'll get together when I get back to LA in two weeks. OK? Don't be upset, you really are sweet.'

Within a matter of seconds I was elated. My engine once again was revving. 'I've got to see you again,' I mumbled breathlessly. 'I've got to.'

She gave me a long lingering kiss. 'I'm going to miss you, Steve. I really am. Goodbye babe. I'll see you in a couple of weeks.

Above: Seventeen years old and ready to rock.

We'll get together. I'll call you when I'm back. I promise.'

Those were the last words that Billie-Jean said as she stepped out of the car and closed the door. She walked swiftly toward the hotel. When she reached the entrance she stopped and waved. Her glittering smile captured me in a moment of grace. Then she turned and disappeared inside.

It's been almost 60 years since that eventful summer afternoon at my parents' house. I'd learned an important lesson. 'Stay out of the fast lane if you haven't got the pace.'

My summer vacation came to a thudding end. It would be my fifteenth birthday in a week. High school adventure lay ahead. I'll always remember Billie-Jean, the beautiful Osage Indian girl from Texarkana, whose heart I so naively tried to capture and failed so magnificently. I often think of her and wonder how she is.

I'm still waiting for her promised phone call.

Hooray for Hollywood

The Oxford Dictionary defines friendship as: 'One joined to another in intimate and mutual benevolence independent of sexual or family love.' Hollywood has its own definition of friendship. It has nothing to do with the Oxford Dictionary.

Hollywood – the land of the Lotus Eaters. No other metropolis in the world is quite as magical. A true fantasy Mecca where dreams can become a reality, but only if you're prepared to stay the course and have within you the ability to create a solid relationship with a very special female – Lady Luck.

If she's not in your bed every night your dreams will become a nightmare. Hollywood can present a perfidious landscape with no place for the faint-hearted. Two-legged predators abound, spinning webs of enticement laced with insincerity. A true and lasting friendship is a rare commodity when there are minions of backstabbers skulking in the shadows. The one hope of scoring big time is to dress up in determination, have your eyes fully open to reality, avoid the bullshit and keep a solid grip on your confidence. Otherwise Hollywood will chew you up and spit you out. It takes balls to stay in the game. Dealing with rejection and false promises goes with the territory. As Harry Truman so rightly said, 'If you can't stand the heat, stay out of the kitchen.'

SHOWCASE

This issue we are thrilled to introduce an unusually talented young actor . . . our own discovery . . . Steve Rowland . . . So we are devoting the entire department to him . . . Next issue, we'll be back with our usual list of gifted youngsters, looking for a break . . .

Steve Rowland once wanted to be a veterinarian, but switched to acting and now is looking forward to getting started in a screen career.

He isn't trading on his father's name (his pa is director Roy Rowland) because he wants to make the grade all by himself.

Above: First appearance in a fan magazine.

FORREST EDWARD (BUDD) ALBRIGHT

Not a whisper of wind moved through the trees on that April day in 1956. The streets and surrounding neighbourhoods lay uncannily still under the dazzling glare of the early afternoon sun, as I nosed my 1954 white Chevrolet Corvette off the Sunset Boulevard blacktop and on to the forecourt of the Union Oil Station at the money end of the Pacific Palisades. With the top off my chariot and the soothing sounds of radio station KDAY massaging my ears, the midday journey had seemed endless, forcing dream-like apathy to enter my concentration. It was more than likely that the couple of cans of Budweiser I'd splashed down before rolling on to the Sunset Boulevard turf had been the real instigators of my mellowing mood.

Cruising along, my attention had momentarily been drawn to

Above: Checking the action in Beverly Hills.

the dashboard and the staccato winking of the gas-gauge. Without warning the car in front of me suddenly slowed, severely brake-testing my quick reactions. It was a narrow escape from a definite crunch. I needed to call time out in order to collect my thoughts. Since my head was pounding from the day's relentless heat and the Corvette had need for a drink, it seemed only logical to pull up at an oasis for a short respite before continuing the journey westward. With brakes once again screeching like a wounded banshee, I reined in at the station's nearest pump, switched off the throbbing engine, and hopped out from behind the steering wheel with self-service in mind. As I unhooked the hose and removed the Corvette's gas cap, irritated words assaulted my ears.

'Hey man, what do you think you're doing? That's not a self-service pump.' Annoyance in the tone spun me around bringing me face to face with a young man dressed in what once had been a Crisco-white pump jockey's uniform. The black, greasy stains, frayed collar and rolled up shirtsleeves said a great deal about the fellow's diligence in keeping things together at the gas station while doing his job. He had the chiselled features of a Midwestern face, flattered by the California sun, crowned with Brylcreemed, darkish hair in complete contrast to a brown-eyed gaze, as steady as that of a battle-hardened sniper.

Something about his earnest expression brought the beginning of an embarrassed smirk to the corners of my mouth. 'Hey man, I'm sorry. I thought this pump was a Do It Yourself.'

'It's not!' he snapped. 'How much ya want?' The hint of a laugh sneaked through a row of perfect teeth as he took the pump from my grasp, breaking the tension.

'Fill it up,' I said, looking around the station setting, hoping to spot some girly talent. 'I'll bet there's a lot of action around here.' My statement was more like a question, as I glanced over the entire area, while affecting the demeanour of James Dean from *Rebel Without a Cause.*

'You better believe it. Why do you think that I picked this gas station to work at? There's activity around here like you wouldn't believe – and I'm not just talking about the chicks.' The tenor in his voice dropped an octave, as if relaying confidential information.

'Sounds interesting,' I answered. 'Clue me in. By the way, my name's Steve.'

'I'm Budd, Budd Albright.'

We shook hands and laughed out loud. Our earlier meeting had hardly been auspicious. With the tank filled, he replaced the hose. 'Hey Steve, do you mind if I check out your wheels?'

'Be my guest,' I said with a hint of smugness in my answer. Budd was like Bulldog Drummond on speed as he eyeballed every miniscule detail of my set of wheels with serious fervour. I was curious to know what fired his interest. 'Follow me,' Budd said, quickly moving off the forecourt, 'I want to show you something.'

As we moved around the south corner of the building, Budd pointed to an identical white Corvette parked neatly against the wall of the service bay. Up to then it had been hidden from sight.

'Hey man, whose Vette is that?' I asked with the excited tone of someone who's just discovered that he hasn't got exclusivity on white 1954 Chevrolet corvettes.

'That's mine.' Budd's answer was swollen with pride.

'Hey, that's cool.' I couldn't hide my enthusiasm as I made quick steps toward the pristine vehicle. From that moment our friendship was off and running.

Forrest Edward (Budd) Albright landed in LA from Cleveland, Ohio standing tall with six feet of athletic charisma and his mind set with movie star ambition. With little bread in his pocket he was forced to set up residence at his grandmother's Santa Monica home. The sleeping accommodation was small, but adequate. Living with Grandma had restrictions, but Budd was grateful for the free lodging, not to mention her wonderful Italian cooking.

Like the minions that came before him, Budd had arrived in sunny Southern California, his eyes clouded with sugarplum visions and a steely determination to achieve acting fame. He was just nineteen years old and carrying enough testosterone to cause a major earthquake. Los Angeles was used to that. However, Budd's name wasn't on the Richter scale. He needed to find a job.

Hollywood in the 1950s was a melting pot for hundreds of

hopefuls, their eyes fixed on stardom and their pockets running on empty. What money they'd managed to scrape together before they'd left home was sure to have disappeared before the first month was out. Therefore income was essential in order for them to stay the course. It was their utmost concern. The clever ones realized the importance of securing work that would give them viability, somewhere frequented by film industry notables – a situation that offered the possibility of being noticed.

For the guys there were a few options that fitted the bill. One was to find work as a car-park attendant, preferably at a top hotel, restaurant or nightclub, those venues frequented by the film industry's power merchants. Waiting tables or tending bar at one of Hollywood's hot spots or classy eateries was an excellent choice for the girls as well as the boys – a great position in which to be discovered as there was always a parade of agents and industry hawks filtering through those establishments, forever on the lookout for new talent.

Budd Albright grabbed a job offer at the Union Oil Station in the Pacific Palisades. He'd been waiting a month before he decided that this was just the right move to launch his assault on stardom. The job suited him as he was dexterous with automobile engines and didn't mind getting his hands dirty.

The Palisades location was in the heartland of salubrious living. High-powered film executives, agents and celebrities lived in and around the area, not forgetting those passing through while traveling to Hollywood work-stations from their Malibu Beach Colony homes.

Most days a diversity of faces would gather in the Union Oil forecourt to gas their chariots or grab a soft drink from the vending machine. Budd found himself a kingpin in the centre of an activity that he hoped would eventually pay off. He was in the perfect situation to make friends as well as important contact with those who could help his career aspirations. He wasn't alone, however. There were additional faces with similar agendas.

Budd had been working at the Union Oil Station only about two weeks when he discovered that he was on a rotation system with other young hopeful who were also struggling to be discovered. Doug McClure, Jack Jones and Billy Gray had been mostly working night shifts and were thereby able to do battle in the Hollywood trenches during the day. Friendship with Budd, whom they considered to be competition, was not high on their list of priorities. Budd would have to make his own moves on the taking of Hollywood. Doug McClure in particular was not interested in forming a liaison.

For Budd Albright the Union Oil Station was the centre point of action throughout the year of 1956. It was also an eye-opening introduction to the Machiavellian manipulations of the Hollywood gentry. Up until then he'd only had a taste of the treachery.

AN AFFIDAVIT FROM BUDD ALBRIGHT

On a steamy southern California afternoon, I was on a work break and checking out the local female talent when a white 1954 Chevrolet Corvette pulled onto the station forecourt and squealed to a stop at the nearest pump. Out jumped a slim young dude dressed in faded Levis and a white tee-shirt. His black engineers' boots seemed cumbersome wearing, considering the toasting temperature of the day. I also noticed a well-worn black leather jacket lying on the passenger seat - a clue to his chosen persona. That was my introduction to Steve Rowland. As I pumped the 'tane' into his tank, my eyes were glued on his set of wheels. Although suspicious, he didn't seem to mind my checking it over. Afterwards, I asked him to follow me around to the side of the service bay where I pointed out an identical 1954 white

Chevi Corvette. When I said that it was mine he immediately dropped his acquired James Dean posturing and rushed over to investigate. The fact that we both had identical white Corvettes was an amazing coincidence and immediately kick-started us into a heavy conversation about the pros and cons of the car's glorious features. We instantly hit it off, but like two peacocks in competition, we were careful to guard our own personal space. Recent experience had taught me not to get friendly too soon.

Our conversation rumbled along, questioning each other about which car had the hotter set-up. The engine in my Corvette had been gone through with the intention of increasing the overall thrust. The head had been given some proper attention from one of Santa Monica's top racing shops. Also installed were three side-draft carburettors that fired the engine through duel exhaust pipes, thus creating a sexy throb. I had to admit that Steve's car, however, still had the edge. It had a stick shift. It was the first Corvette that I'd seen with a 'four on the floor' transmission and a 289 V/8 engine. It was definitely a lethal roadrunner. My machine was quick, but it was shackled with the disastrous power glide automatic transmission. The engine blew up a short time later while racing on Sunset Boulevard against a rapid Buick Century. Although I won the race, my transmission was a write-off and my bank balance couldn't take the heat of a complete rebuild.

Steve and I talked about many things that day. He hung out at the station until I was off work at which time we continued 'conversating' over coffee at a café around the corner. We found that we had a great many things in common. We both loved danger. Steve was motorcycle-mad as well as being into sport car racing. I loved cars and had competed in powerboat racing. In fact Steve and I found that we liked participating in most of the danger sports. We discovered that we both held a passion for the beach, the mountains and desert and for generally living life on the edge. We also held a great affinity for all animals. Although Steve had been born into a motion picture family, he was nevertheless facing the same struggle as I was for acting

Right: A day in the life.

recognition. We were hoping for a break. We loved rock 'n' roll music and we'd managed to attract some attention with our singing capability. We found that we both had the ability to laugh at ourselves and to spit in the face of adversity. Many years have come and gone since that first meeting. Time has changed most things drastically. The world today is a vastly different place from those days of innocence. My memory of the Union Oil Station in the Pacific Palisades is one of fondness. To me, it was the central station of seductive attraction, the hub of happenings. A never-ending flow of hot cars and hot- looking ladies, always in the mix with movie stars, college jocks, surfer dudes and arrogant high rollers. It was my centre point of action in that summer of 1956. The sun was constant. Everyone was tanned and worked out in the gym. Radio Stations KFWB and KLAC pumped out a continual stream of the latest sounds. Doris Day's 'Que Sera

Sera and 'Be-Bop-a-Lula' by Gene Vincent & The Blue Caps crowded the airwaves competing for the nation's number one spot. Everyone, it seemed, was parading for attention and sexual admiration. Even the manager of the Union Oil Station was pitching for pumpage. Every female was fair game and all seemed willing. High school cheer-leaders, models, married women, wives of prominent business men, their young daughters and their mistresses flattered our fertile egos with flirtatious innuendoes, most of the time amounting to nothing more than innocent banter. More times than not, however, sexual chemistry exploded into passionate relationships. Most lasting just 24 hours.

We loved the ladies, but most important, we were in love with life.

As the summer rolled on, Steve would drop by the station more and more. Our conversation was always the same – acting, music, cars and girls. We started spending a great deal of time together, just hanging out and having a laugh. We got to know and respect each other and although our backgrounds were very different, we formed a unique friendship that has defied the cynical 'Hollywood shuffle'. We still see eye-to-eye on most things and continue to argue about the merits of unimportant trivia. It's a throwback to those halcyon days at the Union Oil Station in the Pacific Palisades when one-upmanship was our competitive battlefield and laughter the elixir that oiled our engines. Later when we teamed up on the Sunset Strip nothing was sacred – no female was safe from our cliché ridden pitching spiel. Thinking about it today, I'm amazed that we were able to fill our score cards. I've had many ups and downs, highs and lows in my life since that summer in 1956 and I'm still standing. The longest survivor of all is our friendship. It's been as constant as night following day for more than fifty years.

Seeking Acceptance

In our early days as actors, Budd Albright and I saw ourselves as the breathing definition of cool as we roamed the Sunset Boulevard badlands in our white Corvettes.

We were Hollywood gunslingers out to collect notches for the bedpost, forever shooting from the hip white-hot bullets of joy. We were the pied pipers of pumping pleasure, continually encouraging all types of brainless action to gleefully follow us to the land of delight. We were out of control and proud of it. I'm sure that we were often laughed at, possibly envied, but definitely not always admired.

Though I must have appeared privileged because of my being born into a motion picture family, I definitely was not lax or irresponsible in my attitude toward my chosen profession and to the sacrifices that it demanded.

In the mid-1950s, style and image were far different than they are today. For a young guy to be noticed or lucky enough to have signed to a studio contract, he had to possess certain essentials — the accepted movie star physical characteristics. This thinking was held over in a formatted agenda from an era gone by, but still carried out by the various major studios' star development programmes. The criteria being that newly-signed male contract players must fit the description of a ruggedly handsome action man and possess the charm of a debonair bedroom bandit.

Robert Taylor, Tyrone Power, Clark Gable, John Wayne, Cary Grant, Errol Flynn were just a few of the names that the studios were desperate to clone by signing mostly young dark haired, six foot hunks that photographically fitted the bill. Whether or not any of these newly signed faces had any previous acting experience, or, for that matter, any noticeable acting talent, never seemed to be the decisive factor. The most important aspect being that their filmed persona would project enough magnetism to wet the knickers of the passionate female public who were forever watching out for a new young heartthrob to sexually fantasize over.

Agents and would-be managers scoured the country searching

for potentially saleable talent to present to the major studios in the hope of securing a six-month starting stock contract. With a bit of luck that could be a foot in the door and with hard work and determination the good-looking, raw new signing one day might just crack Hollywood stardom, big time.

Agents such as Henry Willson became specialists in finding and securing studio contracts for what would become the new and compelling faces for stardom. Willson's penchant for changing their given names to the likes of Rock Hudson, Tab Hunter, Troy Donahue, Rip Torn, Race Gentry and even John Smith launched a new era in recognizable motion picture leading men. With his success rate, Henry Willson soon became one of the most powerful agents in Hollywood — perhaps in the world. His far-reaching fame insured that a never-ending stream of wannabes would continue beating an anxious pathway to his welcoming door.

Henry Willson, it seemed, had the Midas touch and therefore was extremely selective of whom he signed for representation. The men he preferred both professionally and socially were, for the most part, one and the same. I was definitely somebody that Henry Willson would never even consider representing. In his eyes, my being five feet eight inches tall was a physical no-no.

The explosive arrival of James Dean changed the Hollywood leading man stereotype from the moment the film East of Eden burst onto the screen.

In Rebel Without a Cause, Jim provided a new template for the modern movie star heartthrob. His compelling personality and charismatic acting talent caught the industry unprepared for the tremendous impact that this five foot eight inch Indiana farm boy would have on the world. Together with Marlon Brando, James Dean's electric persona blew all to hell Hollywood's yesterday concept of a motion picture superstar. A brand new millennium

Right: Researching my role for *Crime In The Streets*.

BC
UCE CO

Right: Wheels of Glory. My 1954 Chevrolet Corvette.

had arrived with all guns blazing.

It was the middle 1950s and Hollywood was teeming with wide-eyed and panting young studs from all over the country. All of them were hoping to become the next James Dean, Marlon Brando or Elvis Presley. Budd Albright and I were fired with ambition. We took our acting ability very seriously. The New York Actors Studio had set the pattern of procedure for one to become a respected thespian in the newly focused eyes of the talent scouts. Hollywood was now searching for method actors and actresses to place under contract. There was a backlash to one-dimensional handsome leading man. That was yesterday's icon. It was the beginning of a new era. Hopefully my chance had arrived.

Word of mouth had me hound dogging to discover the best actors' workshop in Hollywood, at which I could hone my talent. If I was to be taken seriously as an actor, I had to find, audition for, and be accepted into a creditable acting collective, one that had a respected and successful reputation. There was really only one to consider and that was the best one. It had been organized and was conducted by the gifted stage and screen actor, Jeff Corey. Many thought of it as Hollywood's version of the Actors Studio. I had to go through some heavy shit before I was considered worthy

enough to be accepted. Many of Hollywood's biggest names studied at Jeff's workshop while they were struggling unknowns.

I battled through numerous improvisational scenarios with Natalie Wood, Jack Nicholson, Sally Kellerman, Dean Stockwell, Robert Blake and Kathy Case. I didn't know at the time that I was sparring with famous film faces of the future.

Others who attended from time to time were: Dennis Hopper, Troy Donahue, Edd 'Kookie' Burns, Jim Mitchum, Suzanne Pleshette and many others who at this time evade my memory. I recall those classes as fantastic and creative talent expanding events. I eagerly looked forward to those workshop evenings consumed with an inflated impression of my acting ability and a burning desire to impress the many glorious young starlets who were always in attendance. Jeff Corey's workshop held a titanic explosion of talent, creatively and physically. My enthusiasm was on overload.

Gazing at Beauty

Most of those seen walking were female. Many were outrageously attractive and almost always dressed to thrill.

The expansive streets below Santa Monica Boulevard in Beverly Hills were a dazzling maze of dreams. Million-dollar boutiques lined each side of the three main drives offering fantasy attire, jewellery and items of exotica to the many who could afford the prices. Those with a humble bank balance and melancholy eyes strolled the sidewalks, their imagination spraying fountains of gold across their vision importing a champagne lifestyle that invalidated their beer income.

In the 1950s, Rodeo Drive, Beverly Drive and Canon Drive, although alive with buzzing activity, nevertheless secreted a warm village atmosphere. High rollers, industry executives and the wives and girlfriends of important film-land faces grinned with self-satisfaction from behind the steering wheel of exotic vehicles while rolling up and down the avenue. Hired help of the rich and famous drove with surreptitious eyes along the crowded turf in the hope of sniffing out an available parking space conveniently close to their employer's desired destination. On the frequent occasion that someone would fail to discover that precious unloading slot, frustration would ensue, forcing their use of public garage parking, subsequently footwork became their mode of transportation.

The pristine pavement of Beverly Hills clattered and hummed with the hustle of privileged feet shopping for glory. Many appeared to have urgent appointments — others a license to linger sipping coffee and chatting while observing the passing parade through the glass fronted vantage point of the various coffee and cake shops. Most of those seen walking were female. Many were outrageously attractive and almost always dressed to thrill.

The prying blades of sunlight created havoc with my eyes as I cautiously guided my Corvette along Beverly Drive searching for an empty parking space. Having forgotten to take my sunglasses I

Above: Marianne Gabba and I talk some trash with Sal Mineo.

peered into the imposing glare like Mr Magoo on one of his many cartoon holidays.

Although the traffic was comparatively light there was nevertheless enough high dollar machinery touring the Beverly Hills pavement to instil envy in my soul and firm concentration on my driving.

The intrusion of the morning glaze, however, had not totally hampered my vision for female talent-spotting. That was an activity that indulged my fancy whenever I sat behind the wheel cruising the streets of Beverly Hills. It was game on every time, never failing to increase my aesthetic values.

With the Corvette's detachable hardtop stored away for the summer and the sound of Elvis Presley's 'Heartbreak Hotel' turned up to blaring, I was on a mission to capture the attention of the many gorgeous chicks that swarmed the exclusive byways between Santa Monica Boulevard and Wilshire Boulevard — the epicentre of Beverly Hills' glittering shopping Mecca.

My ego was pumping on all cylinders from having just signed to play a featured role in Don Segal's newest film, *Crime in the Streets*. It was an important break in my career struggle, as I would be in there mixing it with a couple of New York heavyweights, John Cassavetes and Sal Mineo. With Don Segal's direction I was sure that the result would prove my acting ability to the various studios' casting agents and thereby put me on the pathway to realizing my dream of eventual stardom.

I was having illusions of becoming the next James Dean as I prowled along the street in close proximity to the rear of a gleaming black Cadillac Eldorado. The summer scent of freshly cut grass floated from the manicured parks that lined Santa Monica Boulevard, overpowering the exhaust fumes and blending a mixture of motionless fragrance with the melody of distant conversations. I was riding high. Like James Cagney in *White Heat*, I was feeling on top of the world.

Above: Talented Tuesday Weld is not just a pretty face, she's gorgeous.

Anxious traffic began to jam up, creating a slow moving parade of gleaming machinery. The silent sizzle of the midday sun pressed against my neck and shoulders, reminding me that I should have worn a hat. The cars in front of me began moving at a snail's pace, giving me the chance to check that things with me were cool. I had a responsibility to look my best now that I felt my celebrity status was waiting in the wings. I was suddenly image-conscious in a white teeshirt. A veil of smugness clouded my reflection from the rear view mirror. Vanity guided my hand as it fingered my hair into perfection. I smiled back at the face in the mirror. Flawless! I ignored the tiny beads of sweat that were welling into a mini tsunami at my hairline and about to make a river run down my forehead. I felt charged by the tongues of heat that licked my face and arms as I followed in slow procession behind the stoic Cadillac, squinting against the shards of silver

A SKYE PUBLI...

Hollywood Stars

arilyn
onroe

hirley
ones

SPECIAL
NEWCOMER
SECTION

Fashion,
Beauty
and Diet
Guide
to a
Glamorous
Figure

Steve
Rowland...
Next
Jimmy Dean?

Debbie
Reynolds...
Fun Without
An Escort!

Bob
Wagner...
Should A
Girl Propose

light that danced off the shiny black paintwork. The sky glazed a whiter shade of blue, as if to encourage the pressing heat. I prayed that a breeze would stir the air and bring relief to the day and enhance my self-satisfaction

Capturing a parking slot seemed out of the question as a symphony of car horns indicated more gathering traffic. The mounting irritation from impatient drivers stranded in the slow-motion parade of cars ahead, forced me to bite the bullet and cool my frustration at having to crawl along on all fours.

Elvis had stopped his lament about the existence at Heartbreak Hotel. I changed the station from KHJ to KFWB, hoping for a soothing musical injection to filter my mood. The calypso tones of Harry Belafonte sprang to life, appropriately crooning about an 'Island in the Sun.' I turned up the volume and took advantage of the slow procession to search the sidewalk on each side of Beverly Drive for girly activity. Having just acquired a major break in my film career, I felt that my confidence was now coming of age. My ego was in flight. The searchlight in my eyes scanned the pavement with radar precision. There was a promenade of beauty, purposefully striding along the sidewalks, consumed with the excitement of their next purchase. My eyes were on stalks, checking out the action with intent. I prayed for a miracle. Available parking! Anxiety consumed me.

The traffic in front of me crawled to a stop opposite Geary's spacious glass-fronted furnishing emporium. That gave me the opportunity to glance off and admire the window's reflection of my newly re-sprayed white Corvette. I felt immensely proud of the special pearl-white metallic paint job. It was one of a kind and sparkled with an expensive lustre that was sure to capture a flood of envious eyes. I leaned back in the seat and stretched my arms skyward. Except for the rivulet of perspiration coursing down my back and forming into a small pool at the base of my spine, I couldn't have felt better. This was one of God's perfect days and I intended to make the most of it.

Whatever had been holding things up on the pavement ahead

suddenly let go and cars started inching forward once again. I duly followed — one eye on the Caddy in front and the other switched on to search mode for female finery.

On approaching the pedestrian crossing at Dayton Avenue, I was forced to stop and allow a criss-crossing gaggle of beauty in sleeveless summer dresses to meander with attitude across the road in front of me. The desire in my eyes must have been obvious to the growing number of bystanders who couldn't help but notice my smiling, self-assured expression as I followed the movement of suntanned legs high-stepping the curbs up onto the sidewalk. I couldn't wait to park and get into the mix.

I hesitated a moment before driving on. The oppressive heat must have hot-wired my thinking as I started across the intersection. My head was surely up my ass or else how could I have missed her. My foot was hard on the brakes, as I recognized the gorgeous creature about to cross the pavement in front of me. I'd seen her face in all the gossip sheets and fan magazines. She was the template for my ideal lady. Her glamorous countenance was pinned up on the walls of my heart. Here she was. All my Christmases had come at once.

Joan Collins was stunning, like a sultry goddess, gliding with the sensual confidence of a woman with exquisite beauty. There was dignity in her stride that suggested grace and tenderness. Seeing her in front of me ignited a sharp intake of breath.

There was evidence that the sun had kissed her raven hair leaving streaks of gold. The cut was stylishly shaped, further enhancing her radiant features. She moved her perfect body with an erotic power inciting an instant spike of passion that rattled a chain through my soul. I sat transfixed in recognition watching her glide past. Turning toward me she allowed a tiny smile to sneak across her face, exposing an underlying sense of humour from the twinkle in her eyes. I wanted so much to make an impression — to have a conversation. God damn it! Where the hell is a place to park when you need one? Shit!

A chorus of car horns began sounding in the key of frustration, forcing me to move on. The Cadillac Eldorado was a few yards ahead following the line of cars at a steady clip. My eyes were focused on the reality of Joan Collins, in the flesh. I was desperate to speak to her. The promised river of perspiration had now decided to cascade down my forehead damming up my eyes. I had to find a place to park — like yesterday.

I revved the engine once more hoping to capture Miss Collins's attention. Dropping the car into first gear, I let the clutch fly back and with squealing rubber I roared off toward the back of the now stationary black Eldorado. Screech!! Kur-rash!! Crumple!! Splat!!!! My late braking proved a disaster. The result of my impetuous action lay in pieces of freshly painted, pearlized fibre-glass body parts and bent metal submerged in a thickening pool of oil and water. There was rage on the face of the Cadillac owner as he theatrically played to the gathered crowd, pointing out the few scratches left on his car's paintwork while loudly berating me for stupidity.

I had no one to blame but myself. I'd wanted to make an impression on Joan Collins and I'd certainly accomplished that, big time. This was gonna prove to be an expensive episode. I looked off at the crowd on the sidewalk. Joan Collins was standing there smiling with owl-eyed amusement.

Above: Joan Collins is a definite ten.

Three for the Road

I'd had a full day of it. It had been a hot one and I'd just come back from much sweat-filled action on the local Beverly Hills Turf to cool my motor in the shaded silence of my hilltop pad. I was shagged out. My ass was dragging.

It was about 5.30 in the afternoon when my butt hit the outside lounger. In what seemed like only minutes, sleep marched in and whisked me off to the land of nod.

Almost instantly I was in Nirvana, entwined with the most beautiful female I'd ever seen — long cascading golden hair that covered me like a blanket as I lay entangled in the curves of her perfect body. As she spoke of love her velvet voice caressed me in a river of melting honey. She held my face in her silken hands and leaned forward. Her sensual, pouting lips parted, as her luscious mouth captured mine, taking my tongue a prisoner with her passion. I was on fire — Then suddenly and for no apparent reason, I began to cough and the cough began choking me. I couldn't catch my breath and I was shivering with cold. I came awake sneezing. It was 9 o'clock and night had crept up on me as I'd slept, kicking me back to reality and spoiling my Utopian dream of sexual conquest.

The Hollywood darkness had grabbed me in a chilly grip. The fantasy had disappeared in the mist leaving me shaking in the shroud of an unobtainable memory. I felt like a black cloud marking time. I knew it was gonna be one of those nights. It had all the earmarks of frustration city. I had to turn it around — and quick. There was no time for any self-pitying moods. The night was young and there were happenings to behold. I had to prepare for battle.

I stiffly got to my feet and went inside for some shower time and a change of threads. The hot, soothing water washed away the negatives, and dressed in my clean clothes, I was ready to party. It was somewhere around 10pm. I snatched the phone and started throwing calls all over town, but I came up empty. No one from the usual crew was around. Even my partner in most crimes, Budd Albright, was missing in action. He was most certainly cooling it in the tangles of some lovely Latin-looking creature,

completely oblivious to the world outside his own seduction. I felt depression creep in, as I desperately tried to flash back to my earlier adventure in dreamland. Not a chance. I had to face it. I was getting bugged out and frustration was taking over rapidly. A lonely night was looming.

On a hunch, I threw a call to Elvis, who at the time, was staying at the Beverly Wilshire Hotel. He and his Memphis mob were occupying practically the entire 9th floor. After much FBI type interrogation by the hotel switchboard, I was finally put through. Not really expecting him to be there, I was struck stone solid when Red West, Elvis's numero uno P.A. answered the phone. Elvis was in. 'Hey man, what's happening?' I said. 'Anything going on? Any action on the scene?'

Red replied that nothing was happening — no chicks or anything. 'Just a boring night all around.' He and Elvis and a couple of the guys were just sitting about goofing off. I said that I was gonna make fast feet to Rodeo Drive to check out my parents' house which was locked up while they were away in Europe. Since I was only going to be up the street I asked Red if Elvis and the boys would like to get together for a little action search out. He said it sounded cool and that they'd meet me at my parents' place.

Left: Elvis as I knew him.

About twenty minutes later, Elvis and Cliff Gleaves, another of Elvis's inner circle, pulled up in front of my parents' house in long black Cadillac limousine style. Elvis was at the wheel. A couple of short blasts of the horn got my attention. I came outside, jumped in the back seat and we took off — three for the road.

At first we just drove around aimlessly, searching the byways for girly activity. There weren't nothin' shaking but the leaves on the trees. I can tell you that. It seemed as if the whole local female population had pushed the fade out button for parts unknown. As we cruised up and down the Sunset Strip and on into Beverly Hills and then on to Wilshire Boulevard, the only chicks that we saw were those smiling at us from the billboards. Where was everybody? It really seemed as if Mandrake the Magician had come along, waved his magic wand, thus causing a massive female disappearing act. We were fast arriving at frustration city and it was only just closing on midnight.

After cruising the turf and coming up empty the three of us finally accepted defeat on the feminine front. However, we weren't quite ready to throw in the towel and give up the night. Elvis pointed the long black chariot towards the beach and pressed down on the gas. We were on the curve of Sunset Boulevard, a few blocks from Beverly Glen and heading west. The Pacific Palisades beckoned.

Our earlier jovial mood had definitely changed into a relaxed and somewhat cynical acceptance of life. We began jiving back and forth on serious subjects. 'What is life all about? Why do things happen the way they do — when they do?' There was a reflective tone in Elvis's voice. I knew that our tickets were punched for a heavy trip. Then Cliff spoke about a big name disc jockey from New York who had said some great things over the air about Elvis. Compared to all the trash that had been spit out by self-important do-gooders, that New York DJ had come on like a true champion. Elvis reacted about how scared you can get when you aren't sure of things — how lost you feel when everything seems to be spinning out of your control.

Suddenly, I had an idea. It was crazy but if it came off, the night would end on a high note. I'd been grooving on the scene with a chick that lived in the Pacific Palisades. Since our wheels were rolling in that direction, I suggested that we pay my lovely blonde creature a surprise visit. She'd freak out. It would be a laugh. She was Elvis Presley mad. Her mouth was constantly in overdrive about how she'd love to meet him. I had made the big mistake of telling her that my uncle, Jack Cummings, was the producer of *Viva Las Vegas* and that I'd met Elvis on the set during filming. I laid it on about how Elvis and I had really hit it off. From that moment on Elvis Presley was all she talked about. She had been driving me crazy for an introduction. I smiled as my thoughts took the shape of a benevolent despot. Fate was about to deal a winning hand.

Elvis loved the idea and Cliff was jumping up and down at just the thought.

The entire limo was rocking as Elvis pushed the pedal to the metal and turned up the sounds on the radio, as if to underscore our mission of delight.

About ten minutes later, we arrived at our destination, the home of Carol Randall. Carol is a fashion model, a lovely girl — real California style. She's blonde, blue eyed, with all the right parts in all the right places. She's completely oblivious to the effect that she has on the passing male population. She's the gorgeous girl next door.

Carol lives in a small quiet street just south of the main drag in the Palisades. The street lies closer to the cliffs than to the hills, thus giving a fantastic view of the Pacific Ocean from every front window. On a clear day you can see Catalina Island lying twenty-six miles off the coast. Carol is definitely a happening chick.

Elvis reined the chariot to a stop just down the block from the target house. I got out and told the guys to keep low in the car while I went to get her. The idea was to surprise her, remember.

Like a thief in the night, I soft-pawed it down the side of her house and silently stole up to her bedroom window. My tapping on the glass must have shaken her, if the sound of her voice was anything to go by. 'Who's there? Who is it?'

'Carol, it's me, Steve,' I whispered.

'What do you want? What time is it?' Carol's sleepy voice was coated in slight irritation. I had to act fast or I'd blow it for sure.

'Come out. I've got a surprise for you. There's someone I want you to meet. Come on.'

'You're crazy!' she said. 'It's two in the morning. I'm sleeping. Go away! Call me tomorrow.' Carol was definitely far from pleased with my visit.

I had to think of something quick or the whole plan would explode in flames. 'Please Carol, come out for a moment, you won't regret it, I promise. Just throw something on and get out here.'

'OK, just wait a couple of minutes. This better be good.'

'Oh, it will be, I promise you,' I said, my voice breaking above the whisper line. 'Just hurry up!'

About two minutes later, the door eased open and Carol Randall, dressed in slippers and a long white teeshirt, draped to her knees, stepped into the air. She was still not exactly happy with my invasion. 'Come on,' I said. 'We have to go out to the street.'

'Wait a minute! Hang on! What are we doing? What's this all about? I'm not meeting anyone like this.' Carol was starting to protest vehemently.

'Come on. You look fine. I guarantee you won't be disappointed. In fact, you'll freak.'

I now had Carol on the move and we were fast approaching the waiting Cadillac. As we reached curb side the darkened window in the driver's door slowly descended, revealing the sensual, smiling face of Elvis Presley.

'Hello Carol,' Elvis's dulcet Memphis tone was purring.

'You're lovely, just like Steve said.' Carol Randall tried to speak, but the words wouldn't come. In fact, her whole face was frozen in disbelief. She just stood in stoned silence desperately trying to catch her breath. Her mouth was locked in opened amazement. Her eyes were on stalks, almost crashing out on to her beautifully chiselled cheekbones. She started to shiver with what I thought must be the early morning air. It was only when the colour deserted her face and her eyes rolled back into shut-down that I began to worry. Luckily, my reactions were quick enough to break her fall as she collapsed like a stringless puppet backwards onto the cement sidewalk. Carol was out for the count. Zonked by her fantasy encounter. It was now nearly 3 a.m.

To say that Elvis, Cliff and I were worried is an understatement. We had to do something and quick before some curious, local blue suit men fell upon the scene. Like post-haste. Cliff jumped out of the car, at the same time telling Elvis to stay cool. We gently lifted Carol to her feet. She had now started to regain reality although she still had at least one foot in never-never land. Slowly we guided her back across the lawn and up the path by the side of her house to the unlocked door through which she earlier had stepped. By now, she was fully back in the land of the living.

'What happened? Where am I?' Carol's voice was an excited rasp. 'Was that really Elvis? Did he really speak to me?' Her excitement was gathering momentum. 'Where is he? Steve, where's Elvis? Where did he go? Please, let me speak to him again. Please!'

Now that Carol was safely inside her house, she was becoming extremely anxious. Cliff and I decided that we'd better split in cut time. The red dawn was starting to sneak an entrance. That could prove to be tricky if someone spotted the waiting limo and became inquisitive.

As we started for the door on swift paws, we decided to put confused Carol out of her misery. 'Yeah baby,' I said. 'That really was Elvis Presley.'

Before I could breathe another word, Cliff came up with a solid closer. 'Oh, wait a minute Carol, Elvis was here but he has now definitely left the area.'

That said, we slipped out into the early morning mist. The night was history. New adventure was waiting.

A Day at the Beach

The main street in the Palisades village was buzzing with enthusiastic, young beach refugees, still dressed for the sand and sea, but refusing to relent and return to their homes.

The late summer afternoon sizzled. A whisper of wind breathed freshness throughout the steaming Pacific Palisades community as if it was God's reward for surviving the day's baking heat. Frothy white clouds were beginning to disappear as the electric blue sky battled against the inevitable grey arrival of early evening. The sun, having morphed into a sullen, bloodshot eye, was rapidly drowning beneath the darkening waves of the Pacific Ocean.

The day's excessive temperatures had sucked their energy, thereby giving them an excuse to linger at the various coffee shops and cafés, sipping ice tea, cokes and root beer floats, as they cooled their libidos and excitedly planned evening adventure.

Lacy ribbons of steam, like lethargic poltergeists were hovering above the cooling sidewalks, while the stoic palm trees lining Sunset Boulevard were beginning to paint long, fingered shadows across the landscape, as a river-flow of traffic made its slow pilgrimage homeward.

From the Allegro music shop, a few yards away, muted strains of Pat Boone's latest chart topper 'Love Letters in the Sand' filtered through the surrounding conversations creating a muffled symphony of contentment.

I was out of puff from the excitement of the morning and was happy to have captured empty space at a small, sidewalk café next to the Thrifty Drug Store. The outside tables offered comfortable seating and shaded refuge from the oppressive heat that clung in the air like the last guest to leave an all-night party.

I had slipped a pair of cut-off Levis over my clammy swim trunks. A borrowed, vomit-patterned Hawaiian shirt, at least two sizes too big, draped my shoulders like a gaudy shroud. My sock-less feet, crammed into well-worn, brown penny Loafers, were raging at the irritating discomfort caused by the few remaining atoms of sand, that had gone under cover between my toes. The salty scent of the sea clung to my suntanned arms and face like a second skin, humming with the throbbing burn of the day.

Affecting a mannered slouch like James Dean in *Rebel Without a Cause* and with an attitude designed to impress, I sat in moody silence slowly sipping a lemon coke, wishing that it were a cold Budweiser instead.

Natalie Wood had changed into a short, white, sleeveless summer dress that covered her two-piece, flowered swimsuit. White-rimmed, Ray-Ban sun-glasses clung to the brim of a pale yellow, stetson-shaped hat that rested confidently on her head, crowning her dazzling features.

Above and opposite: Natalie Wood and I exhibit our gymnastic skills for the fan magazines.

Her Russian heritage sparkled from the depth of her almond-shaped mahogany eyes. Though remarkably beautiful, Natalie had always retained a sweet humility and tenderness coupled with an appealing glow of vulnerability. This produced was an explosive package of sensual, feminine dynamite. Her effect was clearly evident earlier in the day when her appearance at State Beach sent shock waves throughout the gathered social bystanders.

Having returned from changing, Natalie had settled into the seat opposite me. The fading sunlight cast a nimbus around her head, amplifying her exquisite facial beauty. 'Sorry I took so long,' she said. 'I had to make a quick phone call.' Her radiant smile floated across the table like a gentle wind tiptoeing though a virgin wheat field. 'Steve why are you acting so moody? Is something wrong? What's up?' Natalie pulled the flimsy paper from around a straw and carefully pushing it into her waiting

RESTAURANT

Coca-Cola, began to stir the ice. Her quizzical gaze hung in limbo as she waited for an answer.

'I'm cool. Nothing's wrong,' I mumbled, affecting a practiced nonchalance. 'I'm just digging the scenery,' I lied. My brain was out to lunch, locked in the freezing grip of insecurity, afraid to be myself and too shy to admit the truth.

I was absolutely mad about Natalie and overflowed with desire, but emotional rust had blocked up the machinery needed for me to kick out the old fear of rejection. Therefore my brooding attitude was foolishly designed to make me appear interesting and to hopefully convince her that I had magnetic attraction, not just childish charisma.

Natalie and I had shared great moments of fun earlier in the day. She'd sparkled with innocent glamour, while I made the most of my gymnastic ability, calculated to impress her.

We'd arrived at the beach early, before the usual tangle of poseurs laid claim to what they considered to be their territory. Along with us was Earl Leaf, Hollywood's supreme magazine photographer. We were there to play out some fantasies and generally bound about like kids, in and out of the waves, while Earl photographed the action for the fan magazines.

The day had gone great and Earl had stoked the fire of his imagination grabbing some solid shots, as Natalie set flames to my passion.

By four o'clock the sun's fiery blaze had taken its toll and we decided to call it a wrap and head for cooler pastures.

Earl, however, had other business plans and split for his Hollywood homestead, leaving Natalie and me to check out a suitable oasis.

With the top off the Corvette and our faces in the wind, Natalie and I headed away from the beach and up Chataqua Drive, towards the sheltering embrace of the Palisades. I was desperate to grab some quality time, to let her know my feelings. Throughout the time that I'd spent with Natalie my heart had been battered by the force of her beauty and personality, dizzying me in a spin of desire.

There was so much that I wanted to say, but I was spellbound in an awkward silence.

By the time we'd found a place to park and had walked a block to the chosen café, Natalie's charm had superseded my bravery. I could only hear the thumping pulse of my heart urging me to let the truth hang out — to tell her how I felt — to ask to see her again. I glanced at my watch. Time was running out. I had to make a move before it was too late.

Finally gathering my nerve and with kaleidoscopic thoughts raging through my ego, I downed what remained of my Coca-Cola. After a momentary hesitation I took the plunge. 'Natalie — um — uh — there's something I want to ask you. I don't know exactly how to say this, but — uh — uh can we get together again — and maybe go out for dinner or something?' I started fumbling my words. I was desperate to recapture my cool. 'I really had a groovy time today — and — ah — is it OK if I call you?' My mouth was tripping over my brain — racing ahead. 'Listen — um how about next weekend? I'll call you. OK?'

The melody in Natalie's gentle laugh was number one with a bullet. 'Of course you can call me, Steve. I'll have to check to see if I've got anything on. Call me. I'll let you know.' She paused momentarily, as if regrouping her thoughts. 'Listen Steve, there's something I must tell you…' At that moment Natalie's attention spun to the street and focused on a slowly approaching silver-blue sports car. The driver was obviously looking to meet someone. Natalie stood up and began waving frantically at the gleaming carriage, as it nosed to a stop leaving the motor idling. I couldn't help but notice her sudden excitement. Her body language said everything, as she hurriedly gathered her things. Kissing me swiftly on the cheek she gave a breathless goodbye and raced toward the waiting chariot. As they motored swiftly away toward early evening, the sun's fading rays highlighted the handsome, chiselled face of Robert Wagner at the wheel. It was then that I knew exactly what Natalie had wanted to tell me.

Appointment With Zamba

Kathy Case was excited. She knew where we were going and leaned her head against my shoulder in contented approval, her ink black hair, like a moonless night, spilled across my chest.

A rapturous smile radiated from the exquisite face of Kathy Case snuggled in the seat next to me, her glow lighting a pathway through the still clinging darkness. Waves of shadows floated like phantoms across the road in front of us as we sped through the San Fernando Valley northward toward Escondido and Vasquez Rocks.

The clock had ticked four a.m. an hour earlier, as we drove away from Beverly Hills, snaking along the deserted blacktop through Cold Water Canyon over to the valley side of Hollywood. Dwindling patches of fog glided like graceful ghosts along the highway ahead, delaying Sunday morning's shining arrival. We had a stop to make that would take about two hours out of our journey. Before we met with James Dean at the Santa Barbara Road Races, we had arranged an important visit.

Emptying out of Cold Water Canyon on to Ventura Boulevard, we headed north west toward Antelope Valley. Behind us fingers of sunlight had already begun breaking through the fog, painting the sparse landscape with flickering splashes of golden sepia.

Kathleen Case was the most stunning girl I'd ever met. Not only was she gorgeous to look at, but she was strikingly beautiful inside as well. Her alabaster skin, glacier blue eyes and ballet dancer's grace contradicted her great sense of humour and spirit of adventure. Her gentle soul had touched my heart with tips of wonder. In the short time that I'd been running the Hollywood gauntlet I knew instinctively that I would never again meet anyone else like her. I was in love for the first time and the whole world was singing.

We'd been driving for about an hour when at last we crossed over the Sierra Pacific Railroad tracks near Agua Dulce Canyon. Following the road, we wound along uphill, finally turning right on to Escondido Canyon Road. A few hundred yards further on and we'd arrived, accompanied by the ascending heat of a

Above: Big smiles for the cameras.

My Darling,
Is the most
wonderful person. one
could dream of finding
I could not lose
your love or this love
I have for you — ever
Kathleen

dazzling morning. Again turning right we slowed up and cruised passed a chain-link fence, reining to a stop in a barren parking area. Fastened across the open gate hung a sign blazing with the words Nature's Haven. We'd arrived at the unique homestead of Ralph Helfer, Hollywood's masterful wild animal trainer.

Kathy and I, along with Budd Albright, often visited Ralph's amazing training facility, forever fascinated by his remarkable ability in understanding animals. Because of our affinity for all creatures great and small, Ralph always received us with a welcoming smile, allowing us an open invitation to his ranch whenever we liked - that is, as long as we were respectful and let it be known beforehand that we were coming. We all had great admiration for the work carried out at Nature's Haven, therefore touching base beforehand was the very least we could do to show Ralph our respect.

I'd met Ralph Helfer by chance at a pet shop in Los Angeles. I can't recall exactly why I'd gone there. Perhaps it was fate that had lured me away from my normal patch on the Westside of town. It's conceivable that my destiny was preordained. Whatever it was, that accidental encounter with Hollywood's supreme animal trainer led to my becoming caught up with the intricacies of the animal planet and eventually being overwhelmed with love for Zamba, the world's greatest Lion.

Kathy and I got our first introduction to Zamba when he was just six weeks old. We sat shaded from the sun, gently stroking his soft, flaxen fur, reacting with anthropomorphic translations to his every vocal utterance. Kathy was rewarded with the sandpaper surface of Zamba's tongue licking her face. He was no fool. His instinct must have recognized Kathy's joyful spirit.

Kathy and I travelled to Nature's Haven most weekends. On occasion we would bring a few of our animal loving friends along to bear witness to Ralph Helfer's magical ability at understanding even the most ferocious beast. He taught us that each animal has its own distinct personality and to always bear in mind that they are not domestic creatures. Treat them with respect and always

Above: Zamba checks out the action in Beverly Hills while Hugh O'Brian, Kathy and I try to contain his enthusiasm.

remember that they can be dangerous. They could turn vicious at any moment, so be cautious and never turn your back. They can only be trained, never tamed like a household pet.

We took everything that was said on board and acted accordingly, thereby being allowed to spend entire weekends at Nature's Haven, learning the ropes about what it takes to live amongst and to train feral beasts of the wild.

Over the many weeks Kathy and I became close with Zamba. Looking out from his enclosure, as if with conscious awareness, he'd instantly recognize us and begin rubbing his body against the fencing like a contented house cat, soliciting to be stroked. It was a sight that always thrilled my heart. Zamba loved and respected people. We were two people who loved and respected him.

One fine day, along with Ralph Helfer, Kathy and I drove Zamba to Beverly Hills and walked with him on a sight seeing excursion down Rodeo Drive. I was convinced that the lion was star struck when on that occasion he insisted on stopping in order to speak with Hugh O'Brian, the star of the popular TV series, *The Legend of Wyatt Earp*. I'm not sure what they talked about, but they seemed to get along famously.

Glancing at my wristwatch I saw that we'd made good time and that we'd be able to have a cup of coffee with Ralph and lay some love on Zamba before we once again hit the road for Santa Barbara.

Switching off the engine, Kathy and I stepped from the Corvette into a glorious day that smelled of dry brush and contented wildlife. Under a blue ceramic sky, ferocious heat from the Mojave Desert was just beginning to announce intention, although the sun's prickly face had yet to make an all out appearance.

A whisper of wind swirled the dust around our feet, as we approached Ralph Helfer's gracious residence. He was already on the porch, waiting to greet us. The early morning cast spangles of sunlight through the surrounding forest of trees that sheltered his welcoming home.

'Hi, Guys! You want to have some coffee before you check on Zamba?' Ralph was in a garrulous mood. The weight of time spent working under intense sunshine highlighted the earnest smile on his face. His pale eyes twinkled with sincerity.

'Yeah, Ralph, I could sure use a cup. Kathy and I have a long drive ahead of us when we leave here. Right, baby?' I said looking at Kathy.

'Steve and I are heading for Goleta Airport in Santa Barbara to watch Jimmy Dean. He's competing in the Road Races with his Porsche Speedster.' Kathy's crystal blue eyes were beaming with expectation as she slowly sipped the freshly poured coffee.

'Jimmy's a great driver,' I injected. 'He did really well at Palm Springs. Finished first in the novice class and second in the main event. I don't want to miss his first heat, therefore we gotta shake it up.'

'I'm sure that Zamba won't mind your hasty visit this time,' Ralph said with a chuckle, at the same time winking at Kathy. 'Come on! Bring the coffee with you. He's been waiting to see you.'

With a firm grip on our coffee cups we moved off the porch toward the direction of Zamba's functional enclosure. As we approached we could see a mound of golden fur extending from a space between two giant tree trunks, meticulously arranged as to offer the lion a shady retreat from the usually blistering desert temperatures. We hadn't gone more than a few yards when the

lion's instincts had him up and striding toward us with a kingly grace. Arriving at the fencing, Zamba stood silently flicking his tail, his eyes shining with a steady golden glaze, monitoring our approach, shaking with evident excitement. He'd matured quite a bit since we'd last seen him. There was a small billow of dark brown fur beginning to develop under his neck and circling around his magnificent head. His paws seemed enormous.

'Wow, that's Steve and Kathy with Ralph. I haven't seen them for a while. I hope Kathy scratches my ears like she always does. I'm sure that Steve will stroke me under my chin and ask me in a stupid voice if it feels good. What does he expect me to say? Perhaps if I act a bit cutesy and purrrr they'll take me to Beverly Hills again.' The power of imagination is inspiring.

We stayed stroking Zamba longer than planned. I glanced at my watch and suddenly realised that we'd have to put down fast paws ourselves if we wanted to make Santa Barbara in time to catch Jimmy's first race. Turning to Ralph I said, 'I'm sorry, man, but we really have to split post haste or we're not gonna make it. Thanks for the coffee and for chaperoning us with Zamba.' We shook hands and I started for the car. Ralph followed part way. Laying a gentle kiss on Kathy's cheek, he said his farewell, turned and headed back across the expansive area just as Zamba let out a mellifluous roar. I stopped for a moment and looked back. The lion seemed crestfallen. I could have sworn that sadness had captured his furry expression. William Shakespeare's words played across my memory: 'Parting is such sweet sorrow.'

Shimmering curtains of heat bounced off the highway in front of us as we sped southwest toward Santa Barbara. We had been extremely lucky not to have encountered trouble with the Highway Patrol, as I'd been really cranking the Corvette's speedometer into the red. The kaleidoscopic display of winged insects, splattered across the windshield gave an indication of our ramped speed. Luckily the Sunday morning traffic was sparse.

The Corvette's engine hummed in harmony with the rhythm of the road, but our journey was spilling into a losing pace with

Left: Zamba's kiss is like sandpaper on Kathy's skin.

time. I surrendered to road safety and slowed down. It was a glorious morning and I felt curiously alive, as if God had flushed my lungs with oxygen. The long drive had instilled a quality of enchantment that granted me a reprieve from stress caused by my state of anxiety.

Kathy zippered up her brown, roll-neck jacket under her chin and tied her cream coloured scarf tightly over her head, preventing the wind from distressing her hair. We drove in silence. Rushing currents of air exhaled across the Corvette's open cockpit as we ate up the highway making it impossible for spoken words to be understood. The sky had turned a deeper shade of blue. Splinters of sunlight danced across the windshield with the flickering movement of a serpent's tongue. Kathy, with sunglasses protecting her eyes, scrunched down in the seat, shielding herself from the unruly swirls of the air stream.

The dashboard clock announced that we were running late. Hopefully the first race hadn't already kicked off. Once again putting pedal to the metal, we were rocketing along the highway on wheels of fury.

We arrived at Goleta Airport just as Jimmy was finishing practice laps around the 2.2 mile circuit along with the under-1500cc engine group of competitors. When we finally caught up with him in the pits I couldn't help but notice that a sullen attitude had invaded his demeanour. Something had gone wrong with the Porsche while he was out on the track and he was anything but happy. Jimmy immediately went into a huddle with Bill Tunstall, his friend and pit crew manager. After twenty minutes of tinkering with the engine and scrutinizing the under carriage, everything seemed set to go. Jim's body language still showed extreme displeasure as he and Bill pushed the wounded Speedster to the start line for the first race. The flag was dropped and Jimmy, starting from eighteenth on the grid, shot through the pack balls out, like a man possessed. After a few laps he made it up to fourth place before a blown piston ended his day. Jimmy was turbulent with the situation. A disconsolate James Dean,

Right: James Dean looks concerned before his first race at Santa Barbara.

along with Bill Tunstall loaded the stricken Porsche Speedster on to a rented transporter that would deliver the car to Competition Motors in Hollywood and into the hands of Rolf Wutherich for repair work on the broken engine.

Although Jimmy was not really in a talking mood after his disappointment, I tried to leave him with a few words of encouragement before splitting for home. 'Don't fret it. Just chalk it up to the evils of motor racing. There's always another race meeting.'

'Yeah, man, whatever you say.' Jim mumbled under his breath, his face incapable of a smile, as he turned and moved away. Kathy and I were left standing.

Right: Kathy and I were unaware of the tragedy as we attended an event at The Hollywood Palladium on that fateful evening.

James Dean was born to be wild. It was part of his makeup to take chances. Whatever his agenda he had a tremendous talent for motor racing. As far as he was concerned finishing second was not acceptable. He was in it to win it.

Once more in the Corvette, Kathy and I were homeward bound. Weekend traffic had gathered on the road for Sunday drive time. I decided to take it easy and enjoy the moments. Rolling south on Highway 101 time seemed suspended. I sneaked a furtive glance at Kathy's fragile features, reflecting in the reddening afternoon light. My heart soared at her beauty, glimmering with the radiance of a Rubens painting. I had never felt more in love than at that moment.

Thunderous waves crashed against the shoreline as we cruised south along the Pacific Coast Highway. We were under an hour away from home when I decided to pull into a lay-by close to Trancas Beach. Shutting the engine off, I removed my suede bomber jacket and draped it around Kathy's chilly shoulders. We huddled against each other in silence watching the series of waves swell and rush on to the beach, hissing as they retreated, gathering up shells and tiny pebbles and dragging them back from the safety of the shore. Exhilaration flooded my heart. We stayed until the sky relinquished its amber glow and faded into the tapestry of twilight.

Sunday, May 29,1955 had delivered an outstanding day. Experiencing love for the first time had removed the rust from the walls of my heart. For that reason I was optimistic about the future. However, fate is often unkind and seldom generous.

James Dean had only four months left to live.

Dick Williams

MIRROR-NEWS ENTERTAINMENT EDITOR

DEAN'S TRAGIC DEATH CAUSES GIRLS TO FAINT

James Dean's sudden death should be a grim warning to the other fast drivers in the movie colony to take it easy.

Dean was by no means the only filmite to go racing around in a fast foreign car.

One gal who comes immediately to mind is Anita Ekberg. She drives her Jaguar like it was a race horse. Those associated with her generally decline any offer of a "lift" in her car to some destination, because it's such a hair-raising experience.

Nor is Anita alone. The sports-car craze has fascinated the stars and starlets and the idea seems to be that if you have a sports car you've got to gun it up to 50 in the first half block.

Dean's death Friday night cast a swift pall over Hollywood. It is rare when such a relative newcomer commands so much attention.

The word spread like a prairie fire through the giant Moulin Rouge, packed with celebrities for the WAIF Ball, after Mike Connolly, trade paper columnist, arrived to report the news.

The public grieving by the young girls hit the kind of peak it must have had back in the era when Rudolph Valentino passed away. In one small Italian Hollywood restaurant where I stopped by, four or five girls were sobbing, another was in hysterics and I saw one grieving doll escorted quietly out.

Kathy Case fainted when she got the news and Lori Nelson collapsed in tears, according to Variety's Army Archerd.

The reason Kathy fainted was because her long-time "steady," Steve Rowland, had been invited to accompany Dean to Salinas for the week-end road races.

Only the fact that funeral services will be held in Marion, Ind., Dean's birthplace, saves the occasion from probably turning into a maudlin spectacle here.

At the time of his death a new contract was being negotiated for Dean with Warner Bros. which would have paid him $100,000 a picture, Variety divulged. This will give you an idea of the rapidity with which this boy had shot to the top.

There has been considerable speculation around town on whether or not Dean will win a nomination for a posthumous Academy Award for his portrayal of the moody Caleb in "East of Eden."

My belief is that he will almost certainly win a nomination. He should.

Above: The Dick Williams column comments on the tragic news.

Unexplained Events at Club Renaissance

An unnatural silence distilled the surroundings, but I was too switched on to notice a subliminal bank of whispers that was tracking my every step.

I don't know why I felt so strange. An uncanny blanket of sadness draped my shoulders like an ill-fitting shroud of despair. Maybe it was my slanted mind, bugging itself again as it had since I'd last driven by here three Sundays back. Here I was again, but this time I was prepared to kick out all the jams. My body was ready to rock. Tonight promised to be a special night at Club Renaissance.

Nosing the Corvette into an empty slot near the top of the hill on La Cienga Boulevard I cut the engine and sat for a long moment watching little rillets of rainwater hurry bits of paper and discarded cigarette butts along the gutter toward their final journey. The uneasy disorientation that I had felt earlier had now all but disappeared. The time had come. I shoved all remaining negatives out the back and threw a final glance in the rear view mirror, checking that everything looked cool. Then with trepidation, taking care not to smudge my clean Levis, I stepped out into the soggy, evening atmosphere. Wearing my black leather flight jacket gave me assurance. Anticipation of what lay ahead powered my excitement. On foot, but with caution in my steps, I turned right at the top of the hill then quickened my pace along the murky sidewalk. It was only a few yards to the drop zone.

The clock was ticking around nine o'clock somewhere, but darkness had arrived on the scene early along with a relentless summer drizzle, making it seem impossible to breathe. Cars with steamed up windows exploded past, casting up waves of dirty water from the puddles that had formed on Sunset Boulevard. It seemed as if my whole existence had pulled on a shadowy overcoat with the collar turned up, protecting me against the descending gloom.

Across the street, Ciro's nightclub blurred and tweaked through the sweating darkness, shape-shifting into some strange geometry, like a haunted house in a child's nightmare. A momentary thought flashed like a beacon. Ciro's nightclub reigns as a plush entertainment palace catering to film-land's self-polished glitterati. But Club Renaissance is Hollywood hardcore — a discreet watering hole for the new centurions.

I stood for a moment gathering my thoughts. Then with decision in my stride, I edged out of the descending shadows and headed down the slight incline toward the grinning entrance to Club Renaissance.

Like a chimera rising from the ashes of the 1920s stood the crumbling structure that embraces Club Renaissance. Its shabby exterior defies the weather like a faded movie star who's desperate to recapture the glory days.

The constant gentle rain licked at my face like a serpent's tongue, probing for answers to questions that I'd been afraid to ask.

The club's portal squinted at me through the mist. This hideaway has always been considered, by the cream of Hollywood's groove set, to be the hippest den to be seen at — especially on Sunday jazz nights. Tonight was no exception.

The footbridge that spanned the fall-away gulch separating Sunset Boulevard from the club's dimly lit entrance had seen better days. It swayed under the weight of clamouring, shirtsleeved clubbers. All seemed strangely oblivious to the warm, soaking rain. A vocal cacophony of unimportant pseudo-bohemian subjects was being loudly argued. Stoned voices ignited a symphony of discord into the evening's claustrophobic atmosphere. Vaguely familiar faces floated by in clusters like interlopers from an imaginary world. Most were like zombies, having drowned a long time ago in their own tears of self-pity. The sunglasses they wore kept reality out and rebellion at the ready — a collage of angry souls with nothing to be angry at.

With a nervous intake of breath I brushed across the footbridge, past the gathered poseurs and squeezed through the curtain of rain that dripped and drizzled over the club's crowded entrance.

Entering the club's diffused interior was like stumbling into a drunk's subconscious thoughts. The walls were festooned with music posters and weird contemporary artwork, like Salvador Dali on the road to hell.

Club Renaissance was packed and throbbing with an assembly of intensified, vociferous human sounds, blending in with the jazz emanating coolly from the bandstand. The Wes Montgomery Trio was keeping things real.

The two large connecting rooms were stashed to capacity with the breathing, talking class. The cigarette smoke and humidity was suffocating and I found it difficult to focus through burning eyes.

Things had kicked off early and were already in full swing, as I pushed my way deeper inside. A Clifford Brown 'wannabe' had joined the cats on the bandstand and was improvising on Dizzy's 'Groovis Mentis'. All was cool.

For some strange reason I just couldn't catch the beat. I felt out of tune and out of time. My thoughts were still in a kaleidoscopic state of confusion and I was nearing crash city. Once again I felt the loneliness creep in with a mouthful of promises and a bellyful of unhappiness. Insecurity has a funny taste.

Why was I feeling so out of body? Was I trying to kid myself? Pretending that I was only 'here for the beer?' Fear of admitting my true intentions gripped me, as I madly searched for a friendly face and a place to cool my rising anxiety. My eyes caressed the scene. Many of Hollywood's new young guns, in various states of sobriety, pockmarked the crowd. Troy Donahue, Robert Blake, Dean Stockwell, Dennis Hopper and John Saxon were hanging in there, surrounded by a bevy of beautiful young starlets. All were desperately seeking attention — barely aware of anyone but themselves. Colourfully dressed in clinging skirts and low-cut tops, the girls loudly advertised their availability.

Considering the current state of my mind, I offered them no recognition. I definitely didn't want conversation. A wave of nausea swept over me as I franticly searched for an available perch. My God! What was happening to me?

Suddenly the space I was standing in seemed airless. Once again I was finding it difficult to catch my breath. My vision was blurred, with tears of frustration, as the room became a living, breathing thing with lungs of its own — hissing and scratching — tearing at my skin. The noise of exuberance from the evening's players became drowned in static, as if broadcasting from a distant radio station being ravaged by storms.

A whisper of wind exhaled behind me as the famous faces of John Cassavetes and Sal Mineo floated by like phantoms. I was confused. What were they doing here? They were supposed to be in New York. They'd left only two days ago after we'd wrapped up filming on *Crime in the Streets*. Here they were, still dressed in the film's wardrobe. I tried to catch their attention, but they looked right through me and disappeared. My eyes squinted against the smoky surroundings. My head was pounding, as I struggled to reassemble my scrambled perception.

Bursting through the night's confusion, Budd Albright, dressed in tan chinos, and rain-sodden brown Loafers was heavily into a continual action replay with a double of Debra Paget. Once again I was the invisible man — or possibly it was that Budd only had eyes for the Debra double.

I was fresh out of reason. My senses were splintered as I felt myself cartwheeling through galaxies of cascading shards of moonlight. In desperation I clung to a comet's tail. I prayed for an oasis before I lost what was left of my sanity.

From out of the maelstrom an empty table magically materialized. I quickly grabbed a chair, staked my claim and searched around for someone to help quench my thirst. No one showed interest. From a hollow chamber deep within the club I thought I detected the sub-audible echo of my name being called. Turning to look, I felt something tug feverishly at my clothes, pulling me to the rim of an abyss, willing me to step into the silent darkness.

Above: Tony Curtis and I meet up for a fan magazine photo shoot.

Then suddenly, spiralling from a whirlpool of glorious colour, there she was, a gorgeous, smiling goddess of pin-up perfection, her breasts struggling to escape her skimpy, white uniform — golden hair showering her alabaster shoulders. She was a vision straight from a Vargas calendar. A shimmering nimbus of light encircled her head. Alluring words requested my order, as her velvet-coated voice exhaled seductively in my ear. 'Hi baby, I've been waiting for you to turn up. I'll get you anything you want. What would you like?' For a moment I didn't answer. I couldn't. I just stared in disbelief at her dazzling beauty. Then, gathering up my cool and being extra careful not to spoil the image that I had of myself, I took her head in my hands and without uttering a word, pulled her face gently to my waiting lips. Her response was like a gathering storm of ferocious hunger, eager to be satisfied. The banging of my heart could have drowned out the iron-shod hooves of a hundred horses galloping down a steel highway.

All at once a familiar form loomed in the din. He wore a blue alpaca sweater and concern in his eyes. Twisting in among the scrambled mass of ghostly humanity and beer-soaked, hard-topped tables he headed in my direction. Without a word to me, and grabbing one of the empty chairs, Tony Curtis sat down in anger. He offered no friendly banter, as he spat out his irritation. 'Hey, Rosie, what's your game? I thought that we were getting it on tonight? What's this shit with Steve?'

Rosie didn't answer, nor did she acknowledge that Tony was even there. Her mouth had become part of mine. Her tongue searched and probed every corner of my soul. The flames of her passion soothed me with choking precision. The taste of her lips was beyond reality. I was in freefall. Lifting the skirt of her tiny, white waitress uniform and dropping her order pad, she eased around enabling herself to straddle me, as I sat rooted in the chair. She pushed her luscious body against me, riding furiously up and down, desperate to be impaled. The fragrance of her skin drove me into a galloping frenzy, as I frantically pulled her into me, almost crushing the breath from our bodies.

An air of carnival was suddenly gathering momentum in Club Renaissance.

The room was beginning to overflow with sociable vultures, eagerly pushing forward for a voyeuristic view, cheering our erotic performance. Voices were rising in a mixture of excitement and jealous disapproval. An ever-increasing density of formless shapes began to encircle us, like B-movie Indians surrounding a stricken wagon train. One frantic voice, straining above the others, was shouting my name with desperation. The decibel level became ear-shattering thunder. I fought to stay oblivious, but it kept hammering at me, shocking my system. The voice boomed louder, cheering me on. 'Come on Steve. Come on.' Intensity was gathering momentum jarring my brain — tearing apart my moments of exquisite, excruciating pleasure.

Then from the vortex of disembodiment, a tangled mass of tentacles snaked forward, whipping at my body — grabbing and shaking me like a rag doll. A dragon-like roar was breathing fire — screaming above my head. 'Come on, Steve. Come on. Get up.' Somehow through the distant haze I recognized the tone. It had morphed into the strident voice of my roommate, Michael Callan. 'Come on, man, Wake up! Wake up! You gotta get ready. Have you forgotten? Tonight's the big night — the opening of Club Renaissance. It should be a blast. There'll be loads of chicks! Come on! Hurry up. Don't wanna be late.'

'Yeah, OK, Mickey, thanks for waking me. Give me a couple of minutes to get it together.' I was struggling to clear my clouded head. 'On second thought — you go on. I'll see you there.' Mickey was just back from filming in New York and like a dog in heat, was desperate to get into gear and check out the action.

'That's cool Steve. See you there.'

An uncanny blanket of sadness draped my shoulders as I nosed the Corvette into an empty slot near the top of La Cienga Boulevard. I don't know why I felt so strange. Maybe it was the humidity and the early darkness along with a relentless drizzle that gave me the uneasy feeling. I sat for a moment gathering courage. After a quick glance in the rear view mirror I stepped out of the Corvette into the sweaty dampness, careful to avoid smudging my clean Levis. I checked my watch. It was loudly ticking — close to nine o'clock. I had to get moving. A weird feeling gripped me — as if God had left my body. An obvious explanation had to be anxiety fuelling my excitement. I put caution into my steps, as I made my way along the murky sidewalk toward the club's entrance. Maybe it was the descending gloom firing my imagination but I thought I heard someone whisper my name. I shrugged it off. My mind was playing tricks. I didn't notice a dark significance in the ever-thickening shadows. As I neared the misty entrance a black Jaguar, its paintwork reflecting jewelled prisms of light in the early evening rain, splashed to an eager stop at the curb. Crouching like a ghostly sentinel, it lingered in silence. The engine throbbed with the subtle intensity of its jungle namesake, as if awaiting my wary approach. 'Hey Steve. How's it hanging?' The handsome, animated features of Tony Curtis, ablaze with enthusiasm, appeared from the Jag's descending, curb side window. White plumes of breath streamed from his mouth, disappearing almost instantly into the heavy dampness. His vocal intonation pierced the trundling traffic's Sunday clatter. 'Hey listen, I'll catch you inside. There's bound be some great chicks tonight. I just gotta find a place to park. I'll check you later.'

A smile tiptoed across my face.

Hell, I suddenly felt great. Tonight I was gonna kick out all the jams at Club Renaissance.

Memoirs of a Hollywood Hitman

She was as hot as a fresh fucked fox in a forest fire and I, like a testosterone-driven naïve schoolboy, was yearning for a burning.

Dina was the type from which fantasies evolve — shaped to instil salacious desires in every red-blooded male that ever picked up a copy of *Esquire* magazine or thumbed through the pages of *Playboy* or any of the many pulp-fiction publications, craving the photographic pleasures from all those x-rated magazines resting out of reach on the top shelves of Hollywood's myriad news-stands. She was the empowered fantasy of all my dreams.

Her athletic body stood five feet seven inches off the ground and made the most of her allure in skin-tight faded jeans. Frayed cuffs fell loosely over the tops of well-worn rough-out leather flat-heeled cowboy boots. From their apparent condition you'd be hard pressed to know if they'd ever experienced a shine.

Her legs seemed to go on forever, drawing your eyes to the perfection of her narrow hips and the smooth flatness of her stomach, which on most occasions was teasingly exposed beneath a cut-off white tee shirt or a coloured cotton blouse, tied at the waist. Her tawny, sun-kissed hair tumbled loosely across her shoulders framing her exquisite facial features, stirring in the imagination the stencil for Helen of Troy. A radiant glaze danced from her pale green eyes as if defying the discovery of a mysterious secret. She did not possess the inflated breasts of a glamour model. Those nature blessed her with were small and well-shaped — with nipples that stood out and shouted at you 'touch me — feel me'.

A disarming smile creased her suntanned face and invaded my soul on the day that I first caught sight of her sitting alone at the original Hamburger Hamlet on the Sunset Strip, nursing the last sip from a large glass of ice tea. As she stood to leave her smoky pale green gaze floated over me like a shadow across a garden pond, igniting within me an explosion of uncontrollable desire. Her name was Dina Frost and, like most of Hollywood's young and beautiful hopefuls, she was out to make the grade. So was I — and I chased her until she caught me.

The five o'clock Hollywood afternoon was a Sea of Tranquility that lay basking in the warm August sunshine beneath a cloudless pale blue sky. It was Thursday and lust was overflowing my mind as I recklessly drove through the gathering traffic toward the Gaiety Café on the Sunset Strip. I'd spent most of the afternoon at a Santa Monica rehearsal studio where, along with Budd Albright and the rest of our band, the Exciters, I'd been putting together the final necessities in order to be ready for our Friday night opening at the Carolina Lanes Night Club, situated on the outer perimeter of Los Angeles Airport. It had been an intense few hours. My mind was somewhere else.

My libido was pushing overload as I angled the Corvette into a parking spot. I hastily stepped to the sidewalk and hot-footed my way down the hill, past Turner's Drugstore, turning left at the beginning of the Sunset Strip. Breaking into a run, I covered the short distance to the Gaiety Café in cut time. Bursting with anticipation I bounded through the café's smiling doorway, breathing heavily. Danger was already there dressed to thrill and staring into what remained of a lukewarm cup of Java. 'Hey babe! Sorry I'm late. The band rehearsals ran longer that I expected.' I was hoping that the reference to my musical capabilities and the fact that I was booked to open at the Carolina Lanes would stir Dina's carnal juices in my favour.

'Don't sweat it, sweetheart. I've only been here for a couple of minutes before you,' she said, nailing me with a laser beam stare. It was obvious from the state of the half-filled coffee cup that she was laying on a little white lie for my benefit. In that moment I knew that I was in like Flynn. All the weeks of effort I'd thrown down trying to capture her curves were about to come up shining. This time I was sure that I'd landed on 'lucky' and I could hardly believe it.

'Come on. Let's go to my place,' she said, her smile partially revealing a flash of perfect white porcelain. 'I'm only up the street. We can listen to records and capture the last rays before the sun checks out.'

Her words put a spell on me and like a panting puppy I stumbled over my paws as I followed after her, awash in her sensuous wake. My blood was on fire.

It was one of those modern small white houses that backed up against the hill above Sunset Boulevard on Larabee Drive. Although it wasn't a salubrious area, it was nevertheless a very fashionable place to reside. Smiles of approval and positive comments would usually occur whenever the question of where you based yourself rose up in conversation. It was considered a cool deal to live in a pad above the Sunset Strip.

We sat in the Corvette parked outside on the driveway with the motor idling, exchanging furtive glances. I was more than hot to trot, but something bothered me. 'Hey Dina,' I said. 'Are you sure that everything's cool? You're not married or living with anyone are you?'

'Don't worry Steve, everything's cool. I'm not married and I've been broken up with my boyfriend for a while. We don't live together any more. Anyway he's back East doing a TV show. Believe me, it's all cool.'

'OK. If you're sure,' I said. 'On second thought I'd better shift the Corvette to the street.' I backed the car out of the driveway and nosed into a spot a few yards down the block. There have been times in the past when I've felt a current of treachery, but because of my moral anchor I'd always managed to duck out of harm's way. This time however, my desire threw caution to the wind. Passion had taken over the controls. We slid out of the car and headed up the shady, tree-lined street.

As if to verify truth in her last statement, she suddenly pulled me to her and passionately kissed me, probing my mouth with her tongue.

The welcoming front door of her house came into sight and, pressing her body hard against me, we became one as she bundled us backward across a blanket of fresh-cut grass, up a stone pathway and through the entrance into the silence of her residence, kicking the heavy front door shut with the left heel of her booted foot.

Interior steps led from the entrance hall down into an open plan living room that flowed into the kitchen with only a blue tile-topped breakfast bar intervening. The room's minimalist decor was tasteful in a range of neutral colours. Besides a pair of armchairs and an unimpressive sideboard, an oversized L-shaped, cream leather sofa took up most of the region in front of a free-standing white television cabinet. As if in artistic harmony, a large rectangular glass topped coffee table strewn with books and fashion magazines fought for space on the crowded surface beneath a rectangular shaped, orange earthenware bowl, that was overflowing with an assortment of fresh-cut flowers and bits of driftwood. A light beige shag pile carpet covered the room wall-to-wall and followed down the short hallway disappearing underneath three closed doors that obviously opened on to separate bedrooms.

Squinting for focus around the sun-brightened room my eyes fell upon several framed photographs of what appeared to be happy, contented Dina in the arms of a swarthy Victor Mature look-a-like, whose slicked-back hair and flashy smile failed to hide a sinister edge. His meticulously groomed image personified Hollywood's motion picture perception of a 1930s Mafioso, keen with venomous intent. 'Who's that?' I said.

Dina had gone around to the kitchen and was reaching for a

glass in the cupboard above the bar. 'That's Mark, my ex.' Dina placed the empty glass on the counter top and circled around the bar stopping in front of me. 'Listen, Steve, I told you — we aren't together any more. Please sweetheart, don't think about it. It's not important. He's not with me. You are. And anyway like I said, he's not here. He's in New York doing a TV show.' An alarm bell went off in my head. Why were the photos still there? As if to stop me asking further questions she took both my hands in hers — and moving close she brushed my lips with the gentle touch of a butterfly's kiss. 'Come on, Steve. Follow me.' Something didn't add up, but with my rage of desire for Dina, all my sensibility had been flushed away. Obediently I trailed behind her.

We entered though the only door on the left at the end of the short passageway into a magnificent, all-white bedroom that faced the afternoon sun through a single sliding door. On close inspection I saw that on the outside was a small balcony, standing a few metres from the intimidating hillside.

A gigantic cream-coloured satin spread draped the oversized bed that commandeered most of the room's space. Soft brown satin-covered pillows and cushions were arranged across the area close to the headboard. Mirrored, built-in floor-to-ceiling closets stood opposite the bed's foot end. The shag pile carpet morphed into white from beneath a brass separation strip, secured to the floor between the bedroom's doorframe.

Dina sat on the bed stretching upward seductively. She then reached across to a Magnavox stereo unit that rested on a bedside table. The purifying soul voice of Sam Cooke sprang into life at the touch of a button. 'Steve, come sit here,' she said, patting a space next to her. At the same time she hooked the heel of one boot under the bed frame and pulled her foot free from the constraint of the leather. 'Come on, babe. Help me with the other one,' she said, as she lay back on the satin spread and teasingly stroked my stomach with the toe of her foot. The soft thud of her other boot as it landed on the carpet reignited a sudden surge of confidence, erasing all threads of lingering anxiety. I was inspired.

I suddenly felt that sex without danger could never be this exciting.

Dina sat up and pulled the rose coloured teeshirt over her head. The beauty of her exquisite naked breasts increased the intensity of my breathing. I was burning up in an inferno of lust as I hastily undressed and tossed my Levis and tee-shirt into a crumpled pile on the end of the bed. Flicking my Loafers to the floor, but neglecting to remove my socks, I hungrily moved toward her intoxicating beauty. My heart was hammering as I buried my face in the honeyed fragrance of her hair. I moved my lips to her neck, her throat then across her exquisite face until our opened mouths consumed the very seeds of our passion. Dina pushed me back, sat up and unfastened the belted jeans from around her waist. Arching her back she slid them effortlessly down her tanned thighs, finally kicking them to the floor. The sight of her magnificent, sculptured body sent shock waves through my system. At that moment I wasn't sure that I'd be able to confirm my status as a stud. There was a possibility that I'd bitten off more than I could chew.

'Why do you still have your socks and underpants on?' she whispered. 'Let me help you — underpants first.' Dina's head slowly began moving downward, gently kissing my chest, my stomach and then moving her moistened lips back to my mouth, she forced entry with her tongue. Lying across me she gently slipped her fingers under the elastic of my briefs searching for what had now become my tower of power. With the tenderness of a baby's hand her fingers encircled my manhood and softly stroked the fragile skin with gently increasing fervour. My breathing shot into overload. Molten lava flowed through my veins causing beads of perspiration to cascade down my forehead, stinging my eyes. Dina's moist lips glistened as she bent forward ready to taste my strength.

At that moment something jarred me — a noise like a door closing. I pushed Dina off and sat up as if I'd been stung with an electric cattle prod. 'What was that? Did you hear something?'

Fear paralyzed my movement and nausea squirmed within my gut. My heart skipped triple time into my throat.

'I didn't hear anything, Steve. You're imagining things.'

'Dina, I know I heard something. Please check it out!'

'Relax, it's probably nothing.'

Just then a voice sounded out with the aggressive authority of an army drill sergeant. 'Dina I'm back. Are you here? Where the hell are you? Deeeeeenaa!!'

Dina instantly grabbed her clothes from the floor. 'Oh shit! He's back.' Stark fear clouded the greenness of her eyes as she rocketed off the bed and raced to lock the door. 'Steve you'd better get the fuck outta here — now! He mustn't find you here. Get outta here. Go out through the glass door. Go! Hurry! I'll grab his attention.'

In that instant my premonition was confirmed. Sheer panic brought on confusion as I fumbled for my clothes. The fact that my socks had remained on gave me vital seconds as my feet slipped easily into my Loafers. Heavy footsteps clumped down the passage. 'Dina! Goddamn it where are you? Are you in the bedroom?' The cavernous voice seemed as if it had erupted from the bowels of the earth.

'Yeah baby, I'm in here. Give me a second. I'll be right out.' Dina's frightened eyes glistened with a hint of tears as she furiously indicated for me to hurry up.

There was no time for me to slip into my threads. Terror had turned me into a running man. In what seemed a microsecond I was out the glass door, over the balcony and scampering up through the brush that covered the overgrown hillside, Levis and tee-shirt in my hands and terror in my heart. Dragging my clothes I scampered like a rabbit fleeing the muzzle of a shotgun, through thorn-encrusted bushes and up the jagged rock-strewn hillside. Gasping for breath and desperate to stay clear of an exposed position, I snaked on my belly through the heavy undergrowth inflicting painful scratches the length of my body and tearing hunks of flesh from my hands. Worse than the pain was a feeling of vulnerability as descending phalanxes of shadows charged across the hillside introducing the gathering darkness and bringing along a bitter chill. A few yards further on appeared a break in the vegetation — a place where I could stop to clothe my trembling bones. Dressed at last I furtively stood and surveyed my surroundings. Streaks of blood patterned the front of my white tee-shirt. Worse than my discomfort was my sense of fragility and frustration at having been so naive.

Sunset Boulevard stretched below me. The early evening traffic bustled enthusiastically along the Strip, oblivious to my predicament. From my position as a fool on the hill I could just make out the back of Dina's house. I hoped that I'd successfully made a seamless escape and that I wouldn't read about the death of a starlet in the morning papers.

Taking cautionary steps I slowly picked my way down the rough strewn hillside to the cement safety of Sunset Boulevard. The undergrowth had taken a feeding frenzy off my body and I was struggling to remain focused.

Finally with my battered Loafers once more on friendly ground and being careful not to attract attention, I casually moseyed around the corner then swiftly bounded back up Larabee Drive to reclaim my parked Corvette. I fired up the engine. Home was only ten minutes away. I didn't look back.

Six o'clock the following morning thunder boomed in the distance announcing impending rain. I awoke from a restless sleep, scratching like a dog with an infestation of fleas. Fate had played the joker, but I didn't see the funny side. My entire body was blazing in the furnace of poison oak. Calamine lotion would come to my rescue, but my body would retain the nasty pleasure of the astringent fragrance. I'd been yearning for a burning, but I hadn't bargained on a four-alarm fire with all the bells and whistles. I didn't venture out for a week.

PUMPAGE PALACE

Hollywood Hills Drive in Laurel Canyon marches to the right off Lookout Mountain Avenue and slithers northward. Reaching for the sky, it snakes its way over a thin layer of damp sludge, left over from the much-needed torrential rain, that to the unfamiliar eye would seem to have washed away most of the Laurel Canyon hillside. Trees with bristling green boughs, still heavy with rain, sparkle and shimmer as if decorated for an early Christmas season. Their branches crowd the sunlight — allowing only intermittent shards of warm radiance to brighten the shadows, thus creating a lush stillness that hangs in the air as if protecting the sleepy community.

Patches of pavement begin to appear as the road becomes steeper, continuing skyward toward the summit, eagerly venturing on past the skeletal framework of future palatial homes, until at last it disappears up its own ass and comes face to face with a dead end conclusion in the tangled jungle at the crest of the imposing hillside.

The entire neighbourhood seems devoid of activity. No pedestrians have made an appearance. The usual children seen parading the street on bicycles or scampering from house to house have not ventured out to face the clinging dampness. Only the sporadic sound of a barking dog cracks the stillness confirming contentment throughout the peaceful canyon.

About ten yards below the summit, lying hidden behind a camouflage of thorny foliage is the peek-a-boo entrance to a secret passage. If one is of an inquisitive nature and prepared to fight the aggressive shrubbery — then after a few yards of struggle through the maze of underbrush, the expansive panorama of Beverly Hills and the Trousdale Estates will explode into view. The overgrown vegetation fronting the corridor has always provided perfect cover when protecting those fleeing illicit indiscretions or escaping the menace of hostile bailiffs.

A few yards before Hollywood Hills Drive kisses goodbye to its joyful journey skyward, a glass-fronted, solidly-built, modern white house appears like a sentry on tiptoes, supported by the density of the sheer rock hillside. With position above the winding road and head in the clouds, the view from the front room is a majestic canvas covering the entire city of Hollywood and places beyond — the perfect setting for seduction. This was the infamous residence shared by Jim Mitchum and me. It was our playground of passion. For reasons that need no explanation we christened it Pumpage Palace.

With Jim, it was the attack of the tall people. At six feet, four inches and with the face and fists of his father, Robert, Jim could handle most situations. He didn't suffer fools gladly, as many a wise ass found out to their own detriment. Jim's laid-back persona and enormous sense of humour belied extreme sensitivity that at times exposed hidden insecurity and created within him a blanket of moody silence.

Jim could handle any physical confrontation, but when it came to women it was an entirely different story.

Like all of us who were the sons and daughters of industry royalty, we constantly wrestled with the question of whether we were accepted for ourselves or because we were connected to important and influential Hollywood guns.

Jim had been at the front line fighting this battle for a long time and like me, had become a combat weary survivor of a litany of female insincerities.

Jim Mitchum was the physical clone of his father and most women were drawn to him like fleas to a hedgehog.

He wasn't happy about this but he'd learned to take control of his emotions. He'd learned to use this to his advantage. Once during a reflective moment Jim said, 'Girls seem to always want to come home with me to Mandeville Canyon (Robert and Dorothy Mitchum's home). I know the only reason is that they're hoping to meet my old man. I never tell them that he spends almost all his time at our farm in Maryland. Of course once they're there they always end up staying the night.' A lascivious smile sneaked across his face. 'Two can play that game, you know.'

Jim was a general in our army. He always shot straight from the lip and took no prisoners. His sense of humour was killing. Believe me, he needed it when dealing with the legion of Hollywood assholes that were forever trying on various scams and seductions — always for their own benefit.

Jim and I, along with Budd Albright, had a reputation to uphold. Our days of scoring pumpage are legendary in the chronicles of our minds. Together we rode the range of enjoyment forever on the lookout for sexual satisfaction from the amazing assortment of beautiful young female starlets who were more than amenable in fulfilling our lust driven desires.

The river of bullshit overflowed its banks. We told them everything that they wanted to hear. They in turn stroked our egos and breathlessly succumbed to our flattery and promises. Our over hyped self-esteem blinded us to the reality of Hollywood females and their devious intentions. We honestly believed that they all loved us. However, they had other agendas and ambitions and the quality of their performances were more than worthy of an Oscar. When the girls realized that we really couldn't help their careers they were up, up and away.

Our palace sat in a prime location high above the Laurel Canyon settlement. Unless you owned a helicopter there was only one way up and one way down. This worked to our advantage with the ladies when we insisted that it was too late for them to safely drive back down the hill. They'd always listen to reason and were happy to stay the night, making the journey down to sanity the following day.

The neighbourhood was a Shangri-La of social harmony, rife with struggling artists, musicians, actors and actresses, all shooting for the big time and more than willing to kick out all the jams and party for the universe.

Our immediate neighbours, Scott Brady and Max Baer Jr ran in twenty-four hour pleasure mode most nights of the week. The fall out from their separate villas shook the canyon's very foundation. Siren accompaniment and flashing red lights frequently announced the arrival of a black and white vehicle bearing the men in blue.

I recall a particular night when the walls of the Max Baer Jr domicile were bursting to near collapse with the resounding thunder of stoned enthusiasm. Jim, Budd and I were contributing to the chaos that was jamming the vibes way above the legal noise level.

Booze was the main instigator of our outrageous behaviour, designed to impress the flock of nubile chicks that were letting their availability all hang out.

I'd just stepped from the bathroom on unsteady feet, when I noticed a couple of characters in the hallway examining a handgun. It caught my interest so I stopped to ask if they'd let me check it out. With the arrogant panache of a pair of two-bit posers, they each took turns twirling the pistol like B-movie gunslingers before they handed over the 38 calibre Smith & Wesson Snub Nose. 'The gun's not loaded is it?' I slurred my words as I spoke.

'No man — it's cool,' came the reply. 'Go for it.' Not to be outdone and with alcohol clouding my intelligence, I palmed the pistol and immediately pointed it down the hall into the crowded festivity, aiming the piece at various players in attendance. Then like my outlaw character, Phin Clanton in the TV series, *The Legend of Wyatt Earp*, I began spinning the gun like a practised professional, pointing at various objects in the room, pretending to blow them away.

At that moment a luscious young chick, her red strapless dress doing its best to cling to her body, glided into the room on the arm of Meade Martin, a new hot face on the scene. 'Alright baby, hold it right there!' I said in my best Jack Webb impersonation, stopping her in mid-stride. The colour drained from her lovely features. Fear glazed over the blue of her eyes, as she faced the business end of blue steel. 'The name's Friday. I'm a cop.' Da da-da da! The *Dragnet* theme rolled from my lips. Subsequently pointing the Snub Nose in Meade Martin's direction I coolly voiced the words, 'Book him!' Suddenly whirling around in a crouch, I pulled the hammer back and cautiously swept the gun over the area in the dramatic style of television's hottest detective. Freezing a position, I pointed the pistol at a photo on the wall opposite and squeezed the trigger. BLAM! The explosion was deafening. Immediate silence ensued, like a blanket of intrusion, muffling all conversation. A shock wave of confused faces peered down the hallway. The doll in red screamed in panic and fled the room, leaving Meade stumbling behind, rubbing his ears. The two bystanders split post-haste, screaming superlatives at me as they scampered off protesting their innocence.

After a few moments of bravado, undeterred voices highlighted by drunken perplexity rolled into the rumble of merriment once again, broadcasting total indifference to what had just transpired. The eagerness to recapture revelry saved me facing a world of trouble.

I'd had a miraculous escape from inflicting serious injury on the unsuspecting party rockers, never mind the fact that I could have found myself facing serious jail time. Luck was in attendance while disaster had taken the night off.

The incident shocked my system and left me shaking holding a smoking gun, bathed in the spotlight of unadulterated stupidity and reassessing my mental stability.

Our functions were never as loud, or out of control, but Jim and I were definitely deadly to the extreme when it came to scoring pumpage. Our bedrooms were red-hot from overuse and the carpet was threadbare from predatory female feet skipping back and forth from the living room to the bedrooms. The love lines were endless. We attempted to capture the ladies' hearts with clever dialogue mostly acquired from Mickey Spillane paperbacks. They in turn pretended to swoon at our charm offensive. We played the game breaking all the rules.

Jim and I each had a separate bedroom with a bathroom en suite. The walls of both bathrooms were papered with signed photographs of our many conquests. It was our compulsory requirement to obtain a photo of each and every girl that visited our sweet abode. The competition between us was fierce. Whoever scored the most and had the most photos on the wall at the end of each week, bought the beers. The result was always a draw. Pumpage Palace was a complete ego inflation station. It couldn't have been more aptly named.

REMEMBERING CINDERELLA

Fight night had arrived. Heavyweight boxing was on TV. Sonny Liston was hoping to end the world championship reign of Floyd Patterson. The event was a must-see and therefore an ambiance of mounting excitement had invaded the front room of the Mitchum/Rowland hillside sanctuary. Every living fight fan throughout Hollywood smouldered in sweet anticipation since news of the coming event had flashed from the nation's sports pages. The word on the street was that it was sure to be a war between the two fighters, an occasion that as a boxing 'aficionado' I sure as hell didn't want to miss.

Robert Mitchum, dressed in loosely fitted chinos and a short-sleeved polo shirt along with my father, Roy Rowland, decked out in pale blue golf threads, had fallen by our hilltop pad bringing with them a bellyful of enthusiasm and a litre bottle of 12-year-old Chivas Regal Scotch.

Just the ticket for enhancing a mellow mood till fight time. As we were all rabid boxing fans this was strictly a 'boys only' night.

Girly action was definitely off the menu.

Jim had phoned Budd Albright asking him to join us. With action in his feet, Budd arrived from across the canyon carrying groceries and insisted on throwing together his own mouth-watering specialty, Little Italy spaghetti with wild mushroom sauce and a garbanzo bean salad. To the uninitiated it sounded like nothing exceptional, but with the Albright's magic formula, it was guaranteed to sort out all our gastro cravings with culinary excellence.

After putting the straightener on our hunger pangs and splashing down a few glasses of French Merlot, we piled the dirty dishes in the kitchen and cracked open the bottle of Chivas Regal. With a Mose Allison LP on the stereo we kicked back allowing our minds to travel along with his unique phrasing as he sang about the virtues of the Seventh Son.

Levelled out in a warm blanket of alcohol, our blood flowing with contentment, Jim stretched back next to his dad on the large leather sofa and waited in cool anticipation for the fight to burst into life on the goggle box.

My father relaxed into the embracing arms of the denim fabric lounge chair and clicked it into recline. Budd and I sat on the floor, our backs propped against the front of the leather sofa, choosing to cool out the wait with a couple cans of Budweiser.

Robert Mitchum's basset eyes were shining like a beacon as he and my father, both exceptional storytellers, kick-started an exchange of anecdotes that highlighted some hilarious adventures that each had encountered along their road of struggle during the bad ole days.

The room was filled with a fall out of laughter as my father related a tale of total chaos that ensued during the shooting of an early Johnny Weissmuller Tarzan film. It was during the 1930s. The film was being shot on location at Lake Sherwood in the San Fernando valley. My father was the assistant director in charge of organizing the background action.

As Roy told it, a master scene in long shot was being filmed. It involved elephants stampeding through a native village thus chasing off the bad guys that, according to the script, were on the warpath. After a full day of setting up the shot with two cameras and arranging the background players into position, rehearsing with the animal handlers and generally honing everything to perfection, it at last came time to make the shot.

The cameras were ready to roll and everybody was on standby when an overeager second assistant director yelled 'Action — elephants!' It was as though an all-out war had blasted off. The rumble of cannon explosions shook the entire area, igniting a stampede of galloping animals. Suspense ensued as the entire cast and film crew held their breath in anticipation of the elephants' thundering arrival. Everybody took a few steps back as the herd roared into the setting, crushing everything that stood in their path.

Instantly the director yelled 'Cut — cut! God damn it!' Laughter erupted throughout the entire location, as on entering the scene the elephants slowed to a trot, grabbed each other's tails and marched right on through the set and continued off into the distance, sashaying in rhythm. All that was missing was musical accompaniment. Someone forgot to say the elephants had been hired from the local circus. As far as they were concerned they were performing their act as expected.

The rumble of laughter tempered the ambiance, as waves of relaxation rolled throughout the room, like a preamble to the main event.

With the sound turned down on the TV, fight time seemed to crawl on all fours toward the start line. The endless procession of commercials that flickered hypnotically from the soundless screen filtered through my senses.

I began to nod off. The flow of alcohol and Budd's fine Italian meal had already assigned my body to a neutral state. I leaned back and closed my eyes. A blank screen fluttered behind my eyelids. Soft spears of light anaesthetized my thoughts and transported me into a twilight zone, spinning my brain through a dizzying newsreel of past events. Subliminal shapes reopened old wounds.

Memory can be a curse as well as a guaranteed reflection of happiness. In my semi-conscious state, recalling a particular episode, it delivered a bit of both.

Karin Sonnegard wasn't an ordinary Hollywood starlet. She was not only remarkably beautiful, but was gifted with acute ambition. Her image personified the archetypal blonde, Swedish sex symbol — a poster girl for fantasies, a template for wet dreams.

Her photograph, torn from the pages of countless soft porn magazines, papered bedroom walls and men's locker rooms everywhere, firing bullets of lust to the imagination. What made her different was that she appeared to have the appealing glow of humility.

Her gorgeous image was that of a fluffy pin-up with large perfectly shaped breasts that appeared extraordinary, jutting arrogantly from her body's slender framework. Her eyes, so glacier-blue that in certain light they appeared to transport the innocence of a child across her sensual face. A mane of lustrous silver-blonde hair framed her exquisite features before tumbling to her shoulders like a shower of stars.

Karin did not possess the towering framework of notably glamorous Swedish icons such as May Britt and Anita Ekberg. However, with her five feet, six inch stature she delivered a powerful package of pure sexual dynamite that guaranteed a grunt of mad desire in the loins of every hot-blooded male that was able to breathe. Karin could be described in one sentence as a Scandinavian Cinderella with big tits. What I loved best about her was that she appeared to care about me.

Warm wind off the desert had delivered a fresh smog-free afternoon to the Laurel Canyon community. The rain clouds had moved south and gloomy faces once more were smiling. You could say that Hollywood Boulevard was alive with the sound of music.

The smile on my face cast a radiant beam that could have lit a thousand street lamps while the drumming of my heart was marching with the Anvil Chorus.

Karin Sonnegard sat next to me as we headed out toward an evening's adventure. Jim was away filming on location leaving the house a zone-free playground. I'd thought of a few games that I was hoping Karin would be up for playing. As we drove toward Laurel Canyon, my long-playing mouth was full on, powered by excitement. I felt on top of the world. I had a feeling that Karin and I were about to connect. She pushed all the right buttons and our sense of humour blended, injecting within me a feeling of togetherness. It was possible that the room in my heart was about to become occupied.

It was nearing six o'clock when I eased the Corvette into the carport under the house. The last shimmer of sunlight had disappeared behind the canyon hillside, leaving the whisper of a chill in its wake. I'd arranged to pick Karin up early from the Hollywood Studio Club in order to spend more quality time with her. The Studio Club had strict regulations. All residents must sign out and return by midnight to sign in. To the many starlets and industry hopefuls in residence at this exclusively female domicile, the Studio Club's strict policy was like being incarcerated. The most famous resident to make a great escape was Marilyn Monroe.

Enthusiasm was bursting from every pore in my body as the

seductive aroma of Chanel embraced Karin Sonnegard's luscious body, intoxicating my sensibility. The house waited in chilly silence as she followed me up the few short steps, through the front door and into the welcoming warmth of the front room. I had only one thing on my mind and it didn't take a graduate of MIT to realize what I hoped would be on the cards. Nevertheless I had to make sure that I made all the right moves. The possibility of blowing it was certainly on tap. I was prepared to act the perfect gentleman.

My cooking skills have always been minimal, however I managed to throw together a tiny banquet of roast chicken, baked potatoes and salad, accompanied by a glass or two of Italian Frascati that I'd kept chilled for the occasion. Relaxed after the meal, conversation and coffee flowed. We were becoming immeasurably close. Karin never looked lovelier. My heart rate was pushing overload.

An awkward silence followed, as we made our way down the short passage to my sparsely furnished bedroom. My mind has vivid recollections of a ghostly army of moon shadows dancing across the walls and over the white bedspread, announcing the advancing evening's romantic darkness.

Lust was boiling up, as Karin unzipped the back of her summer dress and slipped into the en suite bathroom, closing the door. I immediately shed my clothes, pulled back the bed linen and waited with burning anticipation like a conquering hero waits to survey the spoils of victory.

Gentle kisses in the moonlit room encouraged eager throes of passion. We immediately began making love as though an enemy was at the gate. Oblivious to everything around us, we engaged in loving combat. Karin's athletic legs wrapped around, locking me inside, squeezing my invading force, encouraging a sexual rinsing. I was overcome by the power of her beauty as I struggled to satisfy her voracious appetite — desperate to hold it together, to tame her ferocious hunger. I was propelled into the stratosphere, ascending on golden billows into an endless garden where flowers try on new colours.

My heart soared as each thrust brought forth from deep within her tiny whimpers that erupted into rhythmic squeals of ecstasy, rising to a rapturous explosion that sent me free-wheeling into a state of nirvana.

Love surrounded my heart as we fell loose on the bed, washed in sweat. It took a few moments for me to catch my breath and regain my composure. Karin nuzzled her gorgeous face into my neck, and gently licked my salty skin, punctuating each dab of her tongue with a soft kiss. She allowed her gaze to lovingly scan my face. 'Steve, that was wonderful.' The mere sound of her breathless voice began to stir movement within me once again. I couldn't remember ever feeling happier. I was sure that at last I'd found the girl of my dreams, someone who really cared. We were good together.

My arms encircled her naked body. I pulled her so close that it was as if we shared the same skin. 'I'm mad about you, darling girl. You're so beautiful. I think I'm falling in love.' My voice rang with true sincerity.

'Me too,' she said, 'me too.' The blue of Karin's eyes focused on me with an earnest expression, as she rose onto her elbows and tentatively spoke my name, 'Steve?' She hesitated before going on. 'I want to ask you something.'

'OK, baby. Anything. What is it?'

Responding with intensity, she continued. 'I read in Army Archerd's column in *Variety* that your father's getting ready to direct *Meet Me in Las Vegas.* Would you introduce me to him? Your father, I mean. I'd really love the chance to audition for a part in the film. I'm sure that a personal introduction from you would really help me.' Karin's blue eyes appeared to shine steely-grey, as her brow furrowed into the vulnerable expression of a traumatized puppy. 'Please, baby. Pretty please?'

It was as though the god of war had pierced my heart with a bolt of lightning. Everything fell loose inside me as I realized the extent of her ambition. A wave of tearful frustration began to swell. I had to bag up my emotions or I would surely see my name on the list of heartaches. I was speechless.

Karin Sonnegard wasn't any Cinderella and I sure as hell wasn't gonna provide a carriage for the ride back to her castle. As far as I was concerned she'd already turned into a pumpkin. I phoned for a taxi.

My head felt inside out. I was struggling to surface from the vortex of a sunken dream. The throbbing pulse of excited voices was circulating like a distant army marching in tempo to an irrepressible clang, clang, clang of a bell. I rubbed my eyes. Floyd Patterson was sitting, head bowed in the corner of the ring surrounded by a throng of concerned onlookers. Sonny Liston had his arms raised in triumph as the new heavyweight champion of the world. Scenes of mayhem spiralled from the TV screen, as hordes of well-wishers invaded the ring and were congratulating the winner.

Robert Mitchum and my father were downing cups of black coffee, readying themselves for a sober departure. Jim and Budd were attacking the pile of dishes, trying hard not to flood the kitchen with fly-away soapy dishwater.

The episode with Karin had left me walking wounded. I hadn't seen it coming, in the same way that Floyd Patterson hadn't seen the punch that ended his championship reign.

With Karin I'd led with my heart and paid the price.

Out of the Ashes

The fading afternoon twilight had finally surrendered to the noisy, uncaring face of Friday night.

I sat shivering in the parked Corvette feeling strangely emancipated like an unholy angel — waiting alone amid the blurring confusion of the smug and mischievous, auto-infested streets of Hollywood — vacant in direction and imprisoned in thought. A continual replay seemed like a diluted dream attacking my conscience, causing a minor flip — fracturing my morality and leaving me spiritually contaminated.

I'd been driving around at random for hours desperately trying to dull the pain that was still scraping the inner walls of my heart — praying that the scars would fade in time.

I hadn't been very considerate or understanding during the break-up. It had ended badly with me acting the complete bastard and screaming at beautiful Kathy Case, whom I'd loved and who'd shared my life for three years. The suit of shame was still hanging in my closet.

Our relationship had been history for a month, but I was still brooding over memories of the good times and struggling to shake off my guilt about the way I had walked out, leaving her submerged in an ocean of tears. I wasn't very proud of my actions and even though Kathy now appeared to have seamlessly moved on I, on the other hand, was becoming an emotional cripple. Falling apart at the slightest recollection wasn't an option. I had to pick up the pieces.

Early that morning under a powder blue sky, the warm sunshine predicted the arrival of a glorious day. Prying spears of light poked through my partially shuttered bedroom window and somewhat eased my shame leading me to realize that a world full of possibilities lay within my grasp. As difficult as it seemed I had to focus on the positives and kick the anguish to the curb. Face up and move on.

Steve McQueen and I had shared a bit of history. We first

Above: A night on the town with Kathy Case, Russ Tamblyn and Laura Lee.

met and bonded while working together filming the Four Star television production, *The Bill Longley Story*. This was a legendary tale of a famous outlaw who, just after the Civil War, rode through Kansas with ruthless intent alongside the violent James gang. The part was brought to life by Steve's unique acting talent. An embryo of superstardom was evident.

During the filming Steve McQueen and I discovered that we shared a mutual passion, that being our love of motorcycles — especially dirt bike scramblers. Every moment that we weren't in front of the camera we were motor mouthing about the joys of moto-cross. With ravenous excitement we planned to have an adventurous tear-up out at Pear Blossom off highway 18 in the Antelope Valley area of the Mojave Desert. Sadly however, the plan never came to pass. More important obstacles of everyday living had got in the way and after a time Steve and I lost touch.

Sometime later, however, destiny came to call and I was cast to play a baddie in two back-to-back episodes of Steve McQueen's hugely successful Western TV series, *Wanted Dead or Alive*. While on the shoot outside Tucson, Arizona, Steve and I once again found time to lay down some heavy dialogue about the ecstasy of moto-cross. After ten days on location, surrounded by the exceptional beauty of the Arizona desert, the exciting prospect of a weekend tear-up at Pear Blossom once again inflamed our passion to the max. Two days of motorcycle mayhem would definitely be marked down on our agenda. It headed my list of things to do when I returned to LA.

A few weeks later the location filming was wrapped and Steve was back in town raring to get down and funky with a dirt bike attack on Pear Blossom. However, with the painful break up of my relationship with Kathy Case, my conscience was still facing a mental firing squad and time had slipped by. I forced my angst on hold and clicked the switch of positive action. Setting the painful memory bank on the back burner, I immediately made contact with Steve. After a short phone conversation we decided to put our original plan of attack into motion.

The pre-adventure arrangement was for Steve and I to hook up around 11 p.m. at the Chez Paulette coffee house on the Sunset Strip where we'd sip some brew while we finalized the flight plan.

Fate however, had designed a different scenario.

Clarity had replaced my confusion with anticipation as I slid out from behind the steering wheel and locked the Corvette.

Directly across Sunset Boulevard, the Body Shop's Technicolor lights blinked seductively at the passing trade. Inside the club's low-slung outer structure a mostly male audience savoured the charms of the erotic dancers, ogling their talent with guilty eyes.

With purposeful feet I took a few short steps along the warm sidewalk. Fifty yards further on I turned left and made my way under the dimly lit, shabby archway that embraced tiny shops and boutiques — all smiling with sleepy contentment from each side of a diminutive arcade. On the left at the far end waited the inviting entrance to the Chez Paulette coffee house. With a clear mind and relaxed posture I delivered my soul across the wooden threshold and into the welcoming pastures of Hollywood's coolest coffee den. It was ten minutes after eleven. I no longer felt bleak of spirit.

The Chez Paulette coffee house was a very special oasis that mainly catered to the vanguard of Hollywood's hippest intelligentsia. Max Lewin, the owner, had transformed the narrowly structured room into a Greenwich Village, New York replica, complete with bookshelves filled with poetry and intellectual reading material. Against the wall on the right side of the entrance leaned a well-worn wooden rack for newspapers and magazines, most of which shouted liberal points of view. The moderate dimensions of the room, along with candle glow lighting helped create a warm and relaxed atmosphere. A constant cigarette-induced haze, like a ghostly voyeur, circled aimlessly above the room's wooden tables cementing a state of togetherness among the late night beer and coffee drinkers.

Once inside I was momentarily delivered into a state of

serenity. The tantalizing aroma of blended coffee was overpowering as I searched the crowded room for an empty table and a possible friendly face. I wasn't ready for any deep exchanges, just a bit of superficial banter while I 'amped' myself with caffeine and waited for Steve to show.

My eyes became dazzled as I squinted through the smoky glare. It seemed as if the entire setting was filled with unfamiliar faces that somehow were trespassing on hallowed ground. A grain of resentment creased my face with a hollow smile, as I defensively thrust my hands into the pockets of my black Italian car coat. A momentary sting of sadness awakened a tiny spring of tears as the vision of Kathy's exquisite being exploded in a subliminal memory of the times we'd shared in this very same room.

Above: 'Are you sure?' asks Edd Burns. Steve's lips are sealed.

Max Lewin's diminutive frame hustled behind the crowded bar. He'd been left short-staffed and short tempered. A couple of pretty girls, new to the job, their breasts threatening to escape the buttons of tightly fitted white blouses, were doing their best to wait on the over-anxious customers. Frustration was causing chaos as impatient feet shuffled back and forth across the well-scarred wooden floor baying for service.

As a rule the Chez Paulette was honoured with the presence of Hollywood's newest rising, young guns. The usual suspects being Edd 'Kookie' Burns, Tuesday Weld, Nick Adams, Suzanne Pleshette, Sal Mineo, John Saxon and Vicki Thal.

Tonight however, they were nowhere to be seen. The absence of Mort Sahl, America's brilliant, left-wing political satirist was curiously bizarre. He was practically a permanent fixture most nights of the week.

Through squinting eyes, I noticed that most of the tables appeared to be occupied by an unwashed pseudo-intellectual collective boisterously debating topical issues. The rising volume of their misinformation was causing a current of irritation that rattled those who were seeking a quiet evening retreat.

I checked my watch. It was almost eleven thirty and Steve hadn't shown. As I was about to make a move to a freshly unoccupied table in the far corner, Budd Albright and Jim Mitchum crashed the scene in laughter.

'Hey guys, what's shaking?' I said, spinning around, relieved at the invasion of friendly company. 'What have you guys been up to these past hours? Hound-dogging for chicks?'

'No man,' Jim answered. 'Budd and I have been up at the house going over the script for a new war film. Should have tons of action. Budd's auditioning for a part.' Budd's smile revealed satisfaction. He obviously felt that the work he'd put in would surely pay off.

'Hey, let's check out that place in the back and grab some brews,' I said, indicating the newly vacated corner table. 'I'm all "coffeed" out.'

As we edged our way toward the waiting table thunder struck my forward motion, fusing my senses like a shocking surge of electricity. 'Go on guys. Grab the table. I'll be right there.' Budd and Jim were too busy checking the scene for girly action to notice anything unusual about the break in my stride and continued on toward a welcomed sit down.

Her face paralyzed my soul. She was like a magnificent phoenix rising from out of the ashes. Breathing deserted my body, as if I'd been hit with a sucker punch during an unguarded moment. My eyes were awash in a radiant beam of light that reawakened the darkened caverns of my heart. A current of astonishment defused my movement with the glue of desire, like Ulysses when spellbound by the lure of the sirens.

There were three people seated at the table in front of me. One face was slightly familiar — a young actor named Bob Padgett. Sitting attentively next to him was a nubile blonde female, whose outward persona had all the essentials that make up a wannabe actress. Their presence, however, paled to insignificance next to the breathtakingly beautiful raven-haired girl who occupied the third place at the table.

'Hey Steve, how's it going?' Bob asked, motioning for me to join them. 'Who're you with?' Bob's red polo shirt blazed, like a friendly fire around his excitable personality. Mumbling an answer, I pointed toward the back corner where Jim and Budd were now seated already surrounded with a coven of female attention.

Because of the exuberance of the unfamiliar bohemian gathering I hadn't bothered to check out anything beyond the noise barrier and therefore I'd been unaware of the exquisite creature, sitting camouflaged behind a smoke screen of coffee house activity.

Bob indicated for me to join them as he made the introductions. My pulse sang in harmony with a chorus of angels as I was introduced to Carmen Phillips. Her name declared beauty to the world. I stared at her exotic elegance and tried to protect myself against mounting insecurity with an outward pose of coolness, but I was sure that I hadn't fooled her. Bob yammered on elatedly about a film part that he was hoping to get. I sat in hysterical silence, staring at Carmen's exceptional beauty — drowning in a great ocean of melting things, unable to swim at all. Lucidity was beyond my ability as the roar of river sounds united with the hammering of my heart.

A veil of sadness draped her violet-blue eyes, protecting a mysterious past or perhaps my impression had registered from her narrowing vision, as she defended against the swirling cigarette smoke that filtered seductively from between her luscious lips. She projected an unequalled serenity like an incumbent goddess and I was riding contact high. I felt the attesting madness and

Right: Carmen Phillips declared beauty to the world.

To Steve
Best Wishe
all
4598

ring and roar of the world trailing away off somewhere. I wanted to hold on to those initial moments as if I was a miser desperate to save the first tears of my newly born child. No words passed between us, yet I felt an instant connection as Carmen surveyed me with sensual feline intensity.

It seemed as if only minutes had passed when Bob and the blonde wannabe actress, whose name I can't recall, became impatient and decided to leave. Bob and the blonde stood up and made their moves toward the door. As Carmen made motion to follow, she handed me an empty match cover. The hint of a smile momentarily cast a shimmer of light across her elegantly chiselled features. I didn't need to hear the words — her eyes said it all. 'Call me,' she whispered. Her lips brushed my cheek and then she was gone leaving a lingering fragrance of promise in her wake.

As I turned to join Jim and Budd at their table, Max Lewin hustled up to me with a message. 'Some guy called and told me to tell you that Steve was sorry but he can't make it tonight and that he'll have to take a rain check on Pear Blossom. Whatever that means,' said Max with a disparaging chuckle.

I should have been pissed off, but I wasn't. I was elated. Steve had done me a favour. His no-show had been an unexpected blessing. I owed him one.

Some weeks later Steve McQueen and I finally made the road trip to Pear Blossom, accompanied by Keenan Wynn and Lee Marvin. It had been a great two days of bashing the 'burms' in the Mojave Desert. The guys had been great company and I'd had a blast, but I was looking forward to getting home.

I hoped that the weekend would enhance my reputation throughout Hollywood for being a wild, fun-loving, motor-mad crazy who loved nothing better than getting down and dirty while giving the finger to danger.

The baking sun had pulled on an overcoat of leaden clouds as we made our way along the seemingly endless blacktop. A trace of rain was threatening a downpour. That could prove to be treacherous as we drove into a descending blanket of darkness that shrouded the deserted highway.

The acrid smell of racing fuel clung to my skin, keeping alive memories of the weekend's spirited adventure. Bubbles of tired conversation recalling highlights of the tear-up helped pass the time driving.

Dozing in the seat, my head against the window, anxiety floated across my mind on floors of music. I drifted off to the land of nod. A sudden bump in the road jarred me awake. I checked my watch. We'd made good time. We'd be home in under an hour.

I let my head return to the window and once again closed my eyes. Carmen's gorgeous face filled my thoughts. I felt my heart soar. We'd become immeasurably close in the short time since that night at Chez Paulette. I knew that we shared a destiny together. The room in my heart was no longer haunted.

Left: Being with Carmen made the spectres of the past fade.

Gigging with God at the Lighthouse

The blistering hot August afternoon had recovered its breath. A gentle breeze began gathering a tempo that rescinded the heat's intensity, as it chased the sun westward into the waiting arms of early evening.

It was Sunday and fast approaching five o'clock. I was late for the two o'clock kick off, but I was packing excitement and more than ready to groove into the early hours.

Dressed in penny Loafers, chinos and a faded black teeshirt, I hastened my descent from the undulating sidewalk, down the well-worn steps that led to the entrance of no. 30 Pier Avenue, Hermosa Beach, California, the revered home of the world-famous, West Coast, modern jazz laboratory, the Lighthouse.

Legend has it that this kick-ass structure was spawned from the belly of one of the many working concerns that through the years have displayed beacons of guiding light to hapless ships caught up in distress while fog-bound off the southern coast of California. It's the real deal, not an imposter.

The hurricane in my eyes suddenly surged to my feet as I stumbled in haste, stabbing myself with extreme embarrassment in front of a reclining group of solid senders. I hoped that they hadn't noticed my fuck-up — but that was wishful thinking.

Lounging about outside the doorway in various shapes of stoned enthusiasm, were a cluster of shirtless jazz heads catching the last of the sun's rays, while engulfed in the soothing sounds that sneaked through the architecture and out into the slowly departing afternoon heat. The smiles on their faces as they checked me out said it all.

The receding afternoon sun blazed through my Ray-Bans, the fierce glare forcing me to squint, as I hurled myself down the few remaining steps.

I was plugged into the whole deal as I carefully slipped through the weather-worn doorway into the stifling darkness that momentarily blinded me. The velvet tongue of musical cool kissed my ears as the exuberant improvising of superb musicianship put flame to my aesthetic values.

The club's interior décor is a mental trip into 1930s Hawaiian modern. The paintings clinging to the walls follow a South Pacific theme. Numerous seascapes and paradise locations, painted by hopeful artists in better years gone by, along with framed photographs of famous faces, stare back like ghosts in shrouds of faded glamour — a definitive contrast to the clinical perfection of the collected musicians jamming on the bandstand.

The atmosphere was buzzing with an undercurrent of excitement, as if something unusual was lurking in the ether, waiting for the exact moment to create a startling entry. Puzzling, vocal thunder rattled throughout the darkened club, but at that moment I couldn't quite catch its drift.

The Lighthouse was only licensed to accommodate a capacity of about 200, with table seating for 180. The long bar gathers the overflow. I instantly switched on to the fact that this afternoon the club could be in serious violation. The room was overflowing with festivity. Every inch of space was stacked to bursting, with throngs of eager jazz lovers — all hoping to discover that elusive lost chord. The air conditioning was throwing down its own groove as it strained to deal with the overpacked humanity.

There was something exceptional happening. People were jamming the setting with bristling anticipation.

Sprinkled throughout the room were several of Hollywood's major young players, heavily engrossed in the musical virtuosity of the assembled musicians, as they, one by one, took turns igniting appreciation from the gathered crowd. An eclectic group of the jazz world's top exponents were gathered on the tiny bandstand, blowing up a fierce wind of complexity.

I spotted Russ Tamblyn at a table near the front and squeezed forward to ask for a sit-down while he waited for some expected friends to arrive. He obliged reluctantly. I told him not to fret, that I was only cooling it for a couple of minutes while I checked out the gathered players making end-runs around the notes.

Major contenders of the modern jazz school of cool were blowing up a subtle wind. Shelly Mann along with Howard

Rumsey was throwing down the groove on drums and bass. Lou Levy's superb piano enhanced the driving rhythm along with the guitar genius of Jim Hall. Shorty Rogers, Maynard Ferguson, Bud Shank, Art Pepper, Jimmy Giuffre and Bill Harris were all individually improvising on a chosen theme.

With clockwork regularity every Sunday, a gathering of Hollywood's hippest jazz heads materialize to embrace the sounds and check out the action on tap. There's usually an open invitation to anyone who fancies an adrenalin rush, to sit in and blow away their cobwebs, jamming up front with the big boys. You never know who's gonna turn up and wig out.

I stood cool in my shades as I clocked the room checking for famous faces. Nick Adams and Natalie Wood were tucked up close to the bandstand.

At the next table dressed to thrill in a black halter top and matching peasant skirt was Anne Francis. Her blonde sex appeal was flooding over Troy Donahue and Ben Cooper who, along with a pair of token starlets, were digging the happenings. Budd Albright was alone at the bar sucking up a frozen Coffee Cioqui. 'Hey, Budd,' I shouted, 'where are all your Latin lovelies today?' He threw a smile at me and raised his glass letting me know that he was expecting company.

As I eased my way up front I stopped to throw a few words at Bob Fuller and Dennis Hopper, interrupting them in the act of downing a couple of bottles of Corona Special. My head was on a swivel as I cased the scene for a possible move on to some spare female talent. There was a pair of sex symbols showing it off in the far left corner of the room. With carnal intentions but faking disinterest, I moseyed in their direction. My heart was pounding with rising expectation of what could possibly lie ahead.

All of a sudden I felt myself being swept along to the pounding rhythm and intricate, musical manoeuvres pumping from the

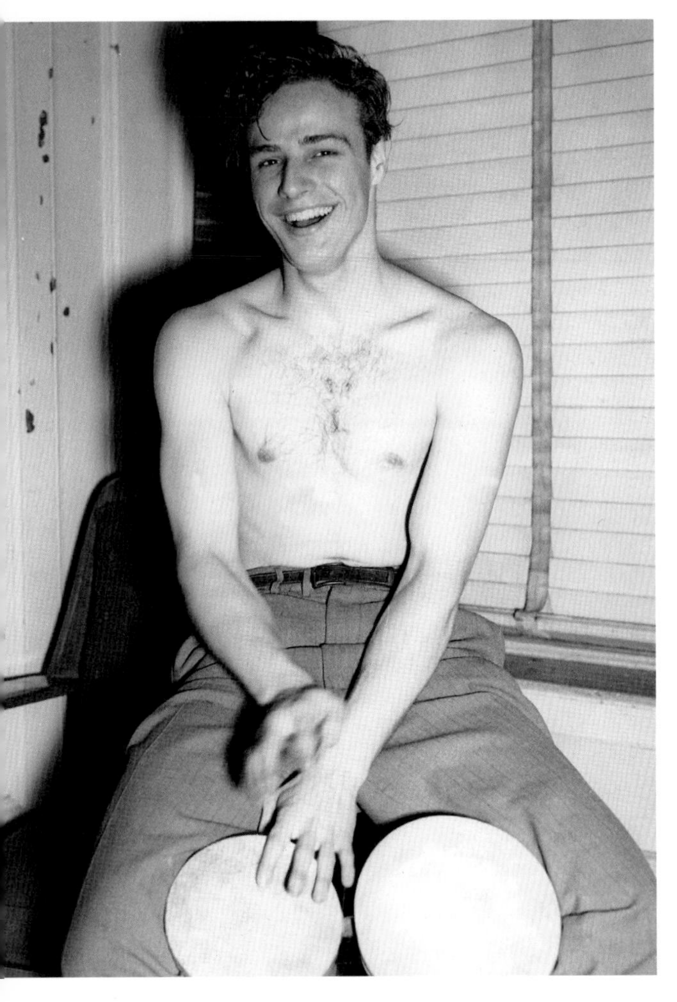

Above: Give him bongos or congas, Brando will find the right groove.

bandstand. Temperatures were hitting into the red. The atmosphere was cracking like arcing electricity and about to explode. My forward motion stopped as the whole room began to groove in a cacophony of thundering excitement. The room's sea of faces was straining their eyes toward the bandstand. Some of the crowd were standing on chairs, desperate to catch a piece of whatever it was that was going down on stage. From where I stood my vision was blocked by a section of the excited congregation. With mounting frustration I negotiated furious footwork back towards the bar in the hope of sneaking a peek from a raised vantage point.

Suddenly and without warning the house lights went out, as if some crazy killjoy with a special agenda had pulled the plug for childish kicks. A ball of confusion erupted and rolled through the club with blind hysteria. Except for the bar area and the red glow of the exit signs, the room was in a cocoon of blackness. An embryo of a riot was beginning to hatch. Then from out of the turmoil began the slow magnetic pull of a solid Afro-Cuban groove. The pulsating throb of highly tuned conga drums exploded with a sensual rhythm that caused a collective hush throughout the darkened club. A bubbling cauldron of rhythmic power began 'maxing the beat' — louder and louder. Voices in the room were chasing a rising tornado as the entire band of players kicked in with storm-fraught intensity.

Just as the volume rose to a shattering crescendo, the house lights burst on to spontaneous applause, and female hysteria. For a mini-second my eyes were dazzled by the brightness. I peered through squinted eyes to check the happening up front, but cigarette smoke clouded my vision, making the action difficult to decipher.

The groove rocked in once more with a churning precision. Like sensual thunder, it shook the room with sexual vibrations. Then, like the parting of the Red Sea, some bodies magically moved aside, allowing me a clear view of the bandstand.

My eyes couldn't collect the reality of what confronted me. I was in shock as if stunned by the presence of God. I froze in disbelief.

There on the bandstand, like a benevolent Buddha, dressed in Levis and an open neck shirt with sleeves rolled up was Marlon Brando. He was as cool as a night breeze over Alaska.

In all the hysteria he hadn't missed a beat. With his hands in motion he caressed the congas, playing as if willing his adoring flock to follow him into the loving arms of immortality. It was an amazing display of his exceptional talent. The emotional impact of that scene mellowed me out and shut me down till closing.

It was six a.m. when my feet hit the concrete and pointed me in the direction of my parked Corvette. The red dawn was slicing the sky like a samurai sword as the sun crept up from the dark horizon. Monday was sure to be another scorcher.

A few remaining die-hards having spilled out of the club, were milling about in the street, reluctant to go home to face their own reality. 'Hey man, do you want to go to a party?' I heard the voice shout from behind me. Turning to look I saw that it was the two lovelies from the club that I had earlier hoped to score with. I gave them a thoughtful moment, but after the astounding events of the evening, I knew anything that they had on offer would only be a sleazy anticlimax.

Behind the wheel and travelling north away from the beach communities, cruising the empty streets towards Hollywood, I kicked the sandman to the curb and turned up the radio. Keeping sleep at bay, I began to sing along with Bobby Darin's hip delivery. Tonight I had experienced Marlon Brando in divine moments of grace. I knew that I would carry the memory forever.

The Doctor's Office

Rain had paid a heavy visit to Beverly Hills the night before, leaving the quiet streets covered with a damp and gleaming lustre.

Although the early morning city sky was still bruised and swollen with liquorice-black clouds and a low rumble of thunder threatened a torrential replay, the air abounded with a brilliant freshness that made breathing an exhilarating pleasure. The usual oppressive smog had taken a sabbatical, leaving an overall invigorating feeling of cleanliness that ignited a subliminal rush of freedom and unveiled a stunning panoramic view that could be seen for miles in every direction. About two hundred kilometres to the north, above the freshly snow-capped San Bernardino mountains, a narrow strip of sapphire blue sky was churning against billows of stubborn grey cloud, determined to establish a definite foothold on the slowly dissipating stormy canvas.

What was left of the rainwater had thinned to a gentle trickle washing the gutters clean while travelling toward an eventual journey's end in the bowels of the elaborate Beverly Hills sewer system.

My watch was ticking six a.m. as I nosed the Corvette into an underground parking slot beneath the Bedford Medical Building on South Bedford drive in the commercial heart of Beverly Hills. It was too early for Sax Fifth Avenue or any of the glitzy boutiques on Wilshire Boulevard and Rodeo Drive to open, therefore the sidewalks were empty of the usual pampered Beverly Hills shoppers and traffic was light on the ground.

I'd been feeling like shit. World War III had erupted at the back of my throat creating a painful exercise in swallowing. My whole body ached and I was fighting off a massive attack of sneezing, resulting in a soggy paper trail of used Kleenex that spilled out of the ashtray and on to the empty passenger seat next to me.

Above: A scene with Rhonda Fleming from MGM's *Gun Glory*.

Right: Playing a baddie in MGM's *Gunfighters of Casa Grande*.

I was due in wardrobe at MGM studios at eight o'clock to be geared up for a major role in the new Stewart Granger film, *Gun Glory*. Filming was set to begin the following week on location in Garberville, Northern California and since this was to be an all action Western, as well as an important break for my career, I definitely needed to be in tip-top physical condition and ready to rock from day one. Playing any role in a Western demands heads-up attention and stamina. Since this was my first big step-up in class, my overall performance would definitely be under scrutiny. I couldn't afford to blow it. Fighting off the flu was something that I could well do without.

Doctor Louis Motchan was in his early forties and gifted with

Above: One of the many posters for *Gun Glory*.

an expansive personality. As well as having superb medical knowledge, his ability to keep our family's individual engines running was an achievement in itself. Lou was a great guy and not only had he been our family doctor for as long as I could remember, but he was considered a close family friend as well. Therefore he readily agreed to see me at his office two hours before his normal working day was due to begin. He knew how important my getting that career break could prove to be for my future and he was prepared to play his part in doing whatever necessary to help things run as smoothly as possible.

The situation was simple. It required a shot of penicillin thereby putting the skids under the advancing menace of the flu.

Doctor Motchan's practice was on the second floor of a five floor spacious medical building. The tastefully decorated waiting room was shared by two doctors, Louis Motchan and an equally gifted medical practitioner, whose name I can no longer recall. The room's generous dimensions had an air of gentility. Buttermilk coloured hessian material papered three quarters of the interior walls. Bottle-green William Morris wallpaper covered all the remaining sections, stopping at a two inch, dark-oak dado strip that surrounded the room adding a touch of class.

Copies of *Vogue* and *Field & Stream*, along with day-old newspapers were spread across a coffee table's polished surface. Several issues of the latest *Confidential* gossip rag, along with various copies of *Sports Illustrated*, were carelessly stuffed inside two small metal magazine racks. Judging by their dishevelled condition, many nervous hands had hastily rifled through the pages while waiting anxiously in anticipation of what ailment the doctor might discover during their appointment.

Struggling with the pain of swallowing and fighting for a channel of air that would relieve my blocked sinuses, I entered the room sneezing. Through watery eyes I negotiated a sit-down in the nearest chair just as a second sneeze rattled my structure. 'God bless you,' came a childlike feminine voice from across the room. 'Are you OK? You really look uncomfortable.'

Because of the explosive power of my sneezing entrance I hadn't noticed anyone sitting in the waiting room. Furthermore I hadn't expected to see anybody there before the start of office hours.

'Thanks,' I said, keeping my head down and casting a shy smile in the direction of the attractive female form, sitting on the left side of the settee browsing through the pages of a glamour magazine. 'You got it right,' I answered. 'My head feels like it's been hammered for fifteen rounds by Rocky Marciano.' My nasal intonation rang with an embarrassing tone throughout the room, ruining any hope that I may have had in projecting a cool appearance. I dropped into the nearest chair and quickly picked up a day-old newspaper, hiding behind it while I tried composing myself before attempting further conversation. My head felt as if it was submerged in a bucket of water. It required all my concentration to hold off a further barrage of sneezing.

After a couple of moments I quietly lowered the paper and furtively let my eyes travel across the room, clocking her physical charms. Possibly the fact that I was not feeling at my best had created a loss of confidence. Usually whenever I'd happen upon a cool chick I'd kick right into smooth conversation. However, trying to get stuck in while sounding like a foghorn was certain to play havoc with my charm offensive.

I desperately tried to think of a clever phrase that would grab her attention.

There was something very familiar about her, but I couldn't put my finger on it. A pulse of energy ignited a spark within my body and I felt the rise of carnal stimulation.

At first glance her overall appearance wasn't particularly stunning, but there was something very vulnerable and sensitive about her manner. Although my muscles ached and my eyes were sore there was no denying the power of her sensuality. 'What's brought you here this early?' I asked, trying my best to remain cool. 'Are you here to see Dr Motchan?' She dipped the magazine that she'd been scanning and washed me in a mirrored pool of limpid blue eyes. 'I think I'm getting a cold,' she answered. 'I need to get a check-up before I go away. I'm visiting a friend this weekend — gotta drive to Palm Springs.' There was a quality of enchantment about her yet I sensed a hint of sadness and melancholy in her smile.

She put down the glamour magazine and picked up an issue of *Field & Stream*. Laying it across her lap she began flipping through the pages coming to a stop at an article of interest, her attention being momentarily distracted by something that had caught her eye.

Although her head was wrapped in a multi-coloured bandana, I could tell by the mousey-blonde swirls of hair that ventured around her temples exposing dark roots that she was badly in need of a hairdresser. A black rain-smock was still clinging around her shoulders partially concealing a red and white striped satin blouse that did its best to restrain the allure of magnificent breasts that were bursting to escape. The satin shirt was tucked into a pair of well-worn faded blue jeans. A silver and turquoise-blue buckle secured what I could see of an Indian-beaded leather belt. Stack-heeled, well-scuffed leather boots displayed damp patches across the front and along the sides indicating that she'd obviously attacked a few puddles on her way to the waiting room. Her pale skin was devoid of any noticeable make-up. There was something shockingly tender and mysterious about her presence.

A vice-like pressure began squeezing my head, pulling me to the bottom of a fathomless lake. I tried to think of something witty to say that would make her laugh and kick start our conversation again, but I felt as if my brain had been deposited in a watery grave.

A large sneeze erupted before I could cover my nose forcing me to dig in the tight front pocket of my Levis and grope for a Kleenex. I could feel wet residue clinging around my nose and on my chin. I felt as though I'd been dragged upside down the full length of Niagara Falls. 'Bless you!' she said, this time with obvious concern in her voice. Dropping the copy of *Field & Stream* she continued. 'Are you sure you're all right? Your eyes look really red.'

'Yeah, I'm cool. Thanks,' I croaked, doing my best to appear nonchalant. 'God I hate getting ill. It pisses me off.' I wiped my face, returned the wet, crumpled Kleenex to my pocket and slumped down in the chair.

'Here, let me give you another tissue. Looks like you're gonna need one,' she said smiling, pulling a fresh tissue from her purse and holding it out towards me.

'Thanks for coming to my rescue,' I said. 'Hey — it's a good thing that you're here. I might've drowned otherwise.' A gentle ripple of laughter confirmed that she found humour in the irony of my statement. I felt a flash of confidence return. It was apparent that she sympathized with my obvious discomfort, but nevertheless I sensed that we'd bonded. I felt inspired and suddenly thought of a million things to say, hopefully to make her laugh. I was beginning to like her and hoped for the chance to find out what lay beneath the surface.

At that moment Lou Motchan's smiling face appeared in the room as he opened the connecting door and motioned me into his office. 'Alright, Steve, I'm ready to see you. I'm sorry that you had to wait.' With reluctance I eased my body up from the chair. On hesitating feet I moved toward the door. Lou turned and started down the short corridor, indicating for me to follow. Although time was not on my side I was eager to steal a couple more moments of conversation in the hope of establishing a definite vibe between us. Anxiety followed me across the room. Hesitating at the door I desperately turned the pages of my memory trying to place her face before I spoke.

'Thanks for the Kleenex,' my voice honked through my blocked nose vents. 'It was nice meeting you.' I suddenly realized that I didn't know her name. 'Aha — uh — hey, listen, I'd love to talk to you some more. How about if we meet up after we're through here — grab some coffee up the street at Tiny Naylor's? What-do-ya think? Is that cool with you?'

She looked across at me. A wry smile creased her pale lips. 'Possibly,' she answered. It was a haunted expression that studied me for a moment. 'It depends on how much time I have after I'm finished here.'

'OK, I'll check you out afterwards.' My heart was beginning to pump fresh blood through my veins as I followed Doctor Motchan into the examination room. I somehow was starting to feel better. 'Lou, who's that chick sitting out there?' Excitement was taking me over. 'Is she one of your patients?'

'No, she's seeing my colleague. She's his patient.'

'Who is she? What's her name?' My curiosity was boiling over.

'Come on Steve, you're putting me on. You must have realized who that is.' Lou's eyes sparkled with amusement at my ignorance. 'Didn't you recognize her? That's Marilyn Monroe.'

I almost shit myself. No wonder she'd seemed so familiar, but she sure as hell didn't look like she did on the screen or in the newspapers and magazines. For a moment I almost felt cheated.

I can't remember feeling the lumpy pressure of the penicillin as Lou injected me. The anticipation of sharing coffee with Marilyn had fired my engine. My pulse was roaring in overdrive as I slid off the table and hastily pulled up and buttoned my Levis. After hurriedly exchanging a few parting words with Louis Motchan, I practically fell over my shoes in a full-on adrenalin rush as I raced back to the waiting room. Marilyn Monroe wasn't there. She'd slipped out a side exit and was gone with the wind.

Right: Vulnerability surrounded Marilyn Monroe.

THE THINKING BODY

Pied Pipers

The year was fast galloping to a close. Christmas and 1962 were already standing in the wings preparing to make their grand entrance.

It had been an exciting couple of months for Budd Albright and me. We had suddenly become trendy icons on the scene due to the surprise success of our thunderous nightclub act that we had launched with fanatical exuberance on to unsuspecting Hollywood. Although our music was merely a cross between ordinary rock'n'roll, flavoured with the twisting beat of Joey Dee and the Starliters, our flamboyant presentation was original and eclectic. There were many occasions when our fever-fuelled, sexually enhanced performance sparked the crowd into a rush of riotous proportions.

The twist was a dance phenomenon that was sweeping the nation. It was causing mayhem and in some instances ambulances were in necessary attendance, as overexertion had caused anxiety attacks among the many elderly dancers who'd overdone the twisting as they fought to impress those judging the numerous dance competitions. It seemed as if the entire world wanted to 'Twist Again Like They Did Last Summer'.

Recordings of Chubby Checker, Johnny Otis, Joey Dee and the Starliters among others were storming up the national charts with explosive results. The big question screamed from the headlines of Billboard Magazine, the music industry's bible, 'Dance Craze, the Twist. Is it here to stay?'

Word spread on the jungle telegraph. Our musical exploits were gathering favour. We'd become number-one-with-a-bullet in the eyes and hearts of the over active in-crowd who'd crowned us Hollywood's twist kings. Our egos were pushing overload and doing back flips off the Richter scale. Female availability was part of the package and we eagerly took full advantage of all the perks.

There were never going to be any awards or accolades for our vocal prowess, but we definitely created excitement with an

SENSATIONAL TWIST MARATHON
SUNDAY and MONDAY NIGHTS

SUNDAY NIGHT
STEVE GIBSON & THE RED CAPS

MONDAY NIGHT
STEVE ROWLAND - BUDD ALBRIGHT - THE TWILITERS

with
STEVE GIBSON • RENA SANDS • JIMMY SPRINGS
THE THREE FURNESS BROS. • "SNAKE MATHEWS
MILTON McLAURIN • JAMES JOHNSON

NO COVER
Drinks Only 95c During Showtime
46c From 10:30 a.m. 'til 7 p.m.

EXTRA WEEKEND SPECIAL
STEAK DINNER FOR **TWO!**
$5.00 Per Couple
Plus Cocktail. After-Dinner Drink
Must Be Ordered Before 9 a.m.

. . . "America's Most Unique Nite Spot, bringing back top entertainment with unusually excellent food at a surprisingly low price."—Jack C. Smith-Am. Wire
MORRIE SINGER YOUR HOST (Formerly of the "CORNER")

NEW FACES
Call For Reservations—OL. 4-6281
7978 SANTA MONICA BLVD.
Entertainment Starts At 7 p.m. - Thru Closing

athletic display of our twisting dexterity.

As singers we were cruising along a little above average. Elvis Presley and Sam Cooke wouldn't lose any sleep. They could rest easy.

However, that being said, we were definitely the catalysts for a passport to pleasure. Wherever we played, the venue was always jumping with movie star names and nubile females, provocatively dressed to thrill and letting it all hang out with the hope of enticing a Mr Wonderful into their carefully spun web.

Our music created a highly-charged competitive atmosphere amongst the throng of passionate young men, who with carnal intentions were more than eager to splash out money for drinks and goodies in the hope of scoring pumpage.

We knew the drill. So did the club owners who loved us because of our large and loyal celebrity following. There was always standing room only and the cash registers jingled with a symphonic overflow. Those were memorable times in Hollywood.

Some years had slipped by and I'd become a hit record producer and was living in London, when I suddenly discovered that our original bass player and organist were about to become world famous rock stars. Their individual record sales were shifting in the millions and their stadium concerts were becoming sell-out affairs. Volumes were being written about them. They were beginning to receive rave reviews in the world's music press. For a time everything that they touched turned to gold. Their stars were on the rise and they definitely weren't to be denied.

I often wonder if David Gates and Leon Russell ever think about those riotous nights at the Peppermint West in Hollywood laying down the groove with those mad hatters of twist, Steve Rowland and Budd Albright.

HARRISON CARROLL

Twist Session Ends Up in Free-for-All

The twist session at the New Faces Night Club in Hollywood really twisted up a storm.

Ten minutes before closing time, a husky Oklahoma singer, date of actress Fran Bennett, got into a fight with organist Bobby Hart. It wound up in a free-for-all. Marshall Edson, owner of Ye Little Club, got belted. Twistmasters Budd Albright and Steve Rowland leaped into the fray.

Watching goggle-eyed were Ty Hardin, with his new date, Lynn Aherne, Jo Morrow, Sports Magazine publisher Pete Petersen and various other celebs.

Out of the battle comes another bit of news. Fran Bennett (after the free-for-all started, she retired to the ladies room) got an interlocutory decree of divorce last February from Dr. John Williams, who previously was wed to Eva Gabor.

* * *

Singer Frankie Avalon wound up on crutches in Mexico City after a water-skiing accident in which he was slammed against the side of a motor boat. He suffered a lacerated and badly sprained leg. He'll be allowed off the crutches only for the two hours a night in which he performs.

LUCILLE BALL
Call the Movers

* * *

The jinx continues for Janet Leigh.

Her daughter, Kelley, has come down with the measles. Janet, who missed the disease when she was a kid, had to take time off from "Bye, Bye Birdie" rehearsals, to get a preventive shot.

* * *

Careers will pry apart the happily-wedded Lucille Ball and Gary Morton. Lucy will be tied up until late June on her Warner movie with Bob Hope, "Critic's Choice." After his engagement at the Dunes in Las Vegas, Gary will embark on a road tour that will carry him through July.

Lucille's portable dressing room on the set is so large it took house movers to transport it from Desilu to Warners. Bob Hope took

Wonderful break for Bob Wagner! Vittorio DeSica has signed him to play Sophia Loren's husband in the star's next movie that starts this month . . . Kim Novak's former beau, wealthy Fernando Parra, dated Vikki Dougan when he was in New York. . . . Alicia Clark, ex-wife of Edmund Purdom, who inherited millions on the death of her bridegroom, sewing machine heir Alfred Corning Clark, is at the Bel Air hotel. She may be returning to New York soon, though, for more dates with perfume heir, Bernard Lanvin. . . . Actress Kathy Marlowe tells me that she'll wed 28-year-old sportsman Gerald Livingston Thompson Sunday at the Rancho Buena Vista near La Paz, Mexico. Her wealthy bridegroom-to-be already has bought them a beautiful new home at Corona Del Mar. . . . When Steve McQueen returns from Europe, his new home on 40 acres of Big Sur property will be ready for occupancy. . . . Ricardo Montalban and wife, Georgiana, have bought an apartment in Paris. . . . Four of Roy Rogers' eight kids will work with him in his act at the Seattle World's Fair. . . . The Late Beat: Lew Ayres with Dolores Gray at the Oyster House. . . . Mary Le Bow with Tony Martino at the Islander. . . . Maureen Bailey with Bill Guasti at the Sportsmen's Lodge. . . Diane McBain with Eric Fleming at Jacks at the Beach. . . . The "Jumbo" cast gave Doris Day a combination birthday and anniversary party on the set. She and Marty Melcher have been married for 11 years.

* * *

TODAY'S PUZZLE: What wealthy producer has lost

Above: Harrison Carroll reports on Steve and Budd's riotous opening night at The New Faces night club in Hollywood.

REWIND BACK TO HOW IT ALL STARTED

Jim Mitchum, Budd Albright and I had been close friends for many years. Like great bloodhounds of destiny we made nightly rounds of the clubs, bars and happening hot spots of Beverly Hills, Santa Monica and Hollywood, on a wide-eyed sniff-out for girly activity. Places such as the Sea Witch on the Sunset Strip, PJ's on Santa Monica Boulevard and Crescent Heights were magnets for the very best female finery that Tinsel Town had to offer. A must to include was Grazaries on La Cienga Boulevard, where two local boys Pat & Lolly Vegas were rocking the room into crowded hysteria. The infamous Lenny Bruce outraged the paying public while doing a stint at Grazaries. His comic genius bought him jail time when he allegedly over-stepped the line of good taste with the immortal words, 'Daddy, daddy what's a degenerate?' 'Shut up and keep sucking.' America in the fifties didn't see the funny side.

Along with live music and a relaxed atmosphere, those establishments all had one thing in common — a plethora of arrestingly beautiful women in attendance.

Trinny Lopez, a young singer with a warm and gifted personality, packed them in at PJ's with his charm and special musical ability. He had the added skill of being able to turn the entire room into a massive sing-a-long with songs such as 'Blowing in the Wind', 'If I Had a Hammer' and 'Walk Right in'.

One of the secrets of Trinny's popularity was his open invitation for any aspiring singer in the audience to take over the microphone and belt out a number of his choice. It didn't matter if the person couldn't carry a tune in a bucket, Trinny would always furnish enthusiastic guitar accompaniment with a smile.

Budd and I usually scored big time with the ladies whenever we grabbed the opportunity to lay down a song or two backed by Trinny. We were pretty average singers, but it didn't really matter.

Chicks always seemed to materialize from out of the woodwork to applaud us with zealous enthusiasm. We were totally amazed at the reaction and took full advantage. The ladies appeared to love us. Our libidos were smoking.

The proof seemed to lie in the fact that whenever we sang we were always surrounded by female adoration. They warmed our hearts and warmed our beds.

It was during one of those nights at PJ's that the embryo of an idea first began to format. It had success written all over it.

The house that Jim Mitchum and I had rented on Hollywood Hills Drive at the top of Laurel Canyon came furnished with the added bonus of an upright piano.

Whenever we weren't filming, chasing after auditions, harassing our agents or generally networking our asses off scratching around for further acting jobs, we were usually together up at the house scamming new ideas on how to supplement our Hollywood profiles. Become outrages, come up with something original, see our names spelled correctly in *Variety* and the *Hollywood Reporter* — that would surely get us noticed by the industry and give us commercial value. We were banging our brains, hoping to come up with an answer.

Most nights Budd stayed over at our house, too tired to drive across the canyon to his crouching domicile. We had a lot of room and a big sofa so Budd ended up one step short of permanent guest status.

Between the three of us we knew practically every gorgeous girl walking — which certainly worked to our advantage with a non-stop river of female beauties flowing in and out of our bedrooms. Great times, but we weren't getting anywhere career wise. The time had come to stop playing and start getting serious.

Budd Albright, as well as his acting credentials, had acquired a recording deal with RCA, but nothing much had happened. Most nights he'd sort out his frustration by putting the piano to good use and pound out a few rock'n'roll numbers to recharge his batteries.

I'd recorded a couple of records with the Liberty label, both of which had received good reviews and a few plays on local radio, but nothing earth-shattering had materialized. Nevertheless I still kept the dream alive of one day having a hit record. Frustration had us both primed and we would take turns impressing each other with our vocal prowess, convinced that with luck and hard work we, as a duet, could become the next big thing. Inspired by the overenthusiastic reaction that we'd received at PJ's we were revitalized and felt that we might just have what it takes after all to make it to the big time, but we needed a plan of attack.

Jim kept the beer flowing, always encouraging us to shake our asses and put an act together. 'Prepare yourselves then take it to the public.' Those were his words. Our ambition began working overtime.

That's when the penny dropped.

Yee Little Club was a small nightclub styled in pseudo-English pub décor. It nestled tightly between two storefronts on Canon Drive, three strides from the corner of little Santa Monica Boulevard in the heart of Beverly Hills. It was predominantly a late night hangout for actors, agents, mob guys and great looking women. Most nights a trio was on hand keeping things cool by laying down unobtrusive jazz, accented by the clinking glass accompaniment of the bar-tender mixing drinks.

Yee Little Club had carved a niche within the annals of the jazz heads. Julie London and Bobby Troupe, the Oscar Peterson Trio, Errol Garner, Barney Kessel, Bud Powell and Andre Previn were just a few of the names that had brought in the customers. At this time however, patronage had been a little thin on the ground.

Budd and I were convinced that this could be the perfect venue to launch our plan of attack on the unsuspecting. We had it all worked out as we sat at a far corner table, entertaining a couple of beauties, trying to dazzle them with our crafted chat up lines. Budd slipped a word into the conversation that he and I were singers as well as actors and that we'd caused quite a commotion at PJ's with our dulcet tones. That grabbed the girls' attention. As we'd hoped, they seemed impressed and immediately wanted to hear us sing. After about five minutes of flirtatious conversation, the girls excused themselves, got up from the table and eased their way to the bar. A secret smile crawled across my face. I winked at Budd. We finished our drinks and waited.

A few moments passed and the musicians came to closure on the number that they'd been playing. The bass player took the microphone and made an announcement. 'Ladies and gentlemen, we have a couple of young recording artists here tonight. We'd like to bring them up to do a number. How about a big hand for Steve Rowland and Budd Albright?' Minimal applause. The patrons stared unimpressed. It didn't matter. Our moment had arrived.

Dressed in a practised coat of cool, our hair carefully in place,

Right: Addicted to rock 'n' roll.

we casually made our way up to the microphone. Budd mumbled a few words in the piano player's ear and suddenly the room resounded with the pounding intro to 'Long Tall Sally'. Budd took off on the first verse and by the time I took over the second, all hell had broken loose in Yee Little Club. Suddenly the club's cool atmosphere exploded into a cacophony of stamping feet and excited voices. Glasses were knocked to the floor as the gathered drinkers hammered the tables with an accompanying rhythm. The number finished to a thunderous reaction pockmarked with shouts of 'More! More! Do another song! Hey, do you guys know "Kansas City"? How about "I Got a Woman"?'

We were overwhelmed as we instantly tore into another number — then another, then one more. We had the room rocking and judging by the reaction, the clubbers loved it. The club started filling up with strangers, who having heard the shouts and commotion from outside in the street began crowding through the entrance, curious to discover the cause.

After three more high-energy classics we thanked the appreciative crowd and returned to passionate kisses from the two gorgeous girls that we'd been sitting with earlier.

On our way home that night with the replay of excitement resounding in our heads we felt omnipotent. Our plan had paid off. The next move was to cement the future.

The owner and manager of Yee Little Club was an all round cool guy. As well as a slick promoter, he was a well-known, respected face around town. His name was Marshal Edson. As luck would have it, he happened to enter the club during the height of the musical frenzy. The hysteria momentarily stopped his forward motion. 'What's going on?' he shouted, as he pushed his way through the crowd.

'Hey boss, it's really kicked off tonight. Those two guys are the culprits,' the bartender said, pointing at us and at the same time struggling to manage the surging request for more drinks.

Marshal Edson's eyes flashed around the room like searchlights. He was no fool. He could see money. He was also not shy in coming forward whenever female activity filled the room. Tonight there was an abundance of talent, most of whom had gathered around us.

'Hey you guys are great!' he shouted as he headed toward our table smiling. 'Let's talk a little business. Do you mind?' Pulling up a chair he wasted no time in getting right to it.

'How about you two coming in on Monday night and doing some songs? If things go well you can have a permanent spot every Monday. I can also get you some more gigs. I got a few connections around town. What do ya say?' As Marshal spoke his eyes undressed the two girls that were draped over us.

'Yeah, OK. Sounds cool,' I said looking at Budd.

'We'll talk money later,' Marshal said, getting up from the table and motioning for the bartender to send over some free drinks. 'See you boys Monday night.'

We set fire to the telephone lines spreading the word on the jungle grapevine that the in-place to be on Monday night was Yee Little Club in Beverly Hills. We let it be known that there'd be hot chicks and cool guys grooving to the rocking sounds of Steve Rowland and Budd Albright, backed by the Jack Nitzsche Trio.

The following Monday night the club was packed tighter than a tin of sardines with many bystanders hanging around outside hoping to get in. We'd managed to attract a mob along with a minority of industry names.

Jim Mitchum and his father, Robert, Mitzi Gaynor with a few friends from Twentieth Century Fox studios and Edd 'Kookie' Burns with Asa Maynor gave added credibility to our opening night.

I'm sure that it was mostly curiosity that drew the crowd that night. It was more than likely that our musical enthusiasm rather than our singing talent was what had created the action that continued to fill Yee Little Club every Monday night for the next two months. Marshal loved the fact that our Monday night appearances always coincided with the flocks of attractive women decorating the room. The possibility of a one-night stand, or simply a romantic encounter, brought guys with money to burn who were eager to splash out buying drinks for the women who were more than delighted to accept the attention.

Budd and I had it made in the shade. We had the best place in the world to pull pumpage — from behind a microphone facing a room full of beauty with a song on our lips.

Our Monday nights had become a success and had given Marshal Edson's club a huge boost in popularity not to mention an increase in financial gain. He was keen to look after us and to get our names on a bit of management paper. That was cool with Budd and me, seeing as he had been helpful in orchestrating our success. While business negations were in progress with Marshal we felt that what we really needed in order to move forward was a band of our own. We'd then be self-contained and able to play larger venues.

After a few weeks of auditioning players we put together a solid group of musicians, two guitars, bass, and drums, adding a sax player a short time later.

The word was out that we were ready to rock. We began by playing at industry parties as well as at many of Hollywood's exclusive social events. We were rapidly becoming the 'darlings' of the party circuit and revelled in the adoration that we were receiving. It was difficult not to get carried away with all the female attention that was gathering around us. We dealt with it as best we could from the bedroom.

The management paperwork had yet to be signed, so Budd and I decided to put on our promoter's hat and chase up a few club owners ourselves.

The line of bullshit that we laid down opened doors and it wasn't long before we found ourselves appearing in clubs and bars all over town. We played in places where the cigarette smoke was so bad that you couldn't see clearly beyond the front tables. Most of the owners and managers spoke as if they had piano wire around their necks and the bar staff looked like fugitives from San Quentin. Every now and then jealousy would rise up when a customer's wife or girlfriend displayed too much enthusiasm over our blatantly sexual gyrations. At such times we'd have to be escorted from the venue for our own safety.

We were gigging constantly, but the pay was shit.

Since the management contract still hadn't been signed I was surprised to receive an excited phone call from Marshal Edson. 'Steve, get a hold of Budd! I want you guys to go over to the Encore Room on La Cienga Boulevard and see a guy called Jack Chambers. He's looking for a rock'n'roll group to spark up his mid-week. You guys fit the bill. But before you go, come up to my house and let's get this management deal signed. I trust you guys, but if I'm gonna look after you, let's get things on paper. What do ya say?'

We left Marshal Edson's Cold Water Canyon home with a signed management contract and the determination to conquer the big time.

The Encore Room was a nightclub that had the appearance of a bygone era. The white-walled architecture and shrouded entrance was straight out of a 1940s crime novel. You could imagine Humphrey Bogart standing in the shadows, his eyes squinting above the match in his cupped hands as he bent to light a cigarette.

An enormous antique doorknob set in the centre of a brass surround, jutted from the middle of the oversized green padded entrance to the club. Once inside, we immediately noticed that the tiny stage had been set up to accommodate a jazz artist. The lighting and sound system was a definite no-no for a rock'n'roll group. The place smelled of booze and the previous night's cigarettes. Dirty glasses and unemptied ashtrays still littered the bar. One or two cigarette butts and remnants of careless ash could be seen on some of the tables. Obviously clearing up was not a priority. The air conditioning must have been on holiday as the room's ventilation was non-existent thus maintaining a stale ambiance.

From out of the afternoon shadows that had formed at the back of the club, ambled Jack Chambers. Casually dressed in a yellow alpaca sweater, black well-fitted slacks and black loafers, his persona was that of a pro golfer. On first impression he was a personable guy but you'd think twice before you'd buy a used car from him.

'Hello, boys. I've been expecting you. Marshal Edson tells me that you're just the guys to light up my Thursday nights. What do ya think?'

'Absolutely,' Budd said, 'but first we need to make sure of a couple of things. Your set-up leaves a lot to be desired. We'll need some spotlights, mics and a good sound system, one that won't overload when the Fender guitars and our vocals are mixed through it. We expect people to get up and dance. They won't want to hear a lot of distortion.'

'We gotta make sure that your sound system won't fuse out and blow the lights,' I said, grinning, trying not to show disdain. The blood drained from Jack Chambers' face. He breathed heavily and leaned back against the bar. Budd and I looked at each other. More discussion would possibly cause Jack to have a stroke. We knew what we had to do if we expected a successful evening.

Budd and I got busy. We rearranged the stage, taped up all the loose wires, bought new light bulbs and replaced those that were burnt out. We then went out and hired a small lighting rig and a proper sound system with monitors and a separate mixing desk for our vocals, one that we could operate from the stage.

With the security of proper equipment in place, we then began networking with tornado ferocity. With the help of Jim Mitchum we called the newspapers, the KTLA television news desk and all the local gossip rags. We hyped them into believing that Thursday night at the Encore Room was the place to be if they wanted to witness outrageous behaviour. Finally we phoned our celebrity friends and every gorgeous girl that we knew. We begged them to come and bring their friends. We promised them a night to remember. We were in the mood to kick ass.

Jack Chambers was nervous on the opening night. He almost wore out the club's carpet as he paced back and forth wringing his hands, beads of perspiration catching the light. It was nearing 9 p.m. and only a handful of people had arrived. Jack went outside and looked in the parking lot. 'There're only a couple of cars. Where are all the people that you guys promised?' The veins in Jack's neck bulged to bursting as he screamed at us from the front of the club.

'They'll be here,' we assured him.

A short time before 10 p.m. we heard commotion break out in front of the club. The clamour of horns honking in frustration mixed with the reverberation of vocal irritation, brought Jack running. There was panic in the parking lot as the two attendants, overwhelmed by the crush of high dollar machinery, tried to deal with the drivers' impatience. The room began filling up as a multitude of faces began streaming through the entrance. Heated discussion was heard as a couple of smartly dressed customers obviously had already had too much to drink and were loudly arguing about their right to secure a front table.

It seemed as though only minutes had passed when the Encore Room began vibrating with a capacity crowd. Besides, there was a gaggle of beautiful females, dressed to cause heart palpitations. Our celebrity friends hadn't let us down. Robert Mitchum and his son Jim had a table at the front. Max Baer Jr, Connie Stevens, Peter Brown, Robert Conrad, Carmen Phillips, Louis Prima and Keely Smith had all turned up for a share of our musical mayhem.

Jack Chambers surely must have felt his blood pressure go into overdrive with the realization of how much money the club was going to make.

We kicked off at 10:30 and within what seemed like only minutes the room erupted into frenzy. Expensive footwear stomped to the beat while those that were more inspired exhibited a flagrant display of sexual manoeuvres as they crowded the tiny dance floor.

The cocktail waitresses had difficulty hanging on to trays of drinks as they struggled to negotiate through the pandemonium. The two bartenders were under attack from impatient customers who couldn't get served fast enough. Jack rushed behind the bar to help out.

As we were finishing our last set to tumultuous applause, a smiling Marshal Edson walked into the club. 'Looks like it's been a successful evening. You boys have the joint jumping.' Marshal's smile said it all as he walked toward the bar to speak to Jack. It was obvious that future negotiations were on his agenda.

The Encore Room took in over two grand that night. Jack was elated and told Marshal that he'd like to have us to play the weekends as well as every Thursday. By the end of the month we were doing five nights a week to a packed house. Some of Hollywood's hottest stars, like Burt Reynolds, Jane Powell and Debbie Reynolds frequently turned up to enjoy the madness. A couple of our contemporaries, Marc Cavell and Jericho Brown were constantly in the audience, digging our music while eyeballing the passing parade of classy females that had become part of our entourage.

Jack Chambers was doing cartwheels. Not only was he raking it in, but his charm offensive was on a constant high rev, raining special attention on the many celebrity faces that were always in

Hollywood's Own
Twist Sensation's
STEVE
ROWLAND
and
BUDD
ALBRIGHT
Invites You
To A
GIANT TWIST DANCE SPECTACULAR
THIS FRIDAY, FEB. 16th — DEAUVILLE CLUB, Santa Monica
Donation—$2.00—Must bring this invitation
(Suits and dresses required)
Produced by Ted Cooper — Wally Eagler
$50.00 PRIZE TO TWIST CONTEST WINNER

attendance, twisting the night away.

While our moon was in orbit Marshal moved us on to bigger, more important venues. It wasn't long before we were the headline act at the fashionable Peppermint West, Hollywood's most popular, high-octane dance emporium, catering to a multitude of twist addicts six nights a week. The door to the big time was swinging open and for a short time we were riding the crest of stardom.

However, the public are fickle and after a while the twist was no longer in vogue. The Peppermint West shut its doors and the crowd moved on. We were out of fashion.

When you're hot, you're hot! When you're not, you're not!

That's show business.

It's Party Time

The summer sun presented an angry face by introducing July with the scorching heat of a witch's cauldron, toasting the residents of Hollywood into wilting submission.

The midday fiery furnace had forged the newly laid blacktop surface on Sunset Boulevard in front of the Sea Witch into soft moulding putty. If you were so inclined you could have left your shoe print imbedded there for posterity. A subtle breeze that had idled over the Pacific Ocean was fighting to gather some puff as it chased behind the afternoon inferno with the hope of bringing on much needed evening relief. The tick-tock on my wrist let me know that it was close on six p.m. I was beat to the street and dragging my ass as I turned right off Kings Road and headed homeward for a breather. I needed to recharge my batteries in preparation for the evening's adventure.

I eased the Corvette into kerbside parking on the hill above where La Cienga meets The Sunset Strip, crawled out and loped down the incline with the eager intention of acquiring an ice-cold six-pack of Budweiser from the Liquor Locker on the corner before crossing Sunset Boulevard to my temporary accommodation at the Sunset Towers West residential. Those who installed the Liquor Locker's refrigeration system must have had the South Pole in mind, for, by the time I reached the apartment, my hand clutching the king of beers was frozen numb and beginning to throb.

Blistering summer days in LA are frequent, but this day brought to mind what burning in hell must feel like.

Once inside, I couldn't wait to undress and hit some cool shower time. My first priority however, was to bust open a cold can of Bud and wash the dryness from my smogged out throat with a soothing flush of the golden hops. After dragging a long swig from the frosty can of soothing liquid I reached over and switched on the stereo. Leaning back I closed my eyes and let the voice of Bobby Darin take me 'Somewhere Beyond The Sea' - to a place where everything was peaceful and uncomplicated.

Pulling my sweat-soaked tee-shirt off over my head I lay shirtless, cooling in the comforting embrace of the sofa, nodding in time to the hypnotic purr of the air conditioner. I closed my eyes. A swirling montage of pastoral images filled the screen behind my lids, shape shifting into the facial beauty of Kathy Case - her voice and gorgeous body still haunting my subconscious mind with terrifying clarity. Interweaving emotions flooded my thoughts, erasing the past in a complexity of colour only to rearrange into a mysterious radiance of unfathomed beauty.

Confusion wrestled me back to an instant state of reality. I'd been a visitor to the land of nod and time had seemed to pass slowly while in fact it had raced away. It was getting late and I had to shift my ass. I pulled down a final mouthful of Budweiser and started for the shower just as a whacked out Budd Albright entered the room. We'd been sharing the apartment since our riotous nightclub act had spiralled upward and rooming together close to the action seemed for us the obvious answer. Another factor being that the lease on Pumpage Palace had run its course and my friend and former house mate, Jim Mitchum had decided to move in with his latest flame.

'Hey man, how's it hanging?' Budd croaked as he flopped down in the nearest chair.

'Christ, it sure has been a scorcher,' I answered, once again heading for the bathroom. 'I'm late. I gotta grab a quick shower and get threaded out. I'm seeing Yvette Vickers. Tonight's the night that I'm hoping to get lucky.'

'Where ya going?' Budd's voice was husky with weariness.

'I'm taking her to The Luau - then hopefully back to her place in Benedict Canyon.' The rushing force of the shower covered the final part of my answer. 'I've really got a thing for her,' I screamed through the hiss of cascading water. 'I sure as hell don't want to fuck up by being late.' My last three words were cancelled out by the telephone's anxious jingle. 'I got it,' Budd yelled from the

Right: Yvette Vickers was very special. She stirred my soul.

other room.

As I hurriedly stepped from the cubicle and began drying off I could hear the excited tone in Budd's voice rise to a crescendo as he hung up the phone.

'That was Evie Johnson. She's having a dinner party tonight and wanted to know if we'd be able to come. She said that she'd only slung it together at the very last minute and apologised for the terribly short notice.'

'What'd ya tell her?' my question echoed from the bathroom.

'I thanked her for the invite and said that I'd definitely be there, but that you were heavily into a new romance and had already made plans. I hope you're not pissed off at what I said. I know you, Steve. You'd pass on any dinner party in favour of Yvette. Right?' I poked my head around the door. Budd looked sheepish. 'I probably should have asked you first, but . . . Anyway you can call her back. Tell her you'll come. She won't mind if you bring Yvette.'

'No, man, it's cool. You're right. I'd much rather party alone. Yvette's special, if you know what I mean.'

Budd's feet were already moving for the bathroom. 'I'll tell you about the happenings tomorrow,' he said, excitement in his delivery. The splashing shower blocked out all further conversation.

Evie Johnson is the ex-wife of Van Johnson, one of Hollywood's top stars. My father directed him in the MGM film, *The Romance Of Rosy Ridge*. Van Johnson was partly responsible for launching the career of Janet Leigh when he accepted the then unknown 21-year-old girl as his co-star in the film. It was a magnanimous gesture rarely shown by a major film star in 1950s Hollywood.

Evie Johnson was renowned for throwing wild Hollywood parties, often inviting up-and-coming young actors and actresses to partake in her hospitality. It was alleged that most weeks Evie made the rounds to the many top action spots seeking out the next Tab, Rock, Debbie, Marilyn, Rod, Burt, Troy etc. She would then effortlessly throw together a gala evening and invite everyone

Above: Evie and Van Johnson during better days.

who was anyone to her huge home south of Sunset Boulevard in Beverley Hills. Evie enjoyed discovering new talent and laying on festive get-togethers. If truth be known however, it more than likely filled a small void in her life as well.

Evie was always a gracious hostess, sparing nothing in creating fabulous evenings. On many occasions these gatherings oozed with sexual vibrations. Every striving young actor and actress was well aware that if they were lucky enough to receive an invite to a gathering at Evie Johnson's they'd make sure to be there. Once through the front door, they'd never know whom they were likely to encounter. However, one thing was for sure, among the gathered guests they'd surely be rubbing shoulders with a few heavyweights who have controlling power in the film industry.

Major stars such as Glenn Ford, Dick Powell, Keenan Wynn, Janet Leigh, Tony Curtis and Rod Taylor frequented these gatherings. Important directors, producers, the heads of casting, all were part of the Evie Johnson inner circle.

These were faces rarely seen in public, preferring to socialize at private functions such as Evie Johnson's where they could relax and let their hair down, secure in the fact that whatever went on at these shindigs remained sealed behind silent lips.

You'd sell your grandmother to get an invite. I was well pissed off at missing out, but I was really into Yvette. She stirred up fire below my waist, but much more important - I was hoping to kidnap her heart.

THE FOLLOWING IS BUDD ALBRIGHT'S REPORT ON WHAT ALLEGEDLY WENT DOWN DURING THE EVENING'S FESTIVITIES.

By 7.30 p.m. I was buzzing west on Sunset Boulevard heading towards Beverly Hills in my Italian Fiat Abarth Zagato sports car. The name sounds expensive and powerful, but in reality, it was an exotic name for a pile of shit. It was tiny – too small for a midget, underpowered, air-cooled, noisy and slow. However, it looked fast and sexy. It was dark blue displaying two white racing stripes that ran from the boot over the roof and down across the bonnet. You could hear it coming from a block away, howling like a junkyard dog on Benzedrine.

As I pulled up outside Evie Johnson's palatial domicile my eyes glimpsed the real deal – large, fast, expensive luxury machinery parked in the street out front, silent and seductively gleaming. I quickly drove further on and stashed my machine around the corner out of sight of the festivities. The last thing I needed were sarcastic eyes ruining my evening with subversive comments about my ride. As I shut off the panting motor, I said a little prayer: 'Please God, let this pile of crap fire up when I come to leave.'

As I strolled up the street towards Evie's residence, I wondered if my clothes were wrinkled from the frantic drive over. Although the promised breeze had done its best to cool things down, the temperature still inspired hints of perspiration.

I was about to turn on to the walkway that led up to the front door when I sensed two shadowy figures approaching from the opposite side of the street. Like two phantoms George Hamilton and Susan Kohner emerged from the darkness with smiles on their faces. They were obviously invited guests for the same evening ahead. I smiled and waited for them to catch up to me.

Susan Kohner is the daughter of Paul Kohner, one of Hollywood's most powerful agents.

A sudden tickle of fear scrambled through my thoughts –'I sure as hell hope that I'll meet a friendly face once I'm inside.' At that moment I had no idea how the night was going to turn out.

Above: Only a fool would disrespect Rod Taylor.

George, Susan and I arrived at Evie's front door together. George pressed the bell. Chimes played a melody that seemed to go on forever as if calling for a gathering of archangels. Suddenly, the door banged open and there stood Brad Dexter (big, bad Brad) waving a drink in his hand. 'You got it. This is the place! Come on in - the bar's down there. Hey George, what's shaking?' Brad had had a few already.

I looked around to see if I was invisible. I might as well have been. Brad put his unoccupied hand on George's shoulder, and motioning for Susan to follow, started down a long dimly lit hallway, completely ignoring my presence. An uneasy feeling crept into my stomach. 'What was I in for?'

The walls along the corridor were covered with expensive oil paintings, some of which had the aged glow of original masters, but I wasn't sure. I didn't stop to look, but followed after towards the distant sound of ebullient activities. We emerged into a huge party room and bar area. The ambiance was more like what you'd face bursting through the door of an Irish pub on St Patrick's Day. It was all happening full on. The room was bustling with what looked like every major name in the Hollywood book of notables. Sitting at the bar was Rod Taylor in deep discussion with Rhonda Fleming. Leaning against the bar next to them and joining in the conversation was Dick Powell. At the other end of the room, Keenan Wynn, Bob Harris and Chad Everett were holding court. Lee Marvin was behind the bar acting out the role of bartender.

Brad yelled out, 'Hey everybody: George is here.' Once again ignored, I desperately looked around trying to spot a friendly face. I needed momentary sanctuary to gather my cool. With trepidation I eased myself into the arena. The chairs and sofas were festooned with faces I'd never seen before, yet somehow they all seemed familiar. The ones that had a more youthful appearance displayed an eager look of anticipation hoping they'd be able to score a contact that would further their journey along the road to fame.

Evie spotted me and instantly hurried over. 'Everybody! Let me introduce you. Meet Budd Albright.'

Bob Harris looked up. 'Hey Budd, how's it dangling?' I nodded in recognition.

Evie took my hand and led me around the room introducing me to everyone individually. 'Budd, say hello to Peter Shaw. Peter is the head of production at MGM. Hey Joe, meet Budd Albright. Budd – Joe Pasternak.' I'd certainly heard of Joe Pasternak. He'd discovered Judy Garland and was the producer of that great MGM movie, *Summer Stock*. Joe Pasternak's list of successful movies is legendary. *The Great Caruso*, introducing and starring Mario Lanza, was another of his superb musicals. Joe Pasternak was a legend. I was about to ask him to catch Steve and me in action at the Peppermint Lounge West. Thank God I thought better of it and kept quiet.

Evie guided me throughout the room, introducing me to directors, producers, wives and girlfriends of the famous. My head was spinning. I looked for an oasis. I needed to reset my brain.

Someone stepped from the bar and jammed a drink in my hand. I mumbled thanks and ambled over to Bob Harris. Bob was a sports car racer from the Pacific Palisades. At least the two of us had something in common. I felt less intimidated talking to him. Bob drove a modified Jaguar XK120. It was yellow with four black racing stripes. Steve and I had tangled with Bob's infamous Jag on Sunset Boulevard a few times. It was hyper fast – big time. The car had won in its class at Santa Barbara, Palm Springs and Riverside. It was a lethal racing machine and Bob was a full on racing driver. He would go on to race for Lotus along with Steve

McQueen, later to become one of Hollywood's top motion picture stunt drivers.

Bob's friendly smile had a relaxing effect as he introduced me to Keenan Wynn. 'Nice to meet you, Budd. Hey, Bob tells me that you like street racing. That right?' Before I could answer, Keenan barked at me, 'What do you drive?'

I took a long sip of my drink before answering with a timid response, 'An Abarth Zagato.'

'An Abarth Zagato!' screamed Keenan, turning to smile at Bob. 'That's a pile of pig shit! It's a goddamn fucking tin can load of

Below: Friendly stars, Keenan Wynn and Van Johnson.

crap - no balls, air-cooled, with a shit transmission. What the hell are you doing driving that?'

I wanted to submerge into my drink. 'It's just temporary,' I said.

'Listen Budd, Bob tells me that you're a good driver. You want to get a real kick in the ass?' Keenan had a slight challenging tone to his voice.

'Sure, why not?' I replied. I was hoping that he'd forgotten about the Abarth.

'Tomorrow, we're all going down to Southgate Raceway. That's a little place where they race go-karts. You wanna come down and try your hand at driving one?' The challenge was still in Keenan's voice. 'Southgate's the place to get the feel of things and to see if you've got what it takes to be a real winner. Bob's been down there a few times. Drove right off the track the first time.'

Keenan roared with laughter. 'He went flying into the hay bales at the end of the front straightaway. You should have seen it.' Keenan laughed even louder as he banged Bob on the back playfully.

Christ, what was I getting myself into? Here I was talking to a guy with the biggest cajones in sports car racing and a crazy actor who drinks Vodka straight out of the bottle. I smiled at the two of them, not sure what to say next.

'Steve Rowland is my roommate. Is it OK if he comes along?

'Sure,' said Keenan 'I know his old man. I made a film with him - one of my best parts. Roy's a cool guy. You oughta get Steve to ask Roy if he'd like to—'

Just at that moment, agitated voices began rising from the direction of the bar. Brad Dexter had brought one of his boozing buddies along to the party and neither Brad nor his friend was feeling any pain. The guys that Brad Dexter hung out with were mostly hard cases who loved to drink and all that went along with it. I wondered why I hadn't noticed the guy before. He was massive, at least six feet four, weighing over two hundred pounds. There was a feeling of suppressed violence about his persona. Completely out of his skull and looking for trouble, he was too

Right: Rhonda Fleming, the template for glamour.

stupid to realize that trouble was right there staring him in the face. Brad Dexter, with a smirk on his face, was leaning on the bar for support. His big friend's arrogance went into overdrive as he loudly began pitching superlatives at Rhonda Fleming who had come to the party with Rod Taylor. Rhonda was obviously annoyed and embarrassed at the unwanted attention that she was getting. Rod turned slowly on his bar stool and looked up at the huge guy hanging over Rhonda, spouting obnoxious remarks.

'I really don't think that the lady wants to talk to you, so why don't you piss off?' Rod spoke softly, as he took a measured sip of his drink.

Ignoring Rod, Prince Charming continued. 'Come on, baby, let's you and me have a little dancee-dancee. Wha-do-ya say?' Brad Dexter, knowing of Rod Taylor's reputation as one tough son of a bitch, suddenly became sober and stood at the bar like a frozen rope.

Rhonda tried to defuse the situation with a laugh, but the big guy reached over and put his arm around her shoulder. 'I think the lady really wants to have a little dance with me - don'tcha baby? It ain't got nothin' to do with you,' he snarled, looking straight at Rod Taylor. He was almost pulling Rhonda off the barstool. His remarks were inviting danger.

'I really wouldn't do that,' said Taylor softly, his voice laced with menace. The entire room suddenly fell silent. Brad Dexter's friend was unwilling to back down in front of everyone and chose to leave his arm around Rhonda Fleming's shoulder. As I said, he'd been looking for trouble and he'd found it. Out of nowhere from a sitting position at the bar, Rod threw a punch that connected squarely on the side of the leering face. The sound was reminiscent of Willy Mays batting a home run in Candlestick Park. Crack! The big guy's head flew back like a crash test dummy.

Anyone else would have realized his mistake and cooled it. Not this asshole. Instead, he reeled back, shook his head and threw a roundhouse shot at Rod – that missed.

Rod now got to his feet. He threw a left hook to the body and followed up with a crushing right to the guy's chin. Bang! Crunch! The obnoxious guy's head almost disconnected from his body. His feet came off the floor, as he literally flew through the air landing backwards on the polished parquet surface. The power in Rod Taylor's fists exploded with such force that Mister Marvellous slid along the floor about ten feet. Only the wall stopped him travelling further. A silent shock of astonishment filled the room.

George Hamilton, his hand clutching a drink, stepped back and raised his glass in a mock salute. 'It's been nice having you here. We really must do lunch one day.'

Evie Johnson had been in another part of the house. Hearing the commotion, she burst onto the scene screaming, 'The antiques, the antiques, for God's sake knock it off before you break up all the furniture - they cost a fortune. God damn it Keenan! What have you started?' she yelled at him accusingly. 'Me? I didn't start a thing,' said Keenan, with an incredulous rasp. 'It was King Kong over there on the floor. He got a bit too friendly with Rhonda and Rod sorted him out.

Evie Johnson was Keenan`s ex-wife. To her, whenever there was trouble, Keenan Wynn was always a suspect. It was a knee-jerk reaction back to the time when they were together as man and wife.

Rod turned to Brad Dexter. 'Get that piece of shit outa here, Brad or you're next - and you'd better apologise to Evie for bringing that asshole here in the first place.'

Brad's eyes were like dinner plates. He was now stone cold sober. 'You got it, Rod. I'll take care of it.' Brad struggled along the hall towards the front entrance supporting his concussed friend. George Hamilton was already waiting at the front door. In his most regal manner, he laid the final 'straightener' on the damaged hulk. 'Good night, sir, I hope you enjoyed the evening. Please don't come again.' The door was opened and Brad Dexter along with his repugnant friend was deposited ignominiously on to the front forecourt.

Back in the party room Rod also apologised. 'Please forgive me, Evie but I'm allergic to assholes. However, I think we managed to miss the furniture.' That said, Rod coolly sat back down at the bar and turned to Rhonda Fleming, 'Now, where were we when we were so rudely interrupted?'

It was like a scene out of a Western B-movie – the most incredible thing I'd ever witnessed. Even more amazing was the fact that when the aggravation was going down, nobody moved or tried to break it up - not even Lee Marvin. Afterwards things settled down and although some of the main faces had left during the skirmish, the party once again continued with exuberance as if nothing out of the ordinary had taken place.

Sometime after midnight, the few remaining guests started to leave. They'd all survived a most entertaining evening to say the least. I thanked Evie for the invite and stopped outside to ask Keenan for the directions to Southgate Raceway. I told him that, all being well, Steve and I would see him there tomorrow.

As I started in the direction of where I'd hidden my car, a voice from behind called out, 'Hey, Budd, which way are you going?' It was George and Susan. I answered that I was going back to the Sunset Towers West. 'If it's not too much out of your way would you mind giving Susan and me a lift to the Beverly Wilshire Hotel?'

A spike of fear stabbed me. Oh shit! 'Of course, George, no problem. Uh …the only thing is uh …' I was gagging for words, 'I have this little Italian sports car and it's… uh … well, it's–'

'Hey, so do I. They're great, aren't they? My Ferrari's in the shop till Monday. Susan and I had to come by cab tonight. It takes forever to get a taxi this time of night in Beverly Hills.' I could hear it in George Hamilton's voice. He was anxious to check out my machine.

'Yeah, George,' I answered, 'they really are great,' as if I knew what the hell I was talking about when it came to Ferraris.

When George saw my car he was speechless for a moment. 'Nice! What is it?'

'It's a Fiat Abarth Zagato.' I tried to make the name sound impressive.

'It looks very small,' Susan commented quizzically.

George seemed bemused as he looked around the tiny car. We all squeezed in. Susan sat in the front bucket seat next to me. George Hamilton, one of MGM's biggest stars, sat behind us in what pretended to be a jump seat. His six-foot frame scrunched in sideways.

What little room there was forced his back into a bent over position, with his head between his legs. His knees practically touched the roof. There was just a thin metal panel between George and the engine that ran red-hot the moment it started up. Accompanying this were dual, throbbing, overloud exhaust pipes that shook the car's entire bodywork. We were set to go. I said a silent prayer. Christ, I couldn't believe it. I turned the key and the damn thing fired right up.

We roared off like a herd of turtles. It was after 1 a.m. and we were on our way to the Beverly Wilshire Hotel, stuffed inside my motorized tin can like sardines on a gypsy's holiday.

As we rattled up in front of the hotel, I could see that the doorman was making moves to call security. He surely must have thought that we were rolling toward destruction.

With the help of the doorman and an agile security guy we finally were able to unravel George Hamilton from the back jump seat. He couldn't move. His back was in spasm, locked in a bent-over position. Susan Kohner announced that she was having trouble hearing as she hobbled into the hotel clutching her ears.

Avoiding obvious trouble, I quickly said goodnight and

thundered off into the early morning mist. I was sure of one thing. George Hamilton and Susan Kohner would remember that joyride for a long time. The Abarth Zagato had surely made a lasting impression.

EPILOGUE

About a year later, I was having lunch at the fashionable Beverly Hills eatery, La Scala. As I got up to leave, I spotted George Hamilton and a lovely blonde honey at a table near the front. As I made my way towards the exit I stopped behind his table, and in my best dulcet tone said, 'Listen, George, if you and the young lady would like a lift somewhere after lunch, I have my Abarth outside.'

George reacted with a serious supply of bemusement as he looked around. For a moment, he didn't quite compute. Then it hit him. 'Budd, how are you?' He rose from his seat and we shook hands. 'You haven't still got that crazy machine have you?'

'No,' I said with a laugh. 'It finally died in the Mount Baldy parking lot – and after a full day of skiing. I had to have it towed back to LA. My lady wasn't impressed. It took us all night to get home. Probably one of the reasons she and I aren't together any more.'

George roared with laughter then, turning to his date, he said,

'Sweetheart, I've got to tell you a story about that car. Budd and I were at one of Evie Johnson's dinner parties and I asked Budd if he would mind giving me a lift…'

As I walked out into the Beverly Hills sunlight, I could hear George and his lovely partner laughing hysterically. It made my day.

STEVE'S AFTERTHOUGHT: THE MORNING AFTER THE NIGHT BEFORE

Budd had undoubtedly witnessed far-out happenings at Evie Johnson's. I almost wet myself laughing at the story and the way he related the events, reliving the special moments in flamboyant style. Bootlegging the dramatic method acting of Rod Steiger's character in *On The Waterfront*, Budd retold the fight scene over and over, elaborating on the pomposity of the unfortunate hard man. I laughed so much that I fell on the floor gasping for breath. I was really sorry that I wasn't there to see it all in person.

Even more hilarious was Budd's tale of his illustrious journey, while delivering George Hamilton and Susan Kohner to The Beverly Wilshire Hotel. The description played like a scene from a Laurel and Hardy comedy.

I was feeling all greatness. I'd had a fantastic evening with Yvette Vickers. I discovered that she's a quality person. She pushed all the right buttons and I couldn't wait to see her again. I didn't like to admit it, but I could have been arrested for my thoughts whenever her loveliness crowded my mind.

SOUTHGATE RACEWAY

Budd shook me awake bright and early with Keenan Wynn's invitation to check out the go-kart action at Southgate Raceway. Although I hadn't gotten home until after two thirty in the morning, at the mention of kart racing I was up and bounding.

Sunday morning brought on grinning sunshine chaperoned by puffs of cotton-white clouds that helped keep the previous day's heat at bay. I could feel it. Today was going to be memorable. I dressed in the space of two minutes and with anxiety rising like Lucifer, I was ready to rumble.

Fifteen minutes after throwing together a quick breakfast of fruit and yogurt and washing it down with a cup of Maxwell House, Budd and I were out of the apartment and on the move, motoring down the Long Beach Freeway towards new adventure at Southgate Raceway. Excitement coursed though our bodies in anticipation of what most certainly lay ahead. We couldn't wait to take on the day. The clock on the dashboard of Budd's car reflected ten minutes to eight. We were chasing excitement as we sped east through the minimal Sunday morning traffic, keeping anxious eyes on the lookout out for the Southgate turn-off.

I was never up that early on weekends unless it was for viewing a sporting event or more importantly, taking a competitive part in amateur motor racing events. Both Budd and I secretly harboured visions of holding aloft the winner's trophy at any one of the many championship race circuits dotted around the country. Each of us had served an apprenticeship in motor racing and we had the scars to prove it.

Budd and I had been out hitting it hard on Saturday night, however we were chasing a dream and the adrenalin had kicked in big time.

As we approached the Firestone Boulevard exit ramp, we could see the Southgate racetrack below us on the right. Turning off we followed a couple of late arrivals through the gates and into the Raceway parking lot. Although we were only invited as spectators, we'd arrived ready to roar.

Once inside the area, we eased through the rows of already parked vans and cars, some of which towed trailers, the karts strapped on securely. Others carried go-karts on the roofs of their cars, fastened on to specially constructed racks. The majority, however were unloading their machinery from small, colourfully painted vans and setting up attached canopies that allowed mechanical preparation to be carried out in a shaded environment.

Budd and I searched for a slot and were lucky enough to find space near the pit area. We quickly ducked in. With the smell of the fuel mixtures and the sharp crack of racing engines starting up, all remaining Sunday morning cobwebs disappeared post-haste. We stepped out into the clamour and anxiously began looking around for Keenan Wynn. Christ! I couldn't believe it. He was already there, bright-eyed and bushy tailed, looking sober as a judge. As we walked toward him he waved us over, a huge, inviting grin played across his face. 'Hey guys! Glad you could make it.' Then turning to a mechanic, who was working feverishly on his kart, he spat some instructions. 'I'm sure I need some shorter gearing. Check it out! I gotta have more grunt to get out of the corners. Wha-da-ya think?' Then turning to us, Keenan said, 'Come on guys, I'm gonna introduce you to Von Deming, one of the head honchos around here.'

We began walking through the crowded pit area in the direction of the workshop. The whole vicinity was alive with the activity of race preparation. You could feel a vibrant flow of competition gaining momentum as the clock ticked towards 10 a.m. — the commencement of the day's competition. I was impressed. I was certain that Budd was in his element as well.

Von Deming's face cracked a forced smile as we approached. His craggy features let it be known that he was probably about ten years older than Budd and me. Short-cut, light brown hair crowned his five feet eight inch height and gave edge to his sullen persona. Von had seen action with the Rangers in the Korean conflict. Only his toughness had delivered him survival. Von Deming's eyes narrowed as he looked us up and down with a cynical gaze, his smile had now all but disappeared. 'So Keenan tells me that you guys want to race go-karts. You sure that you got what it takes?' I could read his thoughts: 'Two more Hollywood pretty boys that wanna play hot shot racing drivers. Like to show off for the girlies – expect to be waited on hand and foot. They probably don't know the difference between a machine shop and a toyshop. I'll bet they're afraid to get their hands dirty.' The reality was that Von Deming dreamed of becoming an actor and hadn't a clue on how to go about it. His resentment was therefore somewhat understandable.

A toothy smile of insincerity once again crept across Von

Deming's face. 'Alright, guys, come on, I'll show you around.'

Having made the introductions, Keenan turned and walked back to his kart. 'You guys will be cool with Von. I'll see ya later. I've got last minute race preparations to sort out.'

Von reluctantly led us on a tour of his operation. 'These are the karts that we let beginners drive around the track. They're pretty slow – you can't get into any trouble 'cause they're not race-prepared.' Von gave us a measured stare as if letting us know that those were the only machines that we could possibly handle.

We walked over toward a canopied area. There were karts above the ground on portable racks being worked on by various teams of mechanics. Von, with smugness in his tone, proudly ran his mouth, showing off for our benefit. 'Over here are the race-prepared weapons. Believe me, they're fast. They come stock from the factory but we set them up for proper handling. The engines have been tuned, the brakes adjusted. The big difference from a stock kart is the race tyres. They give better grip! Now follow me.' We moved to a special enclosed area on the other side of the workshop. 'Over here are the modified karts. These engines have really been worked on – bigger carbs, polished pistons, selected gearing, lighter parts throughout – more compression. Only a single engine, but they go like shit off a shovel.

'Now then,' Von paused and took a dramatic breath, 'if you're really serious and have the talent – you can move up to one of these.' Von pointed out a group of seriously evil looking twin-engine machines. The various drivers and pit crews were all busily into last minute adjustments in preparation for scrutiny. 'Those babies will turn 18,000 rpm and do over 100 miles an hour. They almost get airborne when driven flat out. Every part is completely modified. Factory teams and guys with deep pockets and very large balls race these.' Then with self-satisfaction surrounding his tone, Von added, 'These are what my brother, Bill, and I race.' I looked at Budd. He knew my thoughts ('Asshole!'). Nothing needed to be said.

At that moment a gorgeous raven-haired beauty wearing tight

white pedal pushers and a man's blue denim shirt tied with a midriff knot, floated up and tapped Von on the shoulder. She had the violet eyes of Elizabeth Taylor. As she waited for an introduction, her sensuality seized my senses. Budd stared as if hypnotised. 'Guys, this is my wife, Barbara. Say hello to Budd and Steve.'

It hadn't reached 9 o'clock and already my pulse was banging. I wasn't sure whether it was Southgate Raceway, the karts, the anticipation of racing, or the gorgeous wife of Von Deming, but somehow, I had a strong feeling that all of this was gonna get Budd and me into a whole lot of trouble somewhere down the road. It wasn't long before it did just that. But that's a story that needs to be told by The Albright.

It was nearing 10 o'clock and the start of the first race. Qualifying was over and all last minute tuning put aside. The loudspeaker, which had been blasting out the latest chart hits, was now calling for all drivers in the first heat of the stock class to get into their grid positions. Budd and I moved to a clear spot at the fence. The atmosphere was pure electricity as the mostly novice drivers circled the track preparing themselves for the start marshal to wave the green flag that would set off the race. As they slowly rolled around the circuit toward the start-finish line, they were careful not to break formation or to jump the start. With exuberance, the marshal jumped into the air, waving his green flag for a perfect get away. The karts were off in a roaring cluster, all jockeying for position. Some flew off the track at the first chicane, ending in a tangle of machines and hay bales. A few, being first timers, ran their front wheels up on the backs of the karts in front, ending in obvious disaster. Passing was difficult. One loss of concentration and their racing was history. Cool running was the way to keep it together.

That was the first time that Budd and I had witnessed a go-kart race up close. Before the end of that first heat, we were hooked. We knew that we wouldn't rest until we were there competing in the mix – and winning races. Two more heats of the stock class were run. Then it was time for the first race of the single engine, modified class. Keenan Wynn was on the grid, surrounded by drivers at least 20 years younger. This would be interesting. Not only did Keenan Wynn look old enough to be a father to most of them, he appeared to weigh twice as much as any two of them. That could prove to be quite a handicap when racing against lighter, younger drivers.

The drivers cautiously circled to the start-finish line. The green flag was waved and they shot off around the first left-hander, screaming down the straightaway flat out. It was hard to believe, but Keenan, from starting fifth on the grid, passed three karts and was moving up with the front-runners. All of a sudden, from the far end of the circuit, arose a huge cloud of dust. Yellow caution flags were immediately visible. The leading group passed by for a second time and were cruising slowly under a full caution yellow flag. There was no Keenan Wynn. Then from the PA came the words: 'Kart number four, Keenan Wynn is off the track.' The race remained under full course yellow for what seemed an eternity. Keenan, with his aggressive driving style, had gone off, big-time, taking two other drivers with him.

He'd run up on the rear wheels of the kart in front and thus launched himself airborne about 5 feet over the hay bales and into the field at the end of the circuit. There was mayhem. The track was partially blocked by the two other karts. For a couple of moments it was worrying. Keenan was nowhere in sight. Then, as the dust was beginning to settle, a chimera-like figure appeared, carrying a crash helmet and slowly limping toward the pits. The crowd cheered. It was Keenan Wynn. As he grew closer Budd and I raced over to see if he was OK. He was bleeding from various cuts and had torn a piece from the shoulder of his race suit. He was furious. 'I broke a goddamn tie rod. I could have had those bastards! They're fucking slow going into the corners! I out-braked them.'

One of the many reasons why Evie Johnson and Keenan Wynn had divorced was because Keenan wouldn't stop racing. Whether it was a car, a motorcycle, a boat, or a motorized lawn mower - if it had an engine, he'd race it. Keenan also had a few serious accidents including a near fatal plane crash. Evie couldn't handle the stress. The thought of arriving at the hospital and finding Keenan DOA was more than she could live with.

Fear never entered Keenan Wynn's mind. He possessed a huge pair of balls and was one hell of a macho hombre. He was a complete one-off who lived by the motto, 'Let it all hang out'.

Budd and I watched Keenan limp over to his pit mechanic, turning the air blue with choice expressions, frustrated by his bad performance. We felt that it would be a wise move to leave him alone and let him cool down. Keenan was OK. It was really just his ego that had taken a bashing.

We returned to watching the races.

'It sure is ironic,' Budd said with a slight chuckle. 'Last night at Evie's party Keenan was taking the piss out of Bob Harris — making fun of him running off the track at the end of the straightaway.' Budd laughed louder. 'Not only did Keenan lose it big-time, but he left the track at exactly the same place. I'm sure there's a lesson in that somewhere.'

Go-Kart Mania

After that day at Southgate Raceway, Budd and I were completely captured by the mad lure of kart racing.

In fact, it totally occupied our thoughts throughout the following week. Even scoring pumpage took a back seat. Budd was going through the motions of a man under the influence of high anxiety. For him, the days couldn't pass quick enough. We wanted to be at Southgate Raceway competing with the best drivers. Although we had competed in a few minor sport car races, the only real experience we'd had racing was on the street, highly illegal and extremely dangerous. Nevertheless we'd earned a coveted reputation as top guns.

Finally the week rolled into Sunday. Neither Budd nor I had had much sleep during the night. Anticipation kept us up late dissecting our intended race strategy for the day ahead. It was seven o'clock when we hit the freeway, roaring towards Southgate with pulses pounding through bloodshot vision.

As we approached the parking lot my heart sank. Once again the enclosure was teeming with cars and vans. Another race was underway. We wouldn't get to display our talent today, unless there was some playtime after the final race. However, I was sure that would be doubtful. I felt gutted. Budd's face read like the department of disappointment. To say we were pissed off would be an understatement. 'We should have checked out the situation beforehand. It's our fault,' I said. 'We should have been wise to it.'

'What the hell, as long as we're here, let's make the most of it. Check to see if Keenan's racing.'

It was a Groundhog Day version of the week before. The entire setting buzzed with activity. The grandstand was packed to capacity and there was still half an hour before the start of the first race. 'Budd, let's check out the workshop — see if we can find Von,' I said. Budd eagerly agreed. Even though he'd been a bit subdued with disappointment, I was sure that he was hoping for another chance to eyeball lovely Barbara. Budd agreed that was dangerous ground to be treading.

The only person in the workshop was Bill Deming, Von's younger brother. He was hard at work readying his twin-engine mean machine for the day's racing. We'd met Bill the week before and although he'd been polite, I got the distinct impression that he was completely unimpressed. Bill was the exact opposite of Von – a quiet, six foot, 200 pound serious kart racer. As well as being an outstanding driver, he was also considered one of the best at constructing racing engines. Bill hadn't warmed up to the various Hollywood jocks. He felt they were mostly loud-mouth poseurs that were only there for the dare. His only exception was Keenan Wynn who was always flat out into the mix with the best of them. Bill had a lot of time for him.

Bill Deming looked up as we entered. 'Sorry guys, Von's not here. He's at the café. I'm a bit busy so why don't you look in there?' We took the hint and headed toward the track café just as the start of the first race was being announced. The drivers' names were read out. Among them was Keenan Wynn. Budd and I aborted the café direction and headed for a spot at the fence. The green flag was waved and 20 karts screamed around the first left-hander and down the straight — all bumping for position. Suddenly from the infield, mid-way down the course, there arose a huge cloud of dust. The race was stopped (red flag) while the marshals ran to sort out the tangle of machinery blocking the track and spilling on to the infield. From out of the centre of the lingering dust cloud, like Chuck Yeager in *The Right Stuff*, strolled Keenan Wynn. The crowd erupted with cheering.

I couldn't keep myself from laughing. 'Not again, Keenan!'

At that moment Von Deming walked up wearing a tacked-on smile. 'Keenan's quite a character,' said Von. 'He does a big "off" at least once every race meeting. He always survives unhurt. The crowd love him. He's a good driver — he's got balls.' Budd and I agreed, but it must have been obvious that we were bursting for a chance to have a go ourselves. Von had come with glad tidings.

'OK guys, so you think you've got it, do ya? Well, in that case, be here Tuesday morning — early. We'll have a couple of stock karts set up for you. We'll see what you've got — that is if you can stay on the track.' Just two more days. We could hardly wait.

Tuesday morning arrived under a slate grey sky. Budd and I were at the gate before anyone. We were bursting to get it on. Von arrived, unlocked the entrance and motioned for us to park up by the workshop. There, waiting for us, were two specially prepared stock engine go-karts. 'Go out and take a few laps,' Von said. 'Take it easy. Get used to it first. Remember you're not racing — you're learning, so easy on the throttle. I'll come out in a couple of minutes and point out the proper lines. In the meantime, just go and have fun.'

Budd took off on to the circuit. I nailed the throttle and the kart immediately responded by spinning in a complete circle, thus killing the engine. I felt like a total dork. Von rushed over and helped me push off again. My first lesson had been learned. I drove the next few laps like an old-age pensioner on Mogadon. After a few more circles of the track, I began to gain more confidence and went looking to challenge Budd. Within seconds we were into a pitched battle for track position. First I'd pass, and then Budd would pass me. Several times we tangled and spun off the track into the hay bales. But we seemed to be catching on. The years of street racing on Sunset Boulevard was paying off.

By the afternoon, I was getting it down pretty well. I was taking the corners much faster, concentrating on the racing lines. Roaring down the straightaway Budd and I pictured ourselves as Dan Gurney and Sterling Moss, that was until a motorized spectre went rocketing past in a blur of speed like the Warner Bros cartoon Road Runner without a beep! beep! warning. It was Bill Deming testing his twin engine modified for the coming Sunday race meeting. When I saw Bill slip effortlessly through the chicane and disappear down the track straightaway, it struck me just how much practice I would need before I could even consider racing with the big boys.

We made Southgate Raceway our home for the next few weeks, learning as much as we could with constant practice. Bill Deming at last realized that we were serious. He became interested in coaching us. He relayed from his mass of experience many secrets that would help us to become winning kart racers. Finally our constant practice began paying off. Our quickening lap times were the proof.

Three weeks later Budd and I entered our first race. My heart was in my mouth as I rolled up to the start line amongst the pack. When the flag dropped I nailed it.

I was into the left-hander and shooting down the straightaway like a mad banshee. Inexperience and too much throttle spun me off into the hay bales before I'd completed the first lap. Budd fared better. Starting from the back, he moved up three places and was fighting for a good position when a momentary lack of concentation caused him to spin. Before he got restarted he was a lap behind, yet still managed to finish in the top 15. We experienced our first race. We could only get better with more track time practice.

By the end of the summer we felt that we were more than ready to take on the best. From the start we'd been completely consumed with kart racing. It was our main topic of conversation whenever we were out hanging with our friends. We ran our mouths so much that I'm sure that we made number one on their list of the most boring. A few of our friends showed interest in coming to the track to have a go. I'm convinced that they thought that they were gonna show us up, and thereby shut us up. We deserved their sarcasm.

One by one they began to arrive at Southgate Raceway as spectators. I'm sure that it was primarily to watch Budd and me crash while out racing. However, once there, they too were seized by the lure of karting. Each and everyone, having never tried it, thought it was easy. Simple, all you had to do was climb into a kart and race straight off. Everybody threw down a challenge to us. They definitely didn't realize what they were in for. Each and every one would suddenly come to realize their mistake. Bets were taken reluctantly. We didn't want to take their money.

Von Deming became a gregarious guy. He loved the fact that half of Hollywood's young players were suddenly showing up at the track. I'm sure that he felt by getting next to them it could possibly help his film business ambitions. Through Budd and me, Von was introduced to, and subsequently became friendly with, most of the Hollywood crowd that came to the track in ever-increasing numbers throughout the summer. Von made an effort to give all of them a chance to show what they were made of behind the wheel of a go-kart. It was regular cabaret watching the testosterone-fuelled film and TV actors getting it on — mostly making fools of themselves. Their bravado negated their ability. 'Alright baby! Light me up,' was the cry, as off they roared — usually straight into disaster. Most didn't make one lap before they spun off the track, only to return to the pit area in a blaze of excuses. A few tried it once and realized that karting wasn't for them. One or two had a natural gift for racing.

Keenan Wynn, Paul Newman, Steve McQueen, Tim Considine and Don Grady spent every free moment sharpening their natural racing talent.

You could feel that they would go on to bigger challenges in the future. As well as the movie faces there were a few guys whose names would later be spoken in reverence by all who loved motor racing. Johnny Parsons Jr and Mickey Rupp were but two.

As the weeks rolled on more and more famous faces turned up at Southgate Raceway. The word was spreading like a wind-blown prairie fire throughout the Hollywood hills and badlands. Little titbits started appearing in the gossip columns. Then the

Top: Jim Mitchum discusses the lure of pumpage with ladies man, Ronnie Burns.
Above: Tuesday Weld is wise to my intentions and not interested.

press began to arrive at the track hoping for interviews. There were film and TV stars mixing with the hard core kart racers. It was news. One weekend a TV crew from KTLA arrived. That followed with clips on local evening television. Photos of the famous and not-so-famous began popping up in newspapers and fan magazines. A go-kart frenzy was infecting the blood of Hollywood's young honchos. It became the latest fashionable accoutrement. Southgate Raceway was the place to hang out. On any given weekend, you could count the faces. Jim Mitchum, Troy Donahue, Max Baer Jr, Chad Everett, Mickey Callan, David Winters, Peter Breck, Fabian, Marc Cavell, Jim Drury, Robert Fuller, Jay Sebring, Telly Savalas, Michael Landon — names that appeared on the pages of Spotlight, the industry's casting bible.

Naturally where the cool cats gather, so also come the kittens. A plethora of beauties began filling the Southgate landscape, bringing glamour to the setting. Vikki Dougan, Stefanie Powers, Connie Stevens, Linda Evans, Sally Todd, Beverly Washburn, Jenny Maxwell, Pam Duncan, Tuesday Weld, Karen Conrad and Linda Rogers were just a few of the female fineries that splashed upon the scene creating a wave of pounding pulses. Von Deming was in paradise. Up to then he'd only dreamed of getting next to film business personnel and there he was, along with Budd and me, being asked for help, in teaching go-kart racing to half of Hollywood's young celebrities.

One Saturday Von thought that it would be a fun idea to run a practice race with all the celebrities driving on the track at the same time. Budd and I were included. Chaos followed. Karts flew everywhere. I got knocked off the track immediately. Budd fared better and managed to finish in one piece. The race had created immense excitement, proving to be an enormous success with everyone. A few weeks later Budd and I organized another race. This one proved to be even more successful than the first. This time Budd and I didn't race. We watched instead. Everyone, including Von Deming, was delighted with the day's activities and wanted more of the same as soon as possible. That planted the seeds of an idea in the minds of Albright & Rowland.

Budd and I moved up to the single engine modified class. We were driving a couple of hot-handling Bill Deming specials with a tricked out McCulloch engine on each kart. They were definitely the business. We started placing in the top six — then the top three. At each race we were getting better. We began gaining respect from the serious racers after we had won a couple of finals. They came shaking our hands and checking out our set-ups. Budd and I were definitely scoring attention.

One Sunday after a particularly hard-fought battle, a product marketing man from one of the major kart companies (Go-Kart) cornered us in the pit area, as we were packing up to leave. 'Hey guys, how would you both like to drive one of our karts? We'll pay to set them up — no cost to you.' The guy seemed kosher, but he could have been anyone. We'd had a bag load of assholes coming around since we'd been high profile at Southgate.

Budd was first to react. 'What do you want?

Before the guy could answer, I jumped in. 'Why us? There's a lot of good drivers around — faster than us.'

'Yeah,' Budd repeated. 'Why us?'

'Because you guys bring the celebrities and the celebrities bring the crowd. I can't be more honest than that.'

'OK' Budd said, 'what's the deal?'

'I want you two guys to race the karting circuits with two of our karts. It's not the end of the world if you don't win, but what's important is that you only drive our new lightweight competition karts. Winning would put the icing on the cake. What do you say?'

'Sounds good to me,' I said. Budd agreed. Before long we had a pair of the hottest race karts around. Now all we had to do was get stuck into racing — and hopefully winning.

In the spring of 1963 Budd, Von Deming and I produced the first celebrity kart race day. Our original idea was born after that second day of celebrity racing. It had now grown legs and after many weeks of organizing and coordinating not only with the celebrities that would be competing, but with the press and TV as well, our original idea turned into an actuality. The advance publicity and word of mouth brought the crowd on the day. Southgate Raceway was on overload with screaming girls who'd come to see Fabian, among others, race karts and with any luck sign autographs. There was to be a proper race format with four heats and a final. As an added bonus, there would also be two powder puff races for the girls. Budd and I didn't compete in the celebrity races as it wouldn't have been a fair playing-field. We'd had much more race experience and weren't out to prove anything. We did, however, put on an exhibition that gained us respect from our cynical showbiz colleagues.

Our close friend, Jim Mitchum won the overall celebrity final and they're still arguing as to which one of the girls crossed the finish line first in their race. I have no answer. My memory has deserted me on that score.

It was a fantastically successful day. The crowd was overwhelming. The track café ran out of everything. The event was reported on the local TV evening news. Most of the LA newspapers ran stories and photos. Budd and I along with the whole gang made the cover of the August 1963 edition of *Karting World* magazine (right). It featured the event on the inside pages. The day turned out to be one that would go down in the annals of karting history — never to be forgotten.

Right: The cover of Karting World Magazine, August, 1963.

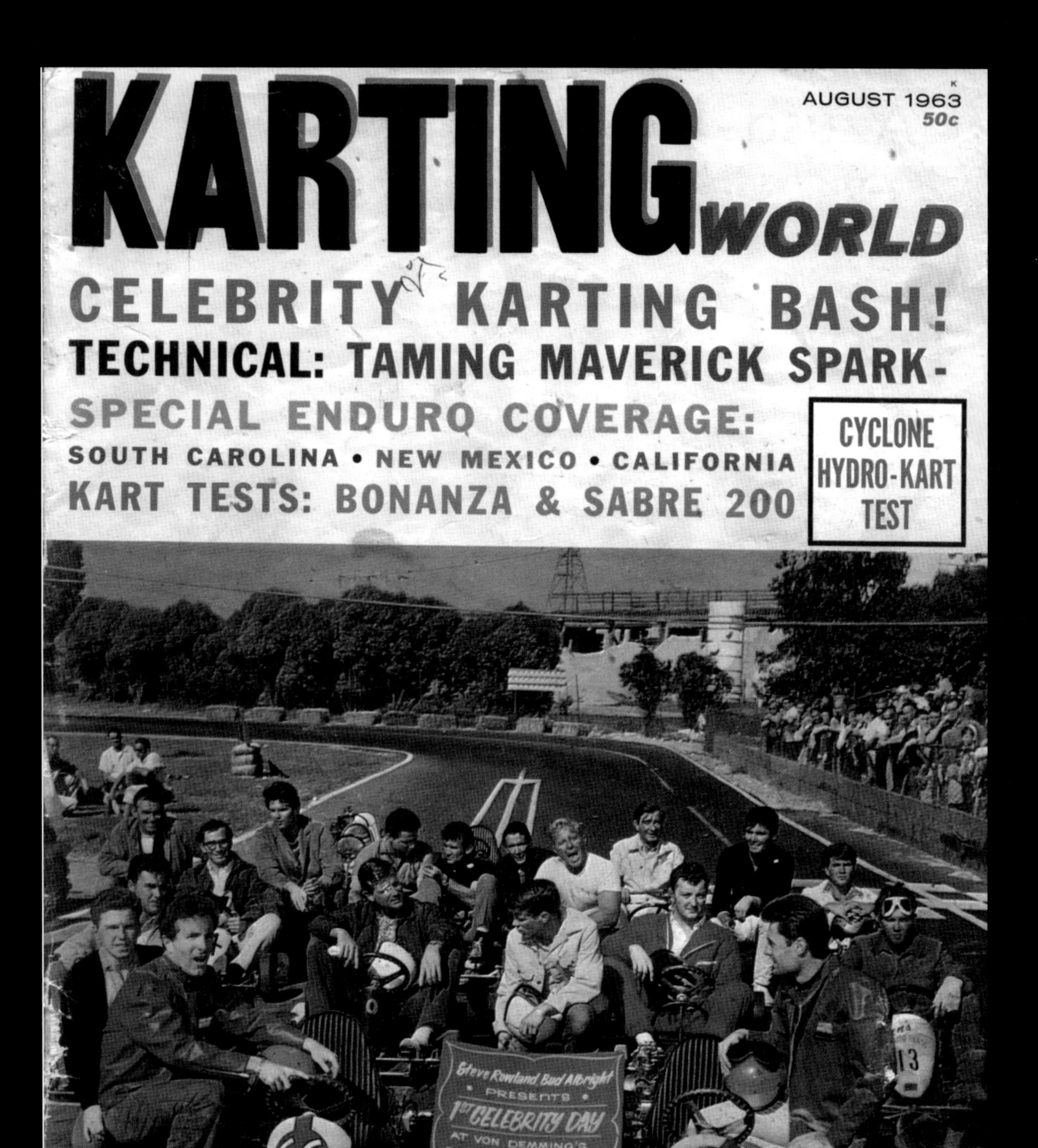
KARTING WORLD

AUGUST 1963

50c

CELEBRITY KARTING BASH!

TECHNICAL: TAMING MAVERICK SPARK-

SPECIAL ENDURO COVERAGE:

SOUTH CAROLINA • NEW MEXICO • CALIFORNIA

KART TESTS: BONANZA & SABRE 200

CYCLONE HYDRO-KART TEST

The Final Wrap

For most of the celebrities, kart racing was only a passing fad. As is always the case, everyone moved on to new excitement.

I had landed a co-star role in the MGM western *The Gunfighters of Casa Grande* and sadly I would be leaving for location in Spain at the end of May. Before I left, however, I had a lot more racing to do. Budd and I moved up with the big boys and started seriously testing ourselves in the unlimited twin-engine modified class. After setting my heart rate to ready, I entered a couple of races where I finished in the top ten and in a couple where I was only able to battle to a mid-pack finish. Had I stayed with it longer, hopefully, I would have been able to do much better.

Paul Newman had a serious talent for motor racing. After film-making, racing was his first love. Throughout his early career, he distinguished himself as a top-rated racing driver culminating in finishing second in the famous Le Mans 24-hour event. A difficult race for the pros let alone an actor in his mid fifties.

Steve McQueen had motor racing in his blood. Whether it was cars or motorcycles, Steve was in there running with the best of 'em, and usually finishing on the winner's podium. He raced moto-cross until the studios put a stop to it. In preparation for his film *Le Mans* Steve spent several seasons racing in Europe. He went on to race saloon cars and won in his class at Sebring, Florida.

Tim Considine was also a gifted racing driver. After those initial days at Southgate Raceway, he started racing Trans Am for Pontiac. He also tested one of the first electric race cars, entering it in the Long Beach Grand Prix.

A couple of guys like Johnny Parsons Jr and Mickey Rupp went the full big time by racing Indi Cars. At Indianapolis, they became top five contenders and revered drivers.

Above: The Jaguars. The rock group was made up from Americans living in Spain. Mickey Hart (centre), became the drummer with The Grateful Dead.

Bill Deming put his superb ability to a different format. He turned to racing powerboats where he became a high scorer until he gave it all up to settle down and run a heating business.

Through Budd Albright's efforts and his industry contacts, Von Deming landed in the honey. Budd's introductions enabled Von to join the closed shop fraternity of motion picture stunt men, where he proved his worth with his fearless driving ability. However, things did not run smoothly, as Von's aggressive nature rose to the surface eventually costing him his position in the industry.

After I left for Spain, Budd continued racing karts in the unlimited modified class. Whenever he was asked how he was doing, he always like to repeat Marlon Brando's famous words from the taxicab scene in *On the Waterfront* — 'I could've been a contender.'

Budd moved on to racing ski boats at Lake Arrowhead in the San Bernardino mountain range, turning professional in 1972. Along with his acting career, he also became a useful film stunt man. However, a misjudged 'high fall' ended his stunt career.

Budd continued to race on the water driving Grand National race boats off shore, racing alongside Don Johnson and Chuck Norris for Team Spectra and Team Vapor Trails until his bones got shaken into submission.

Today, as well as writing scripts for films and TV, Budd is also a photojournalist, following the offshore powerboat circuit. Together with Gary Berwin, they venture out as Strike Team USA.

Today a shopping mall, with all its greedy entities, covers the area that once was Southgate Raceway. All that remain are distant memories.

Left: A bit of bull. Spain, 1964.

EPILOGUE

Above: A beard for a *Dr Zhivago* screen test.

Ten days before I split for Spain, I went on a crusade for sexual healing. I knew that by doing this I'd be burning bridges but thought — what the hell, one last blast. I phoned two special ladies and told them that I was leaving for Spain. I arranged to get together with each one separately. I told them that I really cared and would miss them terribly. I laid on the dramatics. I'm sure that they didn't really believe me, but it must have sparked unbridled passion, for the beast was in them and they made love as if the Russian army was waiting in the lobby. They left me sexually rinsed and praying for salvation.

In June 1963, I began filming in Jerez, Spain on *The Gunfighters of Casa Grande*. After three years working in Spain making three more films, I moved to England where I entered a whole new world of madness — the music business. In my leisure time, and to keep my sanity, I took up the challenge of moto-cross and have been rewarded with a double hip replacement and constant aches and pains. I must still be trying to prove something after all these years, by racing karts with kids half my age, skiing off piste with the crazies, and dating dangerous women.

After living in London for 40 years, I've encountered many fascinating females. They always embellish my action, but I've paid the price. At times I've found myself in injurious situations, but then I've always said that if you're not living on the edge — you're taking up too much room. My ex-wife says that I've never grown up. I agree with her completely.

THE END - TO BE CONTINUED ...

Left: Jackie Levy, the one that got away.

The Original Fan Magazine Columns 1954-1959

Our Gang, Movie Play, September 1954

Hi people. When your editor asked me to write a report on what was happening with Hollywood's younger players, I told her that I was an actor, not a writer.

'But you know all the kids on their way up don't you? Why not give our readers the facts as you see, hear and know them? Dish the dirt and relay the scoops from your point of view. You know the real stories behind the stories, seeing as you're one of the young players yourself. You know who goes out with whom, what they like to do between pictures and after work, their favourite watering holes, restaurants, nightclubs etc. In other words Steve, what are the Terry Moores and Rock Hudsons really like when they're not working. Just write it as you see it. That's all you have to do.'

So here we go.

About this ball of energy, Terry Moore. She really is a dynamo. When she was in the hospital for a serious virus infection, she was told that she shouldn't talk to or see anyone for at least a week. Well, that's like telling the day not to end. She's only set a record for having the most visitors and phone calls ever in the entire history of the Hollywood Good Samaritan Hospital.

While she was there, Don Apel (one of Terry's many) and I were skiing at Holiday Hill. We called her from the mountain to ask how she was feeling. 'I feel terrif' the happy voice on the other end said. 'And guess what? The doctor says I can go home tomorrow. Then next week I can go skiing with you guys OK?'

Well, what are going to do? You can't stop the rain from falling.

On Sunday morning a few weeks ago, I was deep in sleep after coming home very late the night before. Suddenly the phone went, ring-ring-ring! Scream. After knocking over the lamp, the clock, about 20 books and God knows what else, I finally gasped 'hello' into the wrong end of the receiver.

'Good morning, sugarplum. Rise and shine! It's time for church. See you there in twenty minutes. Bye now.' The phone went 'click.' These are the times that try men's souls. Yes, it was Terry Moore.

Saw the wonderful MGM pic *Rhapsody* the other eve. I'm taking bets right now that John Ericson becomes a great big star *muy pronto*. The guy's got it. How about it, gals — what d'ya think? Is he happening or what? How about some letters?

Our Gang

Here is a wonderful new feature! Straight from Hollywood comes this exclusive report of the young stars by one of them

By STEVE ROWLAND

HI, people. When your editor asked me to write a report of what was happening with Hollywood's younger players, I told her that I was an actor, not a writer.

"But you know all the kids on their way up, don't you? Why not give our readers the facts as you see, hear and know them? The dirt, the scoops from your viewpoint. You know the real stories behind the stories because you're one of the young players yourself. You know who goes with whom; what they like to do between pictures and after work; their favorite stopping places, restaurants, nightclubs, etc. In other words, Steve, what are the Terry Moores and Rock Hudsons really like when they're not play-acting. Just call 'em as you see 'em, that's all." (*Continued on Page 58*)

***Left:** My first column as it appeared the 1954 issue of Movie Play.*

Speaking of John. While we were working on *The Student Prince* together, we shared the same dressing room. I got to know him pretty well. And found out that he's quite an impersonator. His Marlon Brando impression is more Marlon than Brando is himself. I think if Johnny Ray heard him, he'd sue. Richard Widmark would think that he was talking to himself in front of a mirror if he happened to see John laying down his R.W. imitation — crooked smile and all.

I ran into John and his doll-like wife, Milly Corey, at Naples, the wonderful Italian restaurant across from Columbia studios on Sunset Boulevard. John was imitating an Italian waiter seating a very stout, elderly woman — noises, grunts and swear words. Enough said. John's got it. He's bound to be a star, wait and see. That is, if he doesn't get sued or chased out of town.

Talked to Lance Fuller the other night at Larry Finley's. He was all by himself sitting way back in a dark corner. None of his usual lady companions were with him. He looked really down in the mouth. Why? I didn't know. He had just been signed to play the lead in two important Universal films. What was the reason he was so low? Well, here's the bit. It seems that he didn't know which one of his string of ladies to take to a big industry party. His list includes such breath-stoppers as Kathleen Hughes, Mamie Van Doren, Julia Adams, Cleo Moore, Diana Lynn, Rosemarie Bowe and five million more. The final outcome was that he turned up stag. I wonder if there's a moral to this tale.

Here's some more quaint tripe. While we were talking that evening, Lance and I decided that the next Sunday, the two of us would get up at four a.m. and head for the deep, dark forests of the San Bernardino Mountains for a day of fishing. What dreamers we'd been. After coming back from the mountains empty-handed, we decided that it would have been easier to buy fish at the corner supermarket. We wouldn't have to get up at four a.m.

and we wouldn't have had to dress for the occasion.

The phone's jingle scared me out of my wits as I had been concentrating on a new script that I was reading and wasn't expecting the jarring jingle. On answering I heard the excited voice of Martha Hyer. Her excitement had good basis, for it seems that while she and Jeff Richards were out sailing the briny, shooting an on-the-boat magazine layout, a sudden storm arose making it impossible for them to return to the harbour. After five hectic hours of complete turmoil in which the boat almost capsized, they reached the dock safely. The only mishap was with the photographer. His camera fell overboard. All the filmed drowned.

Left: *A fearsome four - Kathy Case, Steve Rowland, Rosemary Bowe & Robert Stack.*

A real crazy chick, dressed in slacks, white sweater and moccasins, tore madly across the street in busy Beverly Hills, carrying a French poodle pup under one arm. She was obviously heading for the hardware store on the other side.

'Hey, beauty,' I yelled. 'Where you-all going in such an almighty hurry?'

'Oh hi,' hollered she, holding up the pup in one hand. 'I gotta pick up a new coffee pot. Mine fell off the stove and broke. How are your mom and dad?'

'Great,' I cried, looking back over my shoulder as my car slipped by her. 'How's Tony?'

'Really living the life,' she returned, stumbling up the curb backwards. 'Call us,' were the last words I heard Janet Leigh say as the Beverly Drive traffic swallowed me up.

Merry Anders, that cute little 'How to Marry a Millionaire' doll, really looks as if she's stargazing these days. The reason for all this is her more than casual interest in one Hugh O'Brian. I ran into them together at a Mulholland Drive party a while back. I again bumped into them at the Bar of Music, a great place to go if you're romantically inclined — or not, as the case may be. They were looking dreamily at each other across one of the many candle-lit tables. I sure hope everything works out well. Is there anyone taking bets?

Anne Francis squired a new pet the other day, a cute little Labrador puppy. Anne had found him wandering alone and hungry along the street near her home. He was apparently lost, for he was howling mournfully and seemed not to know which way to go. Anne's big soft heart immediately went thump and she just had to adopt him. He's as black as night and getting bigger by the day. Anne told me that he likes to sleep in the bathtub. His name is Prince Val. I wonder if Anne's landlord allows dogs?

Left: *Janet Leigh and I always had lots to discuss.*

Russ Tamblyn is a real hip kiddy. Man, this cat can make Claire de Lune swing and does a pretty good job when sitting at the eighty-eight. Anywhere there's a melody riding the atmosphere, there's Russ with his ever-lovin' Dolly. (She's not in movies — goes to San Francisco J.C.).

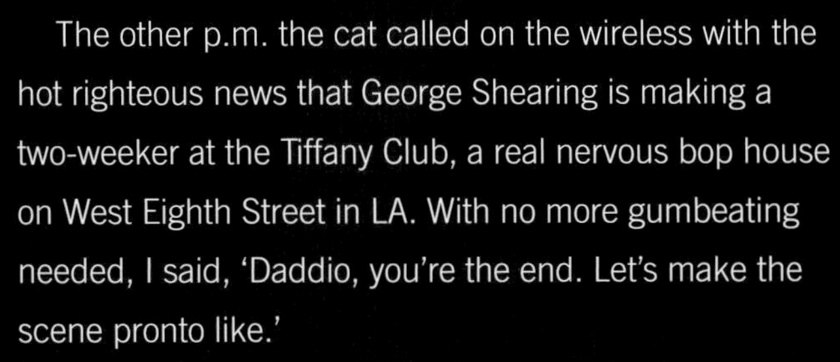

The other p.m. the cat called on the wireless with the hot righteous news that George Shearing is making a two-weeker at the Tiffany Club, a real nervous bop house on West Eighth Street in LA. With no more gumbeating needed, I said, 'Daddio, you're the end. Let's make the scene pronto like.'

Within twenty minutes, the two of us with chicks in tow were sitting mike-side, picking up on George's great new sound. We stayed on way into the late watch. In the next week or so, Gerry Mulligan, along with the frantic Stan Kenton aggregation will be blowing up a storm at the Shrine auditorium. Unless something world-shattering happens, or a fraughty issue arises, we'll be digging it.

Left: *On set with Debbie Reynolds and Russ Tamblyn.*

Rita Morena, the Life magazine cover girl, is on the much-wanted list by the studios. However, she feels she has a problem. She related its sad message to me the other night when I ran into her and Johnny Anderson at the Captain's Table on Third Street and La Cienga. The problem being that she's been offered five wonderful film roles, each from a different studio. They're all scheduled to start shooting at about the same time. She couldn't decide which would be the best choice. After much discussion and three decks of cigarettes had been nervously smoked, we still weren't able to come up with a positive answer and so adjourned for the night.

Among the guests at a wonderful Sunday afternoon at Steve's pool is Rita Moreno.

let's get the gang together!

Leader of Hollywood's sprightly younger set is up-and-coming actor Steve Rowland, SCREEN STARS' Hollywood Showcase candidate for stardom . . . We're betting on him, and you will be too . . .

Always the perfect host, Steve swabs Dorothy Bromiley's back with sun oil. Dorothy's one of Paramount's most promising starlets. Good luck, gal!

Tom Morton of MGM's "Main Street to Broadway," Steve (see him in MGM's exciting "Panther Squadron 8") and Dorothy toast marshmallows.

Tired of swimming, Tracey Roberts, Rob Clarke & Steve toss gumdrops at Rita Mo no's mouth. Rita's in Columbia's "El Alamei

That left, leaving Rita to make up her own mind. The next day she came up with a result. She signed for a film at Twentieth Century Fox. When I spoke to her on the phone she seemed relieved and super excited. It was an offer she couldn't refuse.

Attention! Attention! All points bulletin. Be on the lookout for a beautiful young girl! about five feet four inches tall, dark brown hair, ice-blue eyes, and a fantastic body. Be very watchful, for it is widely known that she will soon be seen in the Columbia movie Human Desire. She'll be co-starring with Glen Ford. This gorgeous gal is very evasive, for she is a combination of three people — Elizabeth Taylor, Ava Gardner and that Italian doll, Gina Lollobrigida. She has a record of more than 40 TV shows, and was to have toured with the Metropolitan Opera Company as a lead ballerina. When last seen, she was headed for stardom. She answers to the name of Kathleen Case. I repeat, Kathleen Case. It is urgent that you watch for her. That is all. Over and out!

Dolores Dorn, the beautiful Warner Bros contractee appearing in *Phantom of the Rue Morgue*, was at the Mocambo with Vic Damone. Dolores says there's no romance, but who knows what evil lurks on the hearts of women? The women know.

I received a postcard from Debbie Reynolds. It travelled al the way from St Louis, Missouri where Debs is appearing in the play *Gigi*. Her card read (quote) 'Hi guy, here I am in St Louis with 'G.G.' and everyone here seems to like the play — at least if attendance means anything. Even the critics loved it. I bought a new Mercury so me and car are driving home, which means I'll be there in a day or so. Love to all. Debbie.' The next day, another card arrived from Debbie. She was in Colorado and would be delayed a day or so. Before I could say woof, Debbie was home and bounding.

Left: *First fan magazine layout. I was hot for Rita Moreno. The pool cooled me off.*

Tommy Morton (you saw him in *Main Street to Broadway*) has opened a dance studio in the San Fernando Valley for professional dancers. He's also been very busy working out the choreography for many of the nightclub acts that will be appearing in Las Vegas and elsewhere.

The guy comes on like another Gene Kelly. You should see him hoof and woof. Wow! Man, this cat is air-born.

The other day, he was over helping me with my planned nightclub act. After an hour or so of concentrated work, he told me to take five while he showed off some of his new routines. I gotta coin an ancient expression, 'They're the most to say the least'. No wonder every studio in town is after his services.

The other pm Tab Hunter, Lori Nelson, Kathleen Case and Yours Truly were at the Plymouth House picking up on all the humans that were trying hard to impress each other. It was at this very time and place that we overheard a very attractive young starlet complaining to her balding escort about another equally attractive young starlet, that happened to be receiving more attention than she was. 'Well you know her,' said the charming child curtly. 'She's lovely. She's alluring. She uses friends.'

Well, that's about all the noise I can relate right now. The rest is too gruesome to reveal. So, as they say in West Utopia — dig you later, alligator.

Our Gang, Movie Play, July 1955

Hear ye, hear ye, hear ye! People personified! It's me again and I'm here with more of the most fantastic happenings. You know, a few people have said that we creatures from the Hollywood swamplands are completely out to lunch. I don't think their jive line is quite qualified, do you? After all, we're just as human as everyone else, at least as far as I know we are. Aren't we? If you figure it out let me know. But before you decide, you better pick up on what I'm putting down. So dive in, the water's warm.

Anne Francis is just too much. She fractures me completely. A few moons ago, Kathy Case and I along with Anne and Bam Price (her husband) got together for a magazine layout. For background atmosphere, we made it to Marine Land, the big aquarium on the cliffs of Palos Verdes. Believe me, humans, the fish were jumpin' and not a line of 'Summer Time' was heard anywhere. The day came on most bright and the Blue Broadway (sky) was open to the world in all its glory. Not a trace of drift smoke anywhere (drift smoke is clouds to those who are un-hip). We were all feeling the merriest, so naturally we had a blast. The photographer copped his pictures and everyone was most content with the whole event.

Along about the early dark, just when the big beam decided to visit the other side of the world, the four of us walked over to the edge of the cliff and looked out over the big blue. You know how groovy everything looks about that time with the sun's sinking face shining on the water and red colour splashed everywhere. Anyway, we sat down on an old log and decided to stay and watch the day turn into night. You know how humans do when for a little while, they're at complete peace with themselves — that's right, they'll start to beat their gums. Well, 'us 'uns' were no exception.

We orated on this and that and the other until Anne Francis herself came up with some words that really put us all in gleeville. She said that she had bought a baby alligator and that it had become a real pet. The only trouble was that it didn't socialize too well with her dog, Val. Naturally, the woofer was curious and naturally the little gator was frightened. The outcome was sniff, sniff, sniff – hiss, hiss – back away. Well, this went on for quite some time. Meanwhile, the alligator that Anne had named Gus, was growing bigger — about two feet bigger. He had now lost his fear of Val while the dog was becoming a bit wary of Gus. Then one dark day the axe fell. Gus caught Val drinking water out of the bathtub. That was Gus's territory. It was just too much for Gus to accept from anyone, especially from Val. That was an invasion of his privacy.

Hiss – snap – down went the jaws over poor Val's nose. 'Howl! Woof! Grrr!' cried the dog as he hastily retreated. The bite had definitely put him completely out of sniffing action. Val was bleeding. Gus was freaking. When Anne arrived on the home scene and discovered what had taken place she was much perplexed. What to do? The next a.m. bright and early, to the zoo she flew with Gus securely packed in an orange crate. Griffith Park Zoo is where Gus is now in residence, living most contentedly with others of his kind. Val's sniff machine

Our Gang

Dig the Absolute in Frantic doings! Bend those ear flaps to Nervous-Man Rowland's hep-gab!

By Steve Rowland

FRANTIC! Frantic with a great big capital F and a nice big red exclamation point. That, creatures, is what Hollywood is. Why is it so, you ask? I don't really know, to tell you the truth, but after you read some of these latest escapades you'll most likely agree that we do descend from somewhere. The question is, where?

* * *

is still out of action and word has it that Gus is under special counselling for nervous alligators. He goes mad at the sound of barking. We were still laughing as nature's light went out and left us in darkness.

Important flash! People and spirits please keep your headsets turned up and keep the hi fi in order 'cause most soon you are gonna witness the greatest sound ever. You're gonna jump. You're gonna stomp. You're gonna wail and scream 'More, more!' Just hang in there 'cause you'll be hearing him *muy pronto.* Hang your ears out for Robert Horton. His big singing voice is coming at you.

Ed Purdom is a real frantic bloke for sure. The other day at the studio I met him head-on. He was falling out of the MGM commissary as I was falling in. 'Steve, old boy,' he said affecting his most broad English tones. 'You ah fouh shuah a real wigging cat with a fauh out wail.' He bowed majestically from the waist. Then with a huge grin, he said, 'I dig yawah style thee most.' With that he handed me a shovel.

The male population of Vic Damone's circle of friends decided to throw a stag party for the ole boy before he gave up his freedom for a lifetime of bliss with one cool chick titled Pier Angeli. Now one of Vic's closest buddies is a young actor who goes by the moniker of Nicky Blair. It was he who made all the arrangements and set the scene to jump off at the Villa Capri, Hollywood's hip stomping ground. The cats that fell on the scene were Tony Martin, Dick Anderson, Jeff Richards, Red Buttons, Keenan Wynn, Russ Tamblyn, Tony Curtis, Dean Martin, John Carroll, producer Joe Pasternak, my father Roy Rowland, Dick Egan, all the press and studio execs, and little ole me. I was really laughing it up. Brother, was this session hectic. In fact, it was so swinging that — well, you know what I'm getting at. The eats were strictly high jive — Italian all round with wine, pizza and all the trimmings. Man, did they please. After everyone had scoffed up a breeze, they all joined in toasting Vic. The cats that assembled were no lush hounds, but don't get me wrong. The champagne was flowing. All the chances went around and everyone spoke words of congratulations for Vic's soon-to-be ball-and-chain situation.

Everyone was singing. It didn't matter whether you could sing on key. Just wail — that's all. Now what more can you say about a stag party than this? It was blast city. Dad and I pulled a Houdini around one a.m. just as a big cat by the name of Rocky Marciano fell by.

The wireless was screaming. It must have screamed at least four times before I became conscious enough to answer its summons. I flipped on the lamp. Oh no — four thirty. Wow! Who on God's green earth could it be at this hour of the morning? 'Yes,' I mumbled into the wrong end of the phone.

'Hi Steve,' spoke the gloomy voice on the other end of the line. I'm sorry to be calling you at such an unholy hour, but I got a problem, or should I say my dog, Honey, is having troubles.'

'Oh, that's all right, Lance. I always enjoy waking at this hour,' I said sarcastically. 'What's shaking?'

'As I said, it's Honey Dog, she wants to have a speak with Duke.' Now at this point, humans, let me say that my dog Duke is just not about to be awakened at any 4.30 in the morning, especially to be asked questions. Finally after I pulled all the covers off him and scratched his stomach and ears a few times, Duke came to life.

'What's your problem?' Duke said, most put out. 'Has the world come to an end or something?'

'No, Duke,' I said, 'Lance Fuller's dog, Honey, wants words with you.'

'What's so important that you have to wake me at this hour? Can't it wait? Oh, dog biscuits! All right, let me have the phone. Hello, Honey. Hi, it's me, Duke. What's your trouble, little bubble?'

'Duke, I'm glad that I got hold of you. Something terrible has happened. I've just returned from the vets today. The man came on real strong saying that I have a bad case of fleas and that he couldn't do anything about them immediately. They're itching me crazy. What shall I do?'

'Oh girl dog, you're flippin out. Get that lazy master of yours to take you to the beach. Tell him you need salt water to rid your fur of those pesky little fellas. You know how they hate salt water. Just one good swim oughta put them out to sea. Now can I make it back to the land of nod?'

'Gee, thanks Duke, you're the coolest. I'll get right on it. Tell Steve that Lance wants another word.'

'Hey Steve, I'm sure sorry that I had to wake you, but you know problems will arise.'

'Well, that's ok, Lance. Anytime. Just one more thing. Do you think that next time Honey could phone after eight o'clock? Four-thirty comes on heavy putting Duke in a bad mood for the rest of the day.'

Mamie Van Doren will be able to swing in any key and speak in counterpoint with Ray Anthony if and when he and she decide to make themselves one. Love — what a fantastic four-letter sound. Hey, maybe I better knock off this jazz before I start bugging out. Anyhow, keep everything moving real cool. OK? I'm gonna blow air on the candle right now, but I'll be digging you all again real soon.

I sure appreciated hearing from you crazy humans. Do you think you could scare up some more ink and let me know what you think about all that's going down? You don't have to shade your writing. Just say it as you mean it. Later!

March 1956

The Glitterville Scene, Dig Magazine

Well now, frantic ones, how's it happening for you all? I hope things are the grooviest. Yeah, it's me and I'm back to lay upon you a whole big mess of righteous noise. You dig? So then, there now, if all your jazz is straight, let's move on into the Hollywood scene post-haste.

Premiers are wild, swinging affairs, but every now and then they can be a real drag. The one that jumped off the other pm was a diluted session that just made it to OK. In other words, it was just alright, if you dig what I'm saying.

The flick that I'm on about was *Giant* and I'm standing confused. Much bread was spent, but to my way of thinking James Dean was the only cat in the film worth sitting through three and a half hours. The only other exception was possibly Dennis Hopper. However, he only had a short time on screen to be cool. But then I'm no movie critic, so no more gumbeating about the merits of motion picture screen values.

The four of us made the glittering premier scene in a rented chariot. Wow, what pretence. Our quartet was made up of my steady doll, Kathy Case and Yours Truly along with Margaret O'Brien and Don Robertson (a producer at RKO). Man, what a group we were - and what a mob greeted us on the landing strip. Because we had made a late arrival, we hopped inside in cut time and hustled along to our seats. We grabbed a sit-down and began digging the screen action post haste. There was no time to eye the rest of the already assembled Hollywood humanity. Therefore, I'm not truly hip as to the who was there routine. Hence, I'll dispense with mentioning it forthwith. Like I said, three and a half hours later, the film came to a thundering finale - thank God. The theatre was loudly resounding with the movie's musical theme. So much so that I feared that the walls of the theatre would crumble to dust. Everybody made fast paws for the exit and we hauled ass right along with them

After much rumbling about we finally retrieved our chariot and split for

Right: *The Hollywood premiere of Moby Dick with Ben Cooper, his lovely lady, Kathy and me.*

Frascati's, in Beverly Hills, where the juice and the eats were the ultimate. It seemed as if all of Hollywood's humanity fell out to cool their engines and to pick up on the piano, bass and bongos, that were laying down a groovy mood. After we arrived, we sifted through the humans and in less than a minute we were caught up in the atmosphere. The faces of Natalie Wood, Dennis Hopper, Tab Hunter, Anne Francis and Perry Lopez were already there. Our crew stayed way into the late watch and really balled it up. Came the two o'clock hour the cat playing bongos made a big mistake. He asked me if I wanted to sit in and blow a bit. The poor fool. He didn't realise exactly what he'd unleashed. I thumped up a storming accompaniment to a couple of numbers, then with a self-righteous shuffle, I returned to my perch. No one said a word. Then Kathy came up with some noise that really knocked me out. 'You know, honey,' she said, 'I also have a few hidden talents. You might not know it, but I'm a pretty good carpenter. I once built my mother a whole set of bookcases. And you know something – your bongoing reminded me so much of when I was hammering nails.'

With that we all fled for the home scene.

Sight of the month: Natalie Wood and Nick Adams sitting in Natalie's dressing room at Warners digging Elvis Presley's new RCA Victor album and trying, oh so hard, not to jump and stomp. That is almost impossible to do when hearing Elvis wail out the notes.

Left: With MGM's lovely singing star, Jane Powell, who's also a culinary expert.

Jane Powell is one mellow singing earth angel as we all know. She's also a super fine cook, as anyone who has ever been to Powellville will agree. But I know something that many of you won't. Janie digs Dixieland jazz. The other pm I fell by her pad to have a small speak-a-thon. The house was rocking so hard that I thought that any second it would choose a partner and get up and dance the Charleston. As I flopped through the front door, I spied Jane digging the swinging sounds the hardest and I was gassed at seeing her so enthralled.

Jane sure knows good Dixieland when she hears it. Dig the following and you'll know what I mean. These are a few of her choices: Tony Almerico's 'Dixieland All Starts', 'The Happy Minstrels' - Art Mooney, 'The Great 16' - Muggsy Spanier,. 'Stompin7 At The Famous Door' - George Girard. After digging these discs, your ears will need a rinse out and your paws will need a retread. My skull is still banging four along with the cowbell.

Over and out.

May 1956

The Glitterville Scene, Dig Magazine

Hey! Just a minute! Hold everything! You can't just dive into this madness without first taking your shoes off. You gotta prepare yourselves for the shock.

Hollywood's a swinging settlement and it's definitely here to stay - crazy as it may be.

I can't think of any human in the world who doesn't dig animals the most. If there is someone out there that's down on those creatures - I don't care to get acquainted. Everybody bounding about on the Glitterville turf dig pets the hardest. There's woofage everywhere.

Standing to the East on the western border of Glendale, two clicks from North Hollywood (a little Los Angeles geography lesson for the foreigners) stands a breathing animal trading establishment that's the end in animal finery. The sign over the door reads, J & M Aviaries. It's an animal emporium with a difference. It specializes in exotica. You can dig it - monkeys, parrots, snakes, tortoises and furry four-pawed creatures from the darkest jungles of the world.

The man and wife who own and manage the shop and menagerie are the very essence of cool. They care about the animals and always do a Sherlock Holmes on every person before selling.

Many of the Hollywood kiddies go on a safari to check out the exotic animal action at J & M. Some have intentions of buying. If you're lucky and happen to fall by at just the right time you might find yourself eyeballing such groovy animal lovers as Natalie Wood and Nick Adams, or possibly Tony Curtis and Janet Leigh - or maybe Tab Hunter and Lori Nelson will be checking out the salt water fish in the aquarium out back. If you dig the atmosphere hard enough to hang around you may even catch Rock Hudson buying his wife, Phyllis, a festive Amazon parrot just to keep their conversation flowing.

Earth-angel Kathy Case and I bought two Panama parrots, and fell hard upon Roger Smith and Victoria Shaw (of the Eddie Duchin Story) to do the same. They goofed and bought a squirrel monkey instead. Russ Tamblyn and his lovely Venetia are always in there eyeing up the baby ocelots and pondering the great weight of what their landlord would say if they brought home one of those sweet spotted kitties.

I'm putting down the groove that all Hollywood have gone ape for the exotic world of J & M Aviaries and the far out creatures that dwell within. Dig this! If you have a parrot in the house there'll always be someone to talk to.

Now hear this. Sherrie North is the swinging ultimate end in the shape dept. It's the truest. Any questions? Well, creatures, play it cool and check her out. You'll find yourselves lost in a land of wonderment.

Later.

Screenlife, September 1956

Music of the Day

It was one of those real bring-down early darks. The atmosphere came on gloomy with grey rain clouds and the whole depressing bit. It was fast approaching six o'clock. I was just sitting around pondering many thoughts in my tin skull, when all of a sudden the wireless started screaming. I stifled its outburst by answering its cry. 'Hi man, how'd you and Kathy like to make it over to my pad tonight? Bring your bongos and some records and we'll have a ball. Cool with you?

Twenty minutes later, Kathy Case and I arrived at Mr & Mrs Russ Tamblyn's domicile. We came looking for action and, man, we were sure to find it. Now this cat, Rusty, has a record collection that just won't quit. He's also quite a thumper on the bongos. Well, anyhow, we all greeted each other, grabbed a cup of Java and settled down for a quiet evening of digging records and blowing a few frames on the Latin skins. Things kicked along real groovy — us just digging the discs and all. Our inspiration was flying high, so Russ and I decided to take off on a bongo duel. We flipped on some Dizzy Gillespie and wailed away. After about a minute Russ snicked on his tape recorder and then things really began to take off screaming. We didn't come down until the following a.m.

Here's a few of the new albums that Russ Tamblyn and Venetia Stevenson have in their collection: *The Four Freshmen and Five Trombones* (Capitol); *Cannonball Adderley and Strings* (Emarcy); *Gerry Mulligan Sextet* (Emarcy); *Chico Hamilton in Hi-Fi* (Pacific Jazz); *Contemporary Concepts of Stan Kenton* (Capitol); *Count Basie Swings and Joe Williams Sings* (Cleff); *Nat Cole Anniversary* (Capitol); *The Man with the Golden Arm* (Decca). Believe me, all these albums are the greatest in coolness.

More Sounds to Wrap Your Ears Around

Hey, creatures! About those new album covers that are housing records these days. They sure are the most to say the least. They're so flashy that they're starting to look like front covers of paperback novels and in many cases they resemble the face of pulp fiction magazines. Wild scenes are sure to be viewed and as for the chicks that adorn so many of these album covers — all I can say is wow and a half!

The companies that have far surpassed the others in cover design are Norgran, Cleff and Verve.

The next time you're at a record palace, dig the following: *Krupa and Rich* (Cleff); *Oscar Peterson Plays Count Basie* (Cleff); *Ellingtonia '56* (Norgran); *The Modern Jazz Sextet* (Norgran); *Al Hibbler Sings Love Songs* (Verve); *Anita* (Verve). By the by, the latter album presents a completely new Anita O'Day. Record companies today sure have it made in the shade. Not only do their sleeves display the greatest in cover art, but the records inside contain the finest sounds around. Get your ears ready and dig this bit of swinging truth. You too can become a jazz head.

A thumping, wild concussion just rocked across my headset's receiver screen. I shall therefore pass on its message. That sweet singing earth chirper Jane Powell has just signed a new record contract with Verve. It looks as though you'll be getting lots of cool music from Powellville in cut time. Now, how can one chick have so much — looks, talent, personality and a Siamese cat?

Here's a bit to ponder. Harry Belafonte is a fabulous ping-pong player. He's got a serve that just won't quit. One thing is for sure. He'll never starve. Believe me, I know from whence I speak, 'cause I lost a half a buck to the Belafonte touch the other day. But I don't think he'll have to consider ping-pong as his bread and butter because his RCA Victor album *Belafonte* is just selling like there's no tomorrow. No wonder he's considered the greatest ever calypso tune spinner. This human can sing, and then some. If any of you creatures haven't dug this album yet, you better make fast paws to do so or consider yourselves completely out of time.

About this cat, Elvis Presley. He sure knows how to live — two Cadillacs, a motorcycle and ten zillion chicks. The Vegas scene split wide open at the seams when he fell on the setting singing up a storm. He is a cool one. RCA Victor can't press enough of his singles and albums to meet the demand.

Just a quick hot flash. Helen Merrill is a gas. Dig her quick and often. She lives on the Emarcy label. She's a singing creature from the county of cool. Helen really spins me round in circles.

The scene was frantic. All the earth children crammed in the record booth were falling out completely. Man, there was fall out of creatures everywhere, stoned by submission to sound. The reason for this occurrence was their reaction to the new Sarah Vaughn album on Emarcy called *Sarah Vaughn in Hi-Fi*. This lady is in the end zone. The kiddies had all gotten her message and had forcibly flipped out. So, babies, if you're hip to a groovy serenade, then you'll all want to dig this album *muy pronto*. If you aren't fractured by it — well you all better take a quick trip to the nearest ear doctor.

There's a frantic cat making it these days in our quaint little West Coast settlement. He's a fine wailing kiddy when it comes to blowing alto sax, baritone sax, flute or just flying on the scene in his red Jaguar coupé. The cat's title is Bud Shank. He was formally with the Stan Kenton Aggregation. I'm sure all of you 'what dig jazz the most' have heard of this chap and will agree that he's the end in making fine sounds come out of metal horns. For those of you who are un-hip to his sound, please do yourself a favour and make fast feet to your nearest record emporium and cop a listen to this fine new Pacific Jazz album, *The Bud Shank Quartet*. As a matter of fact listen to any of his Pacific Jazz albums such as *Bud Shank and Three Trombones*, *The Laurindo Almeida Quartet Featuring Bud Shank*, *Bud Shank and Bill Perkins* (Jazz West Coast). The guy really blows up a storm. There are also many other albums where he's featured as well. Hey, chicks — dig! Like this cat comes on real sharp, you know. Oh, he's a solid one all right, with fine threads and has all the cool moves.

January 1959

The View from Rowland's Head

Look down, look down that lonesome road and you will see a white Corvette pull to a solid stop. A hip creature steps on to the turf, his arms loaded with wrapped up goodies. The cat is definitely in the know. He's dressed in black threads, black shirt and wears a white tie and black boots. Oh yeah, he's too much. He stands on solid ground for a moment and looks about him. Then focusing in the right direction, he moves out on a dedicated mission — to lay the ever-loving groovy truth on the non-believers. He's cool, like Alaska. He's with it, like now. The time is right. He travels towards the large neon sign shining just in front of him. It screams in silent brilliance. The world in hi fi and stereophonic sound. So, people, if you're with it — crazy. You're in tune. The world of truth is about to be yours. Pick up on the message from the man. It's a gas — and like a solid sender, he's here to switch you on.

A Sight to Behold

Remember, frantic ones, I said I was going to lay a solid tale of groove on your brain boxes. Well, dig this and you'll be put wise to nutty city scenes.

It's all about the Carolyn Jones frame. Wow and a half. It's too much and too true. This chick has style she 'ain't never used yet'. Her talent is as fine as wine in the summer time. You can flat believe Elvis got her message when he got next to her during the time they worked together on the flick, *King Creole*. She comes on like that big old ape in the jungle, King Kong. Now allow me to lay this fact on you, Jack. The chick is most mellow in the calf action department. She's got legs like only happen on Vargas calendars. She really turns me on when she does a walk away. You'll find yourself with a large case of runaway eyes when you pick up on her motion. Believe me, you'll be put wise and a half. She's absolutely something else to behold.

New Faces to Discover

There is always an awful lot of talk about the big name cats in town. A great deal is true. Most is a bunch of bull. Nevertheless, there's always a whole lot of talkin' going on. I've been giving all the noise a great deal of thought lately and I've come to the conclusion that there is a large stack of new faces on the scene in Glitter Town that really deserve a talk about. Therefore, that's just what I'm gonna devote this month's column to. I hope you all won't mind the little side trip. Hang in there and I'll put you wise to some of the hippest people that are newly groovy.

Andra Martin is a living fantasy. I happened to be lucky, or shall I say, unlucky enough, to find myself sitting next to her at a movie the other night. When the lights came on and I cast my eyes at the loveliness sitting next to me — well — I flipped four and a half times. I was

THE VIEW FROM ROWLAND'S HEAD

BY STEVE ROWLAND

What's the latest jive from the Hollywood jungle? Here's the blast on all the swinging citizens—from one of the swinging-est.

■ Gather 'round me all you swinging fine nesters of planet earth whilst I come on with more jive from the Hollywood jungle for you to entangle yourselves in. But watch it. It can be tricky. All jazz blown here is strictly ad lib—you know, head-arranged, but the score is the truest. Dig? So now that you're put wise to coming events, hang on to your wigs and don't go cocky on me. We're about to take a fast flight to the scene of fastidious events. Time's a memory. Let's split post haste. Let's crack the supersonic barrier.

Nick Adams, as Hemingway relates, is a frantic fine cat what wails 'way out all the time. This is a known fact. However the other P.M. when the non-fictitious Nick lost a fifty-cent piece in his chariot and couldn't find it—wow he'd had it. The gods descended Mt. Olympus in force.

Nick came falling in the Warners' commissary looking as if that old sleep peddler, The Sandman, had him lassoed or something. He looked as if he'd taken up living under water as a hobby. His eyes came on like a map to the promised land. He fell into a sit-down at my table and began unfolding a tale of purple woe.

Well now, it seems as though somewhere along the line Sir Nicholas of Adams dropped a fifty-cent coin in his black T-bird and it had gone into hiding somewhere in the interior region. He'd looked in vain for it, but to no avail, so he'd given it up as a lost doubloon. Last night, however, while making the home scene after a frantic date with **Lili Gentle,** he suddenly heard it rolling around inside the door on the driver's side. Every time he came to a stop it would roll forward and every time he started up it would roll back. R-R-R-R-click! R-R-R-R clank! He became so bugged with frustration that he stopped right where he was and madly started dismembering the chariot. Out came the seats, the floor mat, the door panel, even the radio. But no fifty-cent piece was anywhere in sight. Now Nick's no quitter, so he kept on a-lookin' anyway—way into the early bright. By this time, the car was strewn all over the turf, Nick's clothes were looking like fugitives from a grease pit, night people were beginning to assemble and gawk, and still no half-a-rock could be found. And here's the note that finished the chorus. Nick's clothes were ruined—a big cleaning bill looms. The T-bird is in the garage. The mechanic is still trying to figure out how to get it back together. Another bill looms. Also, the heat gave him a ticket for blocking traffic and causing a public demonstration. You know how much little things like this cost I'm sure. But here's the real bringdown. The mystery is still unsolved—no fifty-cent piece could be found at all. So, people, you try to figure it out. Maybe you'll get lucky. Oh yeah, I almost forgot. There's a fifty-cent reward.

Oh man! I've been boiling up a storm inside of me ever since I first dug the chick. She flips me completely. She's the grooviest female human going. She is sure one tuff wren, believe me. I've got such fat eyes for her that I'm blind to all surrounding dangers—mainly Arthur Loew, Jr., who also digs her the most. So like, Wow! I'm perplexed. What to do? I'm afraid to call her. Now "ain't" that goofy? But then that's the way I get when I'm hung—all shook up. So I guess **Joan Collins** will never know how I feel. Like the mountain I'll have to stand and weep and hope I won't crack up completely. My feet are in ice water to be sure.

Tommy Sands is one cool solid earth creature in my book. He's the kind of cat this world has too few of. I know this is just a little thing but to me it was too much.

Now we all know Tommy is one busy cat these days, what with records, movies, and personal appearances and all going for him. Yet Tommy found the time on a busy Friday evening to watch a local T.V. record show (*Juke Box Jury*—Peter Potter's) when he heard that I was going to appear on it and have my new record (*Continued on page 61*)

There's a new girl on Steve's private date parade: pert blonde Julie Reding.

Steve's latest record, Say The Word, is busy rocking up spins on the juke boxes.

***Left:** The appearance of The View From Rowland's Head upset a few people.*

onvinced she was an inhabitant of Doll City. But, luck ame up ugly for me when I tried to get next to her. I ound out she's tied with ring and all to Ty Hardin, ABC's ew *Cheyenne* star. He's a faster gun than I am, so I had o cool it.

Ty Hardin, by the way, is a pretty cool cat in his own xistence. He's originally from New York, but the good ld state of Texas has claimed him. He continually argues hat Alaska really isn't larger than Texas, it's just that it as lots of snow and ice piled up. I told him to wait until he melting period. He's also an avid hound dog lover ust like Elvis. Ty is now in the process of raising two Weimaraner pups. You know, those purple coloured dogs with green eyes. They're real ghostly woofers. By the way, like all Texans, Ty plays the guitar and sings. Maybe he'll be renamed the Singing Bronco. Who knows?

May Britt is a slammin' blonde female creature. I'm sure all of you are wise to the fact after digging her in *The Young Lions*. She's another solid Swedish import. Wow, they sure grow fantasy chicks in Sweden. Oh, yeah! So people if you haven't done so, pick upon her newest flick, *The Hunters*. I'm sure you'll get a solid sexy message below the belt.

I don't have to lay very much on you people about this cat because he's already caused a minor earthquake in chickville. He's a giant in the acting department. The proof is that he's already shattered Broadway with his performance in *Compulsion*. Now he brings this same shatter matter to the screen. People dig him. He's got a strong message for you all. Oh yeah, in case you aren't already hip, his tag is Dean Stockwell.

The woodchucks, prairie dogs, groundhogs, ants, beetles and many other various earth dwellers are really keeping anxious eyes and ears tuned sharply so that they are warned in plenty of time of the approaching red demon. The whole valley and canyon animal society have their radar systems working overtime. It's the only way that they can be prepared for Troy Donahue and his red Porsche speedster. Troy flies on the scene like a runaway

THE VIEW FROM ROWLAND'S HEAD

BY STEVE ROWLAND

What's the wild runaway skull noise from Hollywood? Just open your ears to Steve and pick up what's really swinging on the night wind.

rocket that'd escaped from a grade B science fiction movie. This Donahue cat is a real stampeder and he's got the whole chick nation desperate to break down his door in order to get next to him. Some cats just have all the luck.

Oh, man, am I ever hang city bound. Wow and a half. The chick has me flipped so hard I don't even know which end is up. I'm completely dust. The girl's a knock out in every department. She's got those cool groovy dark eyes and long black hair that shimmers in the sunlight. And oh that beautiful cinnamon coloured skin — deliver me. It's too much. Man, Venus de Milo had nothing on this lady in the face and frame department. In other words, creatures, the lady's got it. She's made the screen-scene in two flicks, *South Pacific* and *In Love and War*. At present, she's cooling it in New York on the Broadway stage in the Josh Logan production, *The World of Suzie Wong*. Believe me, people, when I lay this fact on you. I'd swim all the way across the Atlantic Ocean for just a coffee date with this angel. Now, before I take five, let me clue you to her identity. Frances Nuyen is the name to remember.

This little message here is all about a real earth-rocking, canyon-dwelling creature who has landed on all fours and set up camp. Well, you wouldn't know it, but he's completely destroyed the mysterious pink realm of all female creatures. He's laid a solid vibration on the poor things. Man, this cat has sent the dollies flipping and flopping in all directions. All you gotta do to put yourselves wise, is check out the line up of broken hearts lingering at the Chez Paulette coffee house most nights of any week. Wow, it's swing city with sniffles. The Saturday night flow has a deep salty river of tears. It keeps Max, the owner of Chez Paulette, working overtime issuing crying towels to all the weepy ones before following along sweeping up the Turkish Special cigarette butts that are left like a trail of heartbreak. Mystery deepens with an ever-constant smoke screen, coupled with a killing sense of humour. His sarcasm is deadly. As an actor, he's a solid fine professional. You can pick up on his action in the Gregory Peck flick *Pork Chop Hill*. His name is John Alderman and the Big Apple has been his stomping ground. His home away from home while he's cooling it on the coast appears to be split in two — the Chez Paulette coffee house, and the Hamburger Hamlet on the Sunset Strip. You'll always find him at the latter every afternoon around three o'clock. That's a good 'chick digging time' says John. You better believe that he can really spot 'em. As I said before, he's cool — about six feet tall, dark hair, blue eyes, with just the right motion. He'll happen big time if he doesn't do a burn-out first.

Now here's a real Wood City-bound chick to keep your eyes in focus. Her name is Beverly Scott. Man, she's fine and mellow, blonde and green-eyed with tiptop body construction. Do I need to say more? Watch out for her. She'll dazzle your eyesight. Over and out.

Movie Play, August 1959

Gloom City Bound: The Drifter

Freeze out from up above. The man upstairs had turned the temperature machine way down causing things to lay heavy on the cool side. I stood alone in the seven p.m. atmosphere while digging the whole humanity scene that was playing out its little game of life below me. My eyes grew glazed and out of focus with the ever-pounding turbulence in my mind. My thoughts kept travelling back over that broken road to an unrequited love. Sharp spikes kept biting into me and I felt sick all over. I was going through a mental kickback to every romantic novel I'd ever read. You know the scenario — a soul gets on a one-way love train. His ticket's already been punched. Can't laugh, can't sleep, can't eat, the entire soul-destroying bit.

Oh wow, Mr Tune Spinner, please don't play 'I Cried a Tear' or 'It's Just a Matter of Time'. That'll destroy me for sure. Help, I'm drowning and I can't swim at all. She's gone for good and things just aren't the same any more.

Creep in

I just stood there, at the edge of my patio, one step in front of tears, digging below the sad, night-time, car-infested streets of Hollywood, with all its hysterical, madly scurrying civilization. I wondered what new earth-shaking event was taking place at this very moment in any one of the many coffee houses, scattered like pollen throughout flowering Hollywood.

Maybe Mort Sahl was delivering a giant preach-a-thon about the evils of the Hollywood Freeway. I was so lost in myself that I didn't hear the Man coming. His sudden arrival started me, so much that I almost hit splash city into the swimming pool. However, I was quick this time, depriving myself of a dunking. I was slick enough to catch my balance just as he thundered to a shuddering halt at the head of driveway. He held out an envelope, a message for the Drifter. The moment had come to switch on and get with the Hollywood action. Enough time had been spent goofing off here on my private hilltop; too many hours spent feeling sorry for myself.

Contact

Time to move on. Things were beginning to swing up-tempo and I had to be groovin' part of it. I threw on my wailing shoes and unloaded the juice from off the electric company's back. Like the Roadrunner, I stashed my frame behind the wheel of my white Corvette and made like a runaway rocket zooming and twisting down the canyon toward certain neon adventure.

Slowing around a big turn, I caught sight of some chatter action being staged out front of a large white colonial domicile on the left side of the road. Tony Curtis and Janet Leigh were out front laying some words on Keenan Wynn and Lee Marvin, who'd stopped by on their way home from a motorcycle event in the valley. Lee and

Keenan looked as if the whole valley racetrack had taken up permanent residence on their bodies. Man, they were grubby. I threw a quick hello to the foursome and split on down the canyon to Glitterville civilization. The unrequited love scene began playing hearts and flowers in my brain again and I needed to get lost in a crowd.

Action Arrived

I decided to hit on some cake and coffee before going any further. I threw a quick right off to Sunset Boulevard and pulled in behind Pupis, a way out pastry and coffee den opposite from where Sunset Plaza Drive begins to climb. As I stepped on to solid land, I spotted a black Porsche Speedster moving with stealth, obviously seeking a parking slot. As it reined to a stop, I heard, 'Hi man, how's it hanging?' It was Steve McQueen and his groovy fine wife, Neile Adams.

The three of us decided to make the Pupis's interior together — to sit for five and take a taste. As we fell in, I spotted Sandra Dee just slipping over the little patio fence heading toward her car. After about five minutes of throwing coffee in my skull, I laid a later on Steve and Neile and split for the Salem House, a new eatery in Beverly Hills. As I cooled my short at the curb, I heard a loud greet from over my left shoulder. Turning around I dug that it was Mickey Callan and Cora Lynn Chapman. They too were heading for the Salem House as well, so we made it three. Crazy! As we were falling through the door, Bob Wagner, Natalie Wood and Robert Conrad were just heading out. I laid a heavy greeting on the trio and started inside. That's when RJ called me over. He wanted me to dig Alvin, a baby chipmunk that he'd just bought for Natalie. It was cute — with a convict stripe down its back. The monk had been busted for stealing nuts but was now out on probation.

Party City

Just as I was about to make it to a dark corner with Mickey and Cora, someone tapped me up and said that I was wanted on the phone. It was the Man anxious to put me wise about a large blast-athon that Gary Crosby was throwing, at his new Sunset Plaza pad. I said later to Callan and Chapman and split for the Crosby home front.

Man, the electric company was making a fat profit at Gary's modern swing house. I lay back off-stage and dug the setting before committing myself to the gala. Joan Collins, Tommy Sands, Nicky Blair, Jimmy Boyd, Ronnie Burns, Lindsay, Dennis and Phil Crosby, Steve Rowland, Sandra Dee, David and Ellie Janssen, Vince Edwards, John Smith and Mary Ford were heavily into balling it up big time. By then I was too pooped to pop and headed for nod city.

My first contact with conscious earth came via the screaming wireless. I shook my skull twice and found myself once again talking to Mickey Callan. He clued me to the fact that he and Beverly Scott along with Sal Ponti, Marianne Gaba, Lindsay Crosby and Connie Stevens were going to come on like Western heroes and make the Griffith Park scene on horseback. I had no eyes for hoof action, and laid down a polite nay. I had to split. There was more action to uncover 'in them thar hills'.

The Drifter was the view from Steve's alter ego.

Movie Play, September 1959

The Drifter

Quit goofing and get with the functionating below like *pronto.*' Contact had been made. The Man had called and laid down a solid message. I tossed on some clean threads and switched the juice from off the electric company's back. My wailing boots were laced up tight and I was ready to roar like the midnight special. I fired up my white charger and soon I was zooming and twisting down through rain-drenched Laurel Canyon — destination, night time Hollywood adventure.

Party time

The Man had clued me in to a big swing session being held at Bob Turnbull's giant domicile. It's truly a palace of the gods. The pad balances on three paws on top of a plateau at the end of Crescent Heights Boulevard high above Sunset. Believe me, it's up there in cloud city. I had eyes to make it, but now that I was out on the main turf, I decided to grab some much-needed coffee before the climb. It was about 8.30 p.m. The night was young. I edged my short to a resting place at the curb and fell into the Chez Paulette. Wow, many faces of grooviness were already gathered. A bearded John Saxon and Vicki Thal were cooling it at a small back table. They copped sight of my entrance and waved me into a fast sit-down laying on the usual greeting. Vicki put me hip to the fact that John had been so occupied making flicks lately that she'd hardly seen him. I had to laugh at that. These two are like attached at the hip.

About then the door brushed open and Steve McQueen with his mellow wife, Neile Adams, came gliding in. I threw a 'How's it going?' at them. They nodded in recognition and retired to a table where Dennis Hopper and Tuesday Weld were secretly stashed, digging hard one another's identity.

I finished throwing coffee in my skull, laid a later on John and Vicki and headed for the door. Before I split I nudged Max Lewin, Chez Paulette's infamous owner, and clued him to the fact that his good friends John Alderman and Suzanne Pleshette would soon be out on the coast and would be falling by the Chez Paulette to haunt his being. Man, I could almost smell John's Turkish cigarette smoke. I knew that Max could also do without those choking smoke signals.

Just as I stepped into the night I spotted Cora Lynn Chapman all by her lonesome self plodding up the little alleyway outside Chez Paulette, looking to enter. I asked her why she had the hangdog look. She said she was alone and blue because her ever lovin' Mickey Callan was away on a three week *They Came to Cordura* publicity tour. She was lonely. I asked her to come along to the Turnbull hilltop party, but she declined saying that her heart wouldn't be in it. Cora's a doll and a half and that's for sure. I nodded later and hit out for the hilltop circus.

Blast-a-thon and Wailing Times

Yeah man, the gathering was swinging. About 200 soul stirrers had made the setting. They were well into screaming and stomping up a storm to the loud thump-thump of an out-of-tune rock'n'roll band. Humanity was really packed in at this pad. It was like a sardine can with too many brothers and sisters hitching a ride. The whole place came on like one big sideshow. The entire house was shaking and quaking. I stood stoned where I was and laid on searching eyes for a quiet corner where I could stash my frame, dig the happenings and eye the chicks — preferably undetected.

There was an upstairs balcony overlooking the whole deal. Perfect! I cooled it there. The creatures were in a full ball-it-up frame of mind. Thunder, crash, clank! It seemed as if the world was coming to an end. Sal Mineo with Marianne Gaba and Sal's brother Mike made a grand three people entrance. Bob Conrad, John Ashley and Nick Adams boomed in like three soldiers of cool and immediately started digging those chicks that had good legs. Mike Landon and his wife Dodie were in a far corner laying words on Troy Donahue about Troy's big break in the Warner Brothers flick Summer Place. Rafael Campos was flitting all around the area like an out of control balloon that had just had the air released. I caught a wild glimpse of Kathy Nolan and Kenny Miller at the juice bowl. Hoping to refill their glasses, Ben Cooper and Bev Scott stood patiently waiting. A large mass of people gathered in front of me and I lost eye contact with the others momentarily. Wham — bam and a half! I looked again. There was Lindsay Crosby, Jimmy Boyd, Ron Burns, Jim Mitchum and Budd Albright, surrounded by a whole flock of Moulin Rouge showgirls. Some cats have all the luck. I heard a sigh to my left. It came from the dark side of the balcony. It was June Blair looking deeply into Dick Sargent's eyes. A group of people began singing from somewhere below me. I couldn't put the names to the voices exactly, but I think it was Rod McKuen and Marlene Willis. About then, in came Dennis Hopper and Tuesday Weld arguing about something. I didn't catch it. Tuesday split off to a corner and Mark Damon suddenly loomed out of the shadows and headed her way.

Gene Krupa-like drumming picked up the pulse and the festivities really began to rock out. It was Sal Mineo sitting in and taking five on the skins. About then a female tornado entered the room and everything hit slow-down. The chick was sharp, she was solid, she was blonde and had sexy legs, as well as the rest of the essential equipment needed to make her centrefold material. All eyes hit hard on her and stayed focused. She was Dotty Harmony, Elvis Presley's ex and from where I sat, I more than approved of his good taste. She was too much indeed. The Harmony arrived with Ray Anthony along with another super cool chick. The other sweetheart had an equally fine frame, topped with tumbling dark hair. Her name was Shari Sheeley, the solid one that wrote Ricky Nelson's big hit, 'Poor Little Fool.' I couldn't stop myself. Yours Truly entered into the madness and stood laying lustful eyes across the room where Dotty Harmony was standing. The message was sent. There was no need for words. The vibes were picked up loud and clear.

Yeah, all the young ravers were there and more were falling in every minute. Tommy Sands, Sandra Dee, Ricky Nelson, Venetia Stevenson, David Nelson, Edd Byrnes,

Asa Maynor, Peter Brown, Jill St John, Lance Reventlow, were flowing through like a condensed version of young Hollywood's Who's Who.

Suddenly a shout went up and everyone split for outside. Near the swimming pool, a dark shape was quickly moving through the shadows, trying his best to remain undetected. I was curious as to who he was. Hound dogging was in order. Anyway, I'd about had it with the activities so before the bystanders fell back and regrouped, I figured that split city was in order. I struggled down the outside steps, twisted past a few drunken revellers and finally pushed my way to the outer realm and proper breathing space.

Over the heads of some loud incoming party crashers, I again spotted the phantom runner. He was making frantic feet through the bushes and down the hillside as if there were demons in pursuit. I put down heavy paws and floated after him. That's when I saw some red lights, black and white cars and a squad of blue suit men roaring up the hill. I was sure that they had shutdown in mind. I'd hit the spit button just in time. I can't afford any further hassle with the local gendarmes. I hastened my tracks and finally clocked the shadow-concealing figure as he slipped into what appeared to be an ancient foreign coupé. He looked up and I was shocked by a face I thought I recognized. Through the gloom of the dawn's early light I could almost swear that the figure emerging from the shadows was Marlon Brando. Then he was gone and I'll never know.

I knew right then, as the dawn chased down the night that I needed sleep. My ticket had been punched so I moved out toward my hilltop hideout. Mr Sandman had put on his running shoes, but I beat him to the punch. Bed city arrived. It was five a.m.

The View from Rowland's Head

New Day Coming in

My first contact with earth came via the screaming wireless. I shook my diluted skull twice and found myself talking to Mary Jo Sheeley, Shari Sheeley's sharp sister. She laid some important words on me. Don and Phil Everly were coming in town tonight for a week of rehearsal for the *Chevy Show.* Sharon was having a surprise party for the guys tomorrow night. I should fall by. The people who would be making it would be Paul Anka, Eddie Cochran, Dotty Harmony, Connie Stevens, Rick Nelson, Baker Knight, Sandra Dee, the Venet brothers and as many chicks as could be dug up. Solid! I told Mary Jo to hang my name in there. I'd make it.

Right: *Mitzi Gaynor, Kathy Case and Lori Nelson. It's tough at times like this, but you just have to bite the bullet.*

Well, I knew I'd had enough on the sleep front so I got up, threw on clean threads, laid a fast Gillette on my face and hit out once again off the morning mountain top. I was heading for a cruise of the big town and another action trackdown. As I descended into the canyon vegetation, I dug that all was groovy and looking fresh. All of a sudden a thought crashed into my head. I'd thought of a way to beat the Man. I screeched into a fast U-turn and laid rubber all the way back to my pad. Ha! Why hadn't I thought of this before? I let Arty Dogg out of his kennel and both of us went entered the house (mine, not his). I threw some of his dog biscuits at him to keep him occupied and then grabbed the wireless. Wow, the idea was a minor flip. Instead of an in-person check out on the Hollywood front, why not call the various cooling spots and check on who was there and with whom. The Man would never suspect a thing. Mental note: I was being devious and a half.

First call, Kelbo's Hawaiian Barbecue on Fairfax Avenue. Last night's faces — Roger and Victoria Smith, John Ashley and Ann Anderson, Ben Cooper and Bev Scott.

Next call, Top's Coffee Shop at the Park Sunset Hotel on Sunset Boulevard. Rick Nelson, Dotty Harmony, Sal Ponti and Carmen Austin had all thrown coffee in their skulls here while taking time out a few nights back. Crazy! Third call, the Salem House in Beverly Hills. Sal Mineo and Terry Moore were hitting heavy on the eats. In the shadows Gary Crosby and Candy Barr were leaning close together. Wow! Heavy scenes.

A quick call to the Gaiety Delicatessen on Sunset Boulevard where all kinds of good people feed their faces. Barbara Luna, Dave and Ellie Jansen, Mort Sahl and Phyllis Kirk, Rita Dimico, Vicki Lewis, Linda Harris, Ronnie Burns, Kathy Case and Buddy Bregman (where's Anna Maria?), Dorothy Provine with Vince Edwards. The Gaiety is an away station for the famous and infamous, the wannabes and the never-gonnabes. I'd become rich if I had a dollar for everyone that sits at a Gaiety table, posing and talking trash.

Crunch out! The time had come to goof off. After that fourth call I got bugged with the whole nutty thing and decided to put a damper on the action. I flipped on the stereo and laid ears heavy on a stack of Frank Sinatra 45s. Arty on the floor wrapped up in the land of nod. All four paws were kicking wildly in a fruitless chase after one of his dream lovers. I checked the things to remember list before I closed my eyes and joined Arty Dogg in catching zzzzs.

The countdown: remember the party tomorrow for the Everly Brothers. Call George Klein in Memphis. Ask when Elvis will be back in town ready to stomp and wail.

I guess that about wraps it up. Oh yeah, there's a big welcome party being given by Rona Barrett for Bobby Darin next Tuesday at Jack Dennison's. I gotta be sure to make it. Bobby's the bitter end in good people, as most of his harem will agree.

I grabbed the deck of smokes off the table, shook one out, pretended to light it, and settled back listening to Frank singing 'Say It Isn't So'. My mind immediately became flooded in a mirrored pool of "her face" and I couldn't dam up the tears. I've got to stop living in regret. Perhaps I should lay out in a ter-splashed novel, but I haven't got eyes for self-pity. I'd better close down and fade to black.

Afterword

And The Beat Goes On by Budd Albright

After our first meeting at the Union Oil Station in the Pacific Palisades in the spring of 1956, Steve Rowland and I hit it off as if we'd known each other forever. The more we talked, the more I discovered that Steve and I had a great deal in common. Not only were we both struggling actors, but I discovered that Steve was a pretty good singer and about to sign a record deal. I also was a fairly good singer, loved rock 'n' roll and was also chasing a recording contract. As I hadn't yet cracked it as an actor, I was honing my writing skills, acquiring success with a few published articles. Steve was plying his writing talent as a columnist for several fan magazines.

As time went by, Steve and I discovered that aside from chasing our careers, what we really had most in common was our huge spirit of adventure, our love of fast cars, fast women and the lure of danger. Most important was our ability to laugh and not take ourselves too seriously. Although we were extremely competitive, we always had great mutual respect.

We have both experienced the highs and lows of life in the fast lane and never allowed ourselves to be intimidated or wounded by the gossip of Hollywood back-stabbers.

As our separate careers began to flourish we went on a charge through Hollywood, promoting excitement and chasing every gorgeous girl that breathed. Along the way we had a few run-ins with the law, mostly from drag racing on Sunset Boulevard, but we always managed to escape serious trouble. We made a lot of mistakes and probably angered a lot of people along the way, but we enjoyed life to the fullest and were lucky enough to have come out unscathed.

We had the courage to display our dreams in front of a cynical industry that can chew you up and spit you out. We turned frustration into motivation and promoted ideas into positive action.

It was a hell of a ride, my friend. There are no regrets.

This book is written from the heart. It deserves to be a success.

Forrest 'Budd' Albright
Palm Springs, California, June 2007

Right: Budd Albright and I survey the scene at Venice Beach from a lifeguard tower.

2
IFEGUARD OFF
3264

Well, citizens, I see it's sneak out time once again. I'll see you all a
when we next collide. Until then, stay cool and don't drool like a f
Keep your corners well sanded and stay loose from those blue suit
Later, swingers. Steve

Glossary

ADAMS Nick. Blond leading man. 10 July 1931 - 7 February 1968. Best known as Johnny Yuma of the TV series *The Rebel* (1959). Often cast as a 'troubled young man'. Appeared in *Rebel Without A Cause* (1955) alongside good friend James Dean.

ALBRIGHT Budd. 1960s & 70s actor and stuntman. Appeared in *Drive Hard, Drive Fast* (1973) and played Rayburn in first TV series of *Star Trek*. Was a stunt man in the film *There Was a Crooked Man* (1970) starring Kirk Douglas and Henry Fonda. Also one of the West Coast 'Twist Kings', the other being Steve Rowland!

ALDERMAN John. TV actor, writer, director. 6 June 1933 - 12 January 1987.

ANTHONY Ray. Trumpet player and band leader. Born 20 January 1922, Pennsylvania. Played with The Glenn Miller Band (1940-1941) and in the US Navy band (1942-1946). Also with Jimmy Dorsey and Al Donahue bands before forming his own wellknown band. Anthony recorded for Capitol records for 19 years. Once married to actress Mamie Van Doren. His biggest hits were *Dragnet* and *Peter Gunn*. He still plays.

BAER Max, Junior. Actor. Born 4 December 1937, Oakland, California, the son of former heavyweight boxing champion Max Baer. Known around the world as 'Jethro Bodine' in the smash TV series *The Beverly Hillbillies* (1962).

BELAFONTE Harry. Dashing actor, singer, composer, author, producer. Born 1 March 1927, New York, grew up in Jamaica. Made his name as a folk singer in night-clubs and theatres, and on television and records. Recorded the first million-selling *LP Calypso* (1956), which started a craze for traditional Jamaican folk music in the United States. Close friend of Burt Lancaster. Played Joe in the Oscar nominated film *Carmen Jones*.

BENCHLEY Robert Charles. Humorist and actor. 15 September 1889 - 21 November 1945. Theatre critic and modern commentator, one of the first contributors to *The New Yorker*. Actor in *Foreign Correspondent* (1940) and *Piccadilly Jim* (1936). Member of The Algonquin Round Table, a social circle for New York wits including Harpo Marx and Dorothy Parker.

BLAKE Robert. Chunky, 5'4", wise-cracking actor. Born 18 September 1933. Featured in MGM's *Our Gang* series aged five and later appeared in many westerns. Gave haunting portrayal of killer Perry Smith in *In Cold Blood* (1967) and won an Emmy for TV series *Baretta*. Also appeared in *Rawhide* (1959).

BOYD Jimmy. Singer/actor. Born 9 January 1939. Jimmy recorded 'I Saw Mommy Kissing Santa Claus' when he was 12 years old.

BRADY Scott. Pin-up actor. 13 September 1924 -16 April 1985. Appeared in many westerns and crime stories, including *The Gal Who Took the West* (1949) and in *Untamed Frontier* (1952) he beat up Shelley Winters. Achieved minor cult status as bad hombre 'The Dancin' Kid' in the offbeat western *Johnny Guitar* (1954). Other action roles alongside Barbara Stanwyck, Mala Powers and Anne Bancroft and later bit parts in *The China Syndrome* (1979) and *Gremlins* (1984).

BRANDO Marlon. Iconic, brooding actor. 3 April 1924 - 1 July 2004. Billed the greatest movie actor of all time, he scorched the screen in 1949 as Stanley Kowalski in the movie version of Tennessee Williams' *A Streetcar Named Desire* (1951). Other films include *The Wild One* (1953), *Mutiny on the Bounty* (1962), *The Godfather* (1972), *Apocalypse Now* (1979) and Kazan's *On the Waterfront* (1954), which won him his first Oscar for his portrayal of meat-headed longshoreman Terry Malloy, the washed-up pug who 'coulda been a contender'. Director John Huston said his performance of Marc Antony in *Julius Caesar* (1953) was like seeing the door of a furnace opened in a dark room and co-star John Gielgud, the premier Shakespearean actor of the 20th century, promptly invited Brando to join his repertory company.

BRITT May. Blonde femme fatale actress. Born 22 March 1933, Lidingö, Sweden. Spotted as a photographer's assistant in Stockholm by producer Carlo Ponti and director Mario Soldati. Married Sammy Davis Jr.

BROWN Peter. Actor. Born Pierre de Lappe 5 October 1935, New York. Acted in many westerns of the mid-1950s and as eager young deputy Johnny McKay in the classic series *Lawman* (1958) and as a Texas Ranger in action/comedy series *Laredon* (1965). Moved to soap operas and TV films in the 70s.

BURNS Edd (Kookie). Actor. Born 30 July 1933, New York. Role in TV series *77 Sunset Strip* (1958) as hip-talking parking-lot attendant named 'Kookie'. Forever wielding a comb, he attracted a young male following and made a single with singer/actress Connie Stevens, 'Kookie, Kookie, Lend Me Your Comb'.

CAGNEY James. Compact, tough guy actor with a rasping voice and confident strut. 17 July 1899 - 30 March 1986. Best known for 1930s and 40s gangster roles including *Angels With Dirty Faces*. Conversely, he won his only Oscar as song and dance man George M. Cohan in *Yankee Doodle Dandy*.

CALLAN Michael. Popular TV Actor. Born 22 November 1935, Philadelphia, USA. Best known for roles in popular TV serials including *McMillan & Wife*; *Quincy ME* (as Barnaby Jones); *The Bionic Woman*; *The Love Boat*; *T J Hooker* and *Dr Kildare*.

CAMPOS Rafael. Actor. 13 May 1936 - 9 July 1985. Prolific TV actor 1950s onwards. Best known as Pete V. Morales in the classic movie *Blackboard Jungle* starring Sidney Poitier. Was married to singer Dinah Washington.

CASE Kathleen. Actress. 31 July 1933 - 22 July 1979. Best known for films *Human Desire* (1954) and *Running Wild* (1955). Was engaged to Steve Rowland.

CASSAVETES John. Dark, lean, fervent-looking actor and director. 9 December 1929 - 3 February 1989. Known for US TV series *Johnny Staccato*. Also appeared in classic films *Alexander the Great* (1968), *The Dirty Dozen* (1967), *Rosemary's Baby* (1968). Married actress Gena Rowlands.

COOKE Sam. Singer and composer. 22 January 1931 - 11 December 1964. Gospel singer whose first hit single, 'You Send Me' (1957), sold over a million. First major black singer to sign with RCA Records. Other hits include 'Chain Gang', 'A Change is Gonna Come', 'Twisting the Night Away' and 'Having a Party'.

COOPER Ben. Actor. Born 30 September 1930 Hartford, Connecticut. Played seaman Jack Hunter in the film *The Rose Tattoo* (1957) with Burt Lancaster. Seen in many westerns and classic TV series, including *Knots Landing, Dallas, The Virginian, Perry Mason, Bonanza.*

COREY Jeff. Film and TV character actor and acting teacher. 10 August 1914 - 16 August 2002. Appeared in *Joan of Arc* (1948), *Home of the Brave* (1949). Blacklisted but became the premier acting coach in Hollywood with his Professional Actors Workshop. His students included James Dean, Jack Nicholson, Anthony Perkins, Shirley Knight, Jane and Peter Fonda and Kirk Douglas, who came to Corey for help in playing the title role in *Spartacus* (1960).

CROSBY Gary. Stocky actor. 27 June 1933 - 24 August 1995. Son of singing legend Bing Crosby. Appeared briefly with his father and brothers as themselves in *Star Spangled Rhythm* (1942) and *Duffy's Tavern* (1945). From the late 50s appeared in breezy films such as *Mardi Gras* (1958), *Holiday for Lovers* (1959), *A Private's Affair* (1959), *Battle at Bloody Beach* (1961), *Operation Bikini* (1963), and *Girl Happy* (1965) with Elvis Presley.

CUMMINGS Jack. Producer. 16 February 1900 - 28 April 1989. Nephew of Louis B. Mayer. Married Betty Kern, daughter of composer Jerome Kern. Was producer of MGM musicals such as *Broadway Rhythm* (1944), *Kiss Me Kate* (1953), *The Last Time I Saw Paris* (1954), *Seven Brides for Seven Brothers* (1954), *Can-Can* (1960) and *Viva Las Vegas* (1964).

DARIN Bobby. Italian/American singer, composer and actor. 14 May 1936 - 20 December 1973. Huge career with hits including 'Mack the Knife'. In the film *Come September* (1961) he met his first wife,16 year old Sandra Dee. Nominated for Best Supporting Actor in *Captain Newman, M.D.* (1963). Portrayed by Kevin Spacey in *Beyond the Sea* (2004).

DEAN James. Iconic 50s actor. 8 February 1931 - 30 September 1955. He had major roles in only three movies. In the Elia Kazan production of John Steinbeck's *East of Eden* (1955) he played Caleb, the 'bad' brother who couldn't force affection from his stiff-necked father, and played brooding teenager Jim Stark in Nicholas Ray's *Rebel Without a Cause* (1955). George Stevens' filming of Edna Ferber's *Giant* (1956), in which he played the non-conforming cowhand Jett Rink, was just coming to a close when Dean, driving his Porsche Spyder, collided with another car in Cholame, California. His very brief career, violent death and highly publicized funeral transformed him into a cult object.

DEE Sandra. Petite, cute, blonde actress, 'The Queen of Teens'. 23 April 1942 - 20 February 2005. A successful child model, she went on to act with John Saxon in *The Restless Years* (1958) and with Lana Turner in *Imitation of Life* (1959). Her popular teen films were the beach movie *Gidget* (1959) and *Come September* (1961), which also starred her husband, pop idol Bobby Darin.

DONAHUE Troy. Strapping, baby-faced, blond teenage heart throb. 27 January 1936 - 2 September 2001. Starred in *A Summer Place* (1959) with Sandra Dee and as the lead character in *Parrish* (1961). He had a role in *The Godfather: Part II* (1974). Was the inspiration for *The Simpsons* (1989) character Troy McClure. Married briefly to actress Suzanne Pleshette.

EDWARDS Vince. Screen, stage, TV actor, TV director and singer. 9 July 1928 - 11 March 1996. Became a contract actor at Paramount Pictures in the early 50s. In the 60s he played the brilliant but confrontational young Dr. Casey in the television series *Ben Casey* (1961). Recorded a half dozen albums for American Decca records at the height of his Ben Casey popularity, the first of which was *Vincent Edwards Sings.*

EKBERG Anita. 'The Iceberg'. Blonde bombshell actress. Born 29 September 1931, Malmö, Sweden. Ex-Miss Sweden. In Rome, she got her breakthrough in Federico Fellini's *La Dolce Vita* (1960). She stayed in Italy and made around 20 movies during the next ten years.

EVERLY BROTHERS. Harmonizing duo Don and Phil. Born in the coalmining community of Muhlenburg County. Started out as young boys performing in The Everly Family Show. First hit single 'Bye Bye Love' released in 1957 followed by a string of others, including 'Wake Up Little Susie', 'All I Have To Do Is Dream', etc. Later split to follow solo careers.

FISHER Eddie. Crooner. Born 10 August 1928, Philadelphia. Russian/Jewish heritage. In 1953 was given his own fifteen minute TV show called 'Coke Time', sponsored by the Coca-Cola company. In 1955 Eddie married actress Debbie Reynolds, later had affair with Elizabeth Taylor, widow of his best friend, Mike Todd, who died in a plane crash. During the 50s, he was a top-selling pop vocalist. Hits included 'Anytime', 'Wish You Were Here', 'I Need You Now', 'Dungaree Doll', 'I'm Walking Behind You'.

FLEMING Rhonda. Stunning green-eyed, red-headed actress. 'Queen of Technicolor'. Born 10 August 1923, Hollywood. Star of over 40 films. Featured roles in Hitchcock's *Spellbound* (1945), *The Spiral Staircase*

(1946), *Gunfight at the O.K.Corral* (1957) and *Gun Glory* (1957) starring Stewart Granger, directed by Steve Rowland's father Roy.

FRANCIS Anne. Tall, blonde, curvy actress. Born 16 September 1930, New York. Co-starred opposite Hollywood's finest leading men in 1950s classics: *Bad Day at Black Rock* (1955) with Spencer Tracy and Robert Ryan, *Blackboard Jungle* (1955) with Glenn Ford and Sidney Poitier, and the sci-fi classic *Forbidden Planet* (1956) with Leslie Nielsen. In the cult TV series *Honey West* (1965), she combined sexy glamour with judo and karate.

FULLER Robert. Actor. Born 29 July 1933, New York. Appeared in *Gentlemen Prefer Blondes* (1953).

GABA Marianne. Blonde actress. Born 13 November 1939, Chicago. Playboy Playmate of the Month September 1959. Appeared in TV series *Beverley Hillbillies*, *Burkes Law* and *77 Sunset Strip*.

GARDNER Ava. Actress. 24 December 1922 - 25 January 1990. Legendary Hollywood beauty, the 'barefoot' rural southern girl with earthy language who was spotted in a photographer's window. Outstanding in the films *The Killers* (1946), *Mogambo* (1953), *Bhowani Junction* (1956), and T*he Night of the Iguana* (1964). Married to actor Mickey Rooney, band leader Artie Shaw and singer Frank Sinatra.

GIUFFRE Jimmy. Clarinet, sax, flute player and composer. Born 26 April 1921, Dallas, Texas. Played with name bands led by Jimmy Dorsey (1947), Buddy Rich (1948) and Woody Herman (1949). On the west coast he worked with the Lighthouse All Stars and led his own trios. Popular compositions include 'The Four Brothers' and 'The Train and the River'. An academic and composer since the 60s.

GRANGER Stewart. Tall, dashing actor. 6 May 1913 - 16 August 1993. Made more than 60 movies, many as a swashbuckler. Films included *King Solomon's Mines* (1950), *The Prisoner of Zenda* (1952) and *Scaramouche* (1952). He and his then wife Jean Simmons were paired in *Young Bess* (1953), and he later made *Beau Brummell* (1954), *Bhowani Junction* (1956) and *The Wild Geese* (1978).

HARDIN Ty. Strapping actor. Born 1 June 1930, New York. Own TV show, *Bronco* (1958). Films include *Merrill's Marauders* (1962), *The Chapman Report* (1962) and *Battle of the Bulge* (1965). Later became an evangelistic preacher in Arizona and self-styled 'freedom fighter'.

HARRIS Bill. Jazz trombonist with a broad, thick tone, quick vibrato and outrageous sense of humour. 28 October 1916 - 21 August 1973. A swing devotee, he performed with Charlie Barnet, Woody Herman and Benny Goodman. He co-led a couple of groups and toured in Jazz at the Philharmonic in the 50s. Later worked in backing bands in Las Vegas and retired to Florida.

HELFER Ralph. Legendary Hollywood animal trainer and behaviourist. Born on the south side of Chicago. Helfer had a way with animals and deplored the violence he saw in the film industry's use of them. His unique bond with a lion cub he named Zamba grew into a lifetime relationship that included countless guest stints in movies and television shows, and the development of an animal training system based on love, not fear, called affection training. It revolutionized the way animals are trained and treated in the motion picture industry. Zamba's biggest starring role was in *The Lion* (1962).

HICKMAN Darryl. Child actor. Born 28 July 1931. Featured in the classic *The Grapes of Wrath* (1940), also *Men of Boys Town* (1941) and *Tea and Sympathy* (1956). Became a program executive and respected acting coach in LA.

HOPPER Dennis. Unconventional actor, director, photographer, painter. Born 17 May 1936, Dodge City, Kansas. Cast in many TV shows then film roles such as *Rebel Without a Cause* (1955) and *Giant* (1956) with good friend James Dean and *Gunfight at the O.K. Corral* (1957). In 1969 with fellow actor Peter Fonda and writer Terry Southern wrote an iconic counterculture road movie script *Easy Rider*. Hopper directed. Jack Nicholson also featured. More recently Hopper appeared with Kevin Costner in *Waterworld* (1995). This enigmatic actor remains busy.

HUDSON Rock. Tall, handsome actor. 17 November 1925 - 2 October 1985. In 1956 he received an Oscar nomination for *Giant* (1956). He starred in a number of bedroom comedies, many with Doris Day, such as *Pillow Talk*, and had his own popular TV series *McMillan & Wife* (1971). He had a recurring role in TV's *Dynasty*. He was the first major public figure to announce he had AIDS, and his worldwide search for a cure drew international attention.

HUNTER Tab. Blond 'boy next door' actor and singer. Born 11 July 1931, New York. Skilled horseman, had his film debut in *The Lawless* (1950). His single 'Young Love' topped the charts in 1957. His best-known early films were *Battle Cry* (1955) and *Damn Yankees!* (1958). Had his own TV show and is still working as a film producer in Southern California.

JOHNSON Van. 6'1" war hero, film and musical star with signature red socks. Born 25 August 1916, Rhode Island. Played the amiable 'guy next door'. Also appeared in MGM musicals opposite June Allyson and Esther Williams. Serious roles in the 1950s and stage work in the 70s and 80s.

JONES Carolyn. Petite actress. 28 April 1929 - 3 August 1983. First appearance in *The Turning Point* (1952). Dated Aaron Spelling. Breakthrough in the 3-D movie *House of Wax* (1953). She was in the sci-fi classic *Invasion of the Body Snatchers* (1956), *The Bachelor Party* (1957), *King Creole* (1958) and *Career* (1959). Remembered for her role of Morticia Addams in *The Addams Family* TV series.

KAZAN Elia. Director and writer. Born 7 September 1909 in Istanbul to Greek parents. Died 28 September 2003, New York. On Broadway he directed the iconic *Cat on a Hot Tin Roof* and *A Streetcar Named Desire* (he also directed the film in 1951). Proponent of the method approach to acting. Two Best Director Academy Awards, for *Gentleman's Agreement* (1947) and *On the Waterfront* (1954) starring

Marlon Brando. Founded the Actors' Studio in 1947 with Cheryl Crawford and Robert Lewis.

KEEL Howard. Strapping 6' 4" leading man of the musicals. Confident, athletic, handsome, with a fabulous baritone voice. 13 April 1919 - 7 November 2004. Roles in *Annie Get Your Gun* (1950), *Show Boat* (1951), *Kiss Me Kate* (1953), *Calamity Jane* (1953), *Seven Brides for Seven Brothers* (1954), *Rose Marie* (1954), *Kismet* (1955) and *The Day of the Triffids* (1962). TV series included *Hart to Hart* (1994), *Murder, She Wrote, The Love Boat, Fantasy Island* and famously as Clayton Farlow (1981-1991) in *Dallas*.

KELLERMAN Sally. Blonde comedy actress. Born 2 June 1937, California. Known as 'Hot Lips' from her main role in the iconic TV series *M.A.S.H.*

LANDON Michael. Actor. 31 October 1936 - 1 July 1991. Famous for *Little House on the Prairie* as Charles Ingalls, *Bonanza* and *Highway to Heaven*.

LANZA Mario. 'Voice of the Century'. 31 January 1921 - 7 October 1959. Louis B Mayer turned this astounding tenor into a box office idol in the 50s. Famous songs included 'O Sole Mio', 'Be My Love', 'The Loveliest Night of the Year', 'Because You're Mine'. He was mobbed on concert tours and his MGM film, *The Great Caruso*, was the top-grossing film in the world in 1951.

LEAF Earl. 1950s celebrity photographer. Born 1905, died 1980. Originally a journalist for *Time* magazine and *The Saturday Evening Post*. He later snapped the first western photographs of Mao Tse-Tung behind communist lines while North China Manager of United Press. After a stint as a war correspondent he arrived in Hollywood in the early 50s. Worked as staff photographer for *Movie Play, Movie Time* and *Movie Spotlight* magazines amassing a huge portfolio of movie stars, rock stars, and candids. Specializing in celebrity and cheesecake portraits (including his informal shots of Marilyn Monroe), he helped shape the early careers of Shirley MacLaine, Jayne Mansfield and Natalie Wood and left a vast estate of vintage photographs.

LEIGH Janet. Petite 'Scream Queen' actress. 6 July 1927 - 3 October 2004. Discovered by actress Norma Shearer. She appeared in over 50 movies including comedies, westerns, musicals and dramas. Best remembered for the shower scene in Hitchcock's classic thriller *Psycho* (1960). Married once to Tony Curtis, their daughter is actress Jamie Lee Curtis.

LEVY Lou. Pianist and singer's accompanist. 5 March 1928 – 23 January 2001. Levy worked with Sarah Vaughan and others before joining Woody Herman in 1948-9, alongside Stan Getz, Zoot Sims and Shorty Rogers. In the mid-1950s, he accompanied leading jazz and pop singers Ella Fitzgerald, Peggy Lee, Anita O'Day, Frank Sinatra, Sarah Vaughan, Tony Bennett and Nancy Wilson. He also played with Stan Getz, Benny Goodman, Shelly Mann and Supersax and was a respected teacher.

LOPEZ Perry. TV actor. Born 22 July 1931, New York. Played Lieutenant Lou Escobar in *Chinatown* (1974) with Jack Nicholson.

MANN Shelly. Respected drummer and composer. 11 June 1920 - 26 September 1984. Played on boats to Europe in the 30s and worked with several big bands. He drummed for Stan Kenton and Woody Herman and worked with the West Coast experimentalists. He became a studio-based film and TV composer and also had his own group and a nightclub, Shelly's Manhole, from 1960-74.

MARTIN Andra. 1950s TV actress. Born 15 July 1935, Rockford, Illinois. Appeared in *Wagon Train, 77 Sunset Strip* and other TV series.

MARTIN Tony. Sax player and singer. Born 25 December 1912, San Francisco. Starred in hit movies such as *Follow the Fleet* (1936), *Ali Baba Goes to Town* (1937). Biggest hit was 'There's No Tomorrow' (1950), adapted from the traditional Neapolitan ballad 'O Sole Mio'. Married actress Alice Faye and actress/dancer Cyd Charisse.

MATURE Victor. 6' 2$^{1/2}$" hunk. 29 January 1913 - 4 August 1999. One of Hollywood's most popular actors after the war, with roles in *My Darling Clementine* (1946), *Kiss of Death* (1947) and exotic 'biblical' epics *Samson and Delilah* (1949), *The Egyptian* (1954) and *The Robe* (1953).

MAYER Louis B. Movie mogul. Born Ezemiel Mayer 1882 in Minsk, Ukraine, died 29 October 1957, Los Angeles. Along with Samuel Goldwyn and Marcus Loew of Metro Pictures, he formed Metro-Goldwyn-Mayer (MGM). It produced more films and movie stars than any other studio in the world at that time and was home to stars like Clark Gable, Jean Harlow, Judy Garland, James Stewart, Joan Crawford, Spencer Tracy and Cary Grant. Mayer was one of the founders of the Academy of Motion Picture Arts and Sciences.

MCKUEN Rod. Poet, singer/songwriter, producer. Born 29 April 1933, California. Thirty-plus books of poetry published worldwide, has written songs for artists from Sinatra to Madonna and music from film to classical, collaborating with everyone from Jacques Brel to Henry Mancini. Had hits with 'Seasons in the Sun', 'If You Go Away' and others.

MCQUEEN Steve. Actor. 'The King of Cool'. 24 March 1930 - 7 November 1980. Starring roles include *The Magnificent Seven* (1960), *The Great Escape* (1963), *The Cincinnati Kid* (1965), *The Thomas Crown Affair* (1968), *Bullitt* (1968), *The Getaway* (1972), *Papillon* (1973). Once married to Ali MacGraw of *Love Story* fame.

MINEO Sal. Stage, TV and film actor and director. 10 January 1939 - 12 February 1976. Originally a member of a Bronx street gang. At age 16 he played a much younger boy in *Six Bridges to Cross* (1955) with Tony Curtis. Played Plato in James Dean's *Rebel Without a Cause* (1955), Dov Landau in *Exodus* (1960) and Dr Milo in *Escape from the Planet of the Apes* (1971).

MITCHUM Robert. Tall, rugged actor. 6 August 1917 - 1 July 1997. In 1945 he was cast as Lt. Walker in Story of *G.I. Joe* (1945) and received an Oscar nomination as Best Supporting Actor. His star ascended rapidly, and he became an icon of 1940s film noir, though equally adept at westerns and romantic dramas. His apparently lazy style and seen-it-all demeanor proved highly attractive to men and women. Other major films include *The Night of the Hunter* (1955) and *Ryan's Daughter* (1970).

MITCHUM 'Jim' James. Actor. Born 8 May 1941, Los Angeles. The tall oldest son of legendary actor Robert Mitchum, he inherited his dad's sexy, sleepy eyes and taciturn good looks. His first film at the age of 8 was the western *Colorado Territory* (1949) with Joel McCrea, Virginia Mayo and Dorothy Malone. He then played his father's much younger 'brother' in *Thunder Road* (1958), which became a drive-in cult favourite. Other films include *The Last Time I Saw Archie* (1961), *Young Guns of Texas* (1962) and *Hollywood Cop* (1988). He shared a house with Steve Rowland when they were both young actors.

MOORE Terry. Actress. Born 1 January 1929, Los Angeles. Former child model who became a Hollywood starlet. Films include *Mighty Joe Young* (1949) and *Come Back, Little Sheba* (1952) (Oscar nominated performance). She once dated James Dean and has revealed that she was the secret wife of the late billionaire Howard Hughes. She posed for *Playboy* magazine in her 50s.

MORENO Rita. Stunning brunette actress. Born 11 December 1931, Puerto Rico. One of the few performers to win an Oscar, an Emmy, a Tony, and a Grammy. Films include *Singin' in the Rain* (1952), *The King and I* (1956) and *West Side Story* (1961) as Anita, the Puerto Rican girlfriend of Jets' leader Bernardo.

NELSON Ricky. Tall, cleancut singer, actor and teen idol. 8 May 1940 - 25 December 1985. Sang in Howard Hawks' *Rio Bravo* (1959). Many hit records in the 50s and 60s, including 'I'm Walkin'', 'Travelin' Man', 'Poor Little Fool', 'For You', 'Fools Rush In', and 'Garden Party'.

NICHOLSON Jack. Charismatic actor with a shark's grin. Born 22 April 1937, Manhattan. Plays anti-authoritarian characters. Many fantastic roles include Jake 'J.J.' Gittes in *Chinatown* (1974), Randle Patrick McMurphy in *One Flew Over the Cuckoo's Nest* (1975), Jack Torrance in *The Shining* (1980) and The Joker in *Batman* (1989). Has been nominated for an acting Oscar in five different decades.

O'BRIAN Hugh. Tall, handsome, athletic actor/singer. Born 19 April 1925, New York. A former marine, he was discovered by director/actress Ida Lupino. Appeared in action pictures such as *Red Ball Express* (1952), *Son of Ali Baba* (1952) and *Seminole* (1953). Starred in *The Life and Legend of Wyatt Earp* (1955), a western TV classic series, for six years.

O'BRIEN Margaret. Child star. Born 15 January 1937, San Diego. Shot to stardom in *Journey for Margaret* (1942). Unforgettable as 'Tootie' in Vincente Minnelli's *Meet Me in St. Louis* (1944), which won her an Academy Award. Other films include *The Canterville Ghost* (1944), *Our Vines Have Tender Grapes* (1945), *The Secret Garden* (1949) and *Little Women* (1949).

PAGET Debra. Actress. Born 19 August 1933, Denver, Colorado. Her first role in the film noir *Cry of the City* (1948) was followed by westerns, swashbucklers and period musicals, including *Broken Arrow* (1950), *Stars and Stripes Forever* (1952), *Princess of the Nile* (1954) and *Love Me Tender* (1956).

PEPPER Art (Jr). Jazz alto saxophonist. 1 September 1925 – 15 June 1982. In the 1940s played with Benny Carter and Stan Kenton, in the 50s was a leading light of West Coast jazz, along with Chet Baker, Gerry Mulligan, Shelly Mann, and others. Heroin addiction led to prison stints. After rehab, he had a series of highly acclaimed albums.

PHILLIPS Carmen. Stunning dark-haired actress. 10 January 1937 - 22 September 2002. Parts in *It Started with a Kiss* (1959), *Marnie* (1964), *Easy Rider* (1969), *77 Sunset Strip* (1960) and many other TV series. In later life she was an activist for actors' rights and animal rights.

PLESHETTE Suzanne. Smokey-voiced actress. Born 31 January 1937, New York. Played Annie Hayworth in Alfred Hitchcock's film *The Birds* (1963). Appeared in TV show *Route 66* in 1961 and more recently in *The Lion King II: Simba's Pride* (1998) as the voice of Zira. Once married to actor Troy Donahue.

POWELL Jane. Musical actress. Born 1 April 1929, Portland, Oregon. Best known for MGM musicals, playing the girl next door in *Seven Brides for Seven Brothers* (1954), and later stage musicals including *The Sound of Music*, *South Pacific* and *Oklahoma!*

PRESLEY Elvis. 'The Pelvis'. Tall, handsome singer with left-sided grin. 8 January 1935 -16 August 1977. Began singing in Memphis as 'The Hillbilly Cat'. He established early rock and roll music, bringing black blues-singing into the white, teenage mainstream. Girls became hysterical over his blatantly sexual gyrations. When he died he had sold over 600 million singles and albums. The first of his 33 films was *Love Me Tender* (1956).

REYNOLDS Debbie. Wholesome, perky actress and dancer. Born 1 April 1932, Texas. Gene Kelly chose her to partner him in *Singin' in the Rain* (1952). Appeared in many more films, including *The Mating Game* (1959) and *The Unsinkable Molly Brown* (1964). Was married to Eddie Fisher; their daughter Carrie starred as Princess Leia in *Star Wars*.

ROGERS Shorty. Trumpet and flugelhorn player. 14 April 1924 - 7 November 1994. Leading light of West Coast jazz and musical arranger. Rogers played with big bands in the late 1940s and was an arranger for Woody Herman. He was poached by Stan Kenton. His arrangements were tight, innovative and influential. With another group, The Giants, he recorded *The Cool and the Crazy* and *Shorty Courts the Count*. Rogers appeared in Frank Sinatra's *The Man With the Golden Arm*, leading the jazz group. He wrote incidental music for TV series including *The Partridge Family*, *Starsky and Hutch* and *The Love Boat*. Returned to performing with a combo with West Coast legend Bud Shank on alto sax.

ROWLAND Roy. Director, producer, writer. 31 December 1910 - 29 June 1995. Married Ruth Cummings, father of Steve Rowland. Nominated for outstanding Directorial Achievement in Motion Pictures for *Meet Me in Las Vegas* (1956). He also directed *A*

Stranger in Town (1943), *Lost Angel* (1943), *Our Vines Have Tender Grapes* (1945), *The Romance of Rosy Ridge* (1947), *The Outriders* (1950), *Affair with a Stranger* (1953), *The 5,000 Fingers of Dr. T.* (1953), *Witness to Murder* (1954), *Many Rivers to Cross* (1955), *These Wilder Years* (1956), *Gun Glory* (1957), *Seven Hills of Rome* (1958), *The Girl Hunters* (1963), *Gunfighters of Casa Grande* (1964).

SANDS Tommy. Singer. Born 27 August 1937, Chicago. Self-taught guitarist performed at radio station KWKH in Shreveport, Louisiana aged 8. Was signed by Colonel Tom Parker, Elvis Presley's manager. Played the lead in *The Singing Idol* (1957) and his song 'Teenage Crush' shot to number 3 on the Billboard charts. He starred in his biopic *Sing, Boy, Sing* (1958). Once married to Frank Sinatra's daughter Nancy. Later had a nightclub and clothing business in Hawaii.

SAHL Mort. Razor-sharp, unorthodox political satirist, comedian and writer. Born 11 May 1927, Montreal, Canada. He was the first to poke fun at US presidents (but also wrote speeches for Presidential candidates!) and other government dignitaries, shocking and delighting audiences. Had a casual, free-flowing style and nervous giggle and carried a trademark rolled up newspaper. Later he wrote film screenplays for top stars and books and performed in stage productions. Comedians such as Lenny Bruce, Woody Allen and Jay Leno were inspired by him. He was friends with both John F Kennedy and Hugh Hefner.

SAXON John. Dark-haired, baby-faced actor. Born 5 August 1935, Brooklyn. Italian heritage. Worked with major directors including Vincente Minnelli, Blake Edwards, John Huston, Frank Borzage and Otto Preminger. A teenage heart throb he later played mainly solid support roles in *The Unforgiven* (1960), *Death of a Gunfighter* (1969), *Enter the Dragon* (1973), *A Nightmare on Elm Street* (1984), *Fever Pitch* (1985), *Beverly Hills Cop III* (1994), *From Dusk Till Dawn* (1996). In recent years he has been seen in a number of independent films and has appeared in several television series, notably *CSI: Crime Scene Investigation*.

SARGENT Dick. Actor. 19 April 1930 - 8 July 1994. Played 'gawky' film parts initially but best known as Darrin in the comedy TV series *Bewitched* as husband and foil to Samantha played by Elizabeth Montgomery from 1969. An active supporter of gay rights once he had outed himself in 1991.

SHANK Bud. Saxophonist, composer and arranger. Born 27 May 1926 Dayton, Ohio. Played with Charlie Barnet and Stan Kenton big bands in the 1940s. Then with Howard Rumsey's Lighthouse All Stars, as well as his own quartet. A member of the West Coast jazz movement, his cool, exciting, strongly swinging sound made him instantly recognizable. Produced over 50 diverse albums. In the 1970s he joined with Ray Brown, Jeff Hamilton and Laurindo Almeida to form the revered LA Four. Shank popularized both Latin-flavoured and chamber jazz music. He performed with orchestras as diverse as the Royal Philharmonic, Stan Kenton's Neophonic Orchestra and the legendary Duke Ellington.

SMITH John. Film and TV actor. 6 March 1931 - 25 January 1995. He appeared in many films in the 1950s alongside the greats including John Wayne (*The High and the Mighty*), Humphrey Bogart (*We're No Angels*), Mickey Rooney (*The Bold and the Brave*), and Gary Cooper (*Friendly Persuasion*). He had bit parts in several TV series later on.

SMITH Roger. Debonair actor/singer. Born 18 December 1932, California. Spotted in Hawaii by James Cagney. Films include *No Time to Be Young* (1957), *Operation Mad Ball* (1957), *Crash Landing* (1958), *Auntie Mame* (1958), *Man of a Thousand Faces* (1957) and *Never Steal Anything Small* (1959). Played private detective Jeff Spencer in the hip TV series *77 Sunset Strip* (1958). Married singer-actress Ann-Margret in 1967. After diagnosed with myasthenia gravis, a muscle/nerve disorder, he retired from acting, instead producing his wife's stage shows.

SPAIN Fay. Petite actress. 6 October 1933 - 8 May 1983. B-movie drive-in bad girl, played blonde, brunette, tease, taunter and temptress throughout her career. Films include *Dragstrip Girl* (1957), *God's Little Acre* (1958), *The Beat Generation* (1959) and *Al Capone* (1959).

ST JOHN Jill. Smouldering, classy red-headed actress. Born 19 August 1940, Los Angeles. Debut as perky support to John Saxon in *Summer Love* (1958). Best known for role as temptress Tiffany Case in *Diamonds Are Forever* (1971) opposite Sean Connery. Part of Bob Hope and Frank Sinatra's 'in' crowd, she co-starred with Sinatra in *Come Blow Your Horn* (1963) and *Tony Rome* (1967). Once married to crooner Jack Jones. Present husband actor Robert Wagner, whom she married in 1990. More recently appeared in *Seinfeld* (1990) and *The Player* (1992).

STANWYCK Barbara. Actress. 16 July 1907 - 20 January 1990. Talented and versatile actress whose career spanned 59 years (she made 93 movies, amongst them *Stella Dallas* (1937), *Remember the Night* (1940), *The Two Mrs Carrolls* (1947)). Her finest role was probably as wicked Phyllis Dietrichson in *Double Indemnity* (1944). She excelled in comedies and westerns. In the 1980s she played a matriarch in *The Colbys* and starred in *The Thorn Birds*. She was nominated but never won an Oscar. Once married to actor Robert Taylor. The film *A Star Is Born* (1937) is said to be based on Stanwyck's rise to stardom and first husband Frank Fay's descent into obscurity.

STEVENS Connie. Actress and singer. Born 8 August 1938, Brooklyn. Her parents were both jazz musicians. Started her career singing with a group called The Three Debs. She became a teenage icon when she appeared in many teenage movies of the 1950s such as *Young and Dangerous* (1957) and *Rock-a-Bye Baby* (1958) with Jerry Lewis. In 1961 she had a top-ten hit record with 'Sixteen Reasons'. She went on to appear in many top TV series. Once married to Eddie Fisher. In June 1998 opened the Connie Stevens Garden Sanctuary Executive Day Spa in LA.

STEVENSON Venetia. Actress, production manager, producer, production designer. Born 10 March 1938, London. Daughter of actress Anna Lee and Robert Stevenson. Films include *Island of Lost Women* (1959), *Day of the Outlaw* (1959), *The City of the*

Dead (1960), *Studs Lonigan* (1960) and *The Sergeant Was a Lady* (1961).

STOCKWELL Dean. Actor. Born 5 March 1936, Hollywood. Started out as a child actor in the 1940s, with an innocent face, sparkling eyes and curly hair. Made the transition to significant adult roles in *Sons and Lovers* (1960), *Long Day's Journey Into Night* (1962), *Dune (*1984), *Paris, Texas* (1984), *Blue Velvet* (1986), *Married to the Mob* (1988), *The Player* (1992), *Air Force One* (1997), *Buffalo Soldiers* (2001) and *The Manchurian Candidate* (2004).

TAMBLYN 'Rusty' Russ. Agile and musical child actor who also enjoyed a varied adult career. Born 30 December 1934, Los Angeles. Best known as 'Riff', gang leader of the fiery Jets in *West Side Story* (1961), and for his athletic dancing in *Seven Brides for Seven Brothers* (1954). After some low budget horror movies he landed the role of the overtly weird psychiatrist Dr. Lawrence Jacoby in the TV cult series *Twin Peaks* (1990). He still acts, manages his daughter's career and does some choreography.

TAYLOR Robert. Leading man. 5 August 1911 - 8 June 1969. Made many films including *Camille* (1936) with Greta Garbo and *A Yank at Oxford* (1938), the edgier *Billy the Kid and Waterloo Bridge* (1940) and combat films *Standby for Action* (1942) and *Bataan* (1943). He was a flying instructor in the Naval Air Corps during the war and directed naval training films. Other well-known roles in *Quo Vadis* (1951), as Walter Scott's *Ivanhoe* (1952) and *Knights of the Round Table* (1953). His best friend Robert Reagan read his eulogy.

VAN DOREN Mamie. Blonde actress with hourglass figure. Born 6 February 1931, South Dakota. Discovered by Howard Hughes aged 15. Films include *Untamed Youth* (1957) and *Teacher's Pet* (1958) with Doris Day.

VARGAS Alberto. Artist. Born in Arequipa, Peru, in 1896, the son of a successful photographer. Arrived in New York in 1916. His name has become synonymous with pin-up girls, but in the early 1940s he was just a guy hired by *Esquire* magazine to ape previous artist George Petty's sleek women with their telephone posing and large-hat lounging. His own distinctive, delicate watercolour style emerged. His wide-eyed wonder-women rivalled Betty Grable as the ultimate pin-up girl of World War II. Vargas (who signed his *Esquire* work 'Varga') had already achieved some notoriety for his Ziegfeld Follies and movie poster art, but *Esquire* made him famous. His regular *Playboy* slot in the 1960s and '70s elevated Vargas to a status as one of the true giants of American illustration. His magnificent paintings of women have come to embody the fantasies of three generations of women and men around the world.

VICKERS Yvette. Blonde B-movie actress. Born 26 August 1936, Kansas City. Films include *Short Cut to Hell* (1957), *Attack of the 50 Foot Woman* (1958), *Attack of the Giant Leeches* (1959) and *Hud* (1963).

WAGNER Robert. Actor. Born 10 February 1930, Detroit. Always wanting to be an actor, he held a variety of jobs (including one as a caddy for Clark Gable). His fresh, all-American looks landed him a contract with 20th Century Fox. In 1962 he went to Europe to make the movie *The Longest Day* (1962). Married Natalie Wood twice but was shattered when she fell off of their yacht *Splendour* and drowned. Married actress Jill St John in 1991. Successful television series include *Hart to Hart* (1979). Latest roles as henchman in Austin Powers spy spoof films.

WALKER Clint. Towering 6' 6" tall actor. Born 30 May 1927, Illinois. A leader of the 60s TV western craze in his role as Cheyenne Bodie in *Cheyenne* (1955). Also featured in *The Ten Commandments* (1956), *None But the Brave* (1965), *The Night of the Grizzly* (1966) and *The Dirty Dozen* (1967).

WEBB Jack. Actor/director. 2 April 1920 - 23 December 1982. Joe in *Dragnet* was his most famous role. During a brief stint as Head of Production for Warner Bros in 1963 he revised the much loved *77 Sunset Strip* series which then nosedived. Webb was married to torch singer Julie London. The character Brett Chase in *L.A. Confidential* (1997) was based on him.

WELD Tuesday. Actress. Born 27 August 1943, New York. A successful child model, in 1956 she debuted in the low-budget exploitation movie *Rock, Rock, Rock* and decided to become an actress. After numerous TV appearances in New York she went to Hollywood in 1958 and was cast for *Rally Round the Flag, Boys!* (1958). Over the next few years Tuesday became Hollywood's teen queen, playing precocious sex kittens in *Wild in the Country* (1961) (with Elvis Presley), *Return to Peyton Place* (1961), *The Cincinnati Kid* (1965) and *I Walk the Line* (1970). Also appeared in *Once Upon a Time in America* (1984) and *Falling Down* (1993). She married English comedian and actor Dudley Moore. She still occasionally appears in film and television.

WEISSMULLER Johnny. Tarzan. 2 June 1904 - 20 January 1984. He made around 20 Tarzan films throughout the 1930s and 40s.

WILLSON Henry. One of Hollywood's most powerful agents. Discovered Rock Hudson, Tab Hunter and other beefcake actors.

WILLIAMS Esther. 'America's Mermaid'. Actress. Born 8 August 1922, Los Angeles. Made her film debut with MGM in a 1942 'Andy Hardy' picture called *Andy Hardy's Double Life* (1942) as Mickey Rooney's love interest. MGM created a special sub-genre for her known as 'Aqua Musicals', which included *Bathing Beauty* (1944) and *Million Dollar Mermaid* (1952). Retired 1960s. Promoter of competitive and synchronized swimming.

WYNN Keenan. Character actor. 27 July 1916 – 14 October 1986. From a famous show-business family, his father was actor Ed Wynn. Father and son starred in several movies together, such as *The Hucksters* (1947), *Annie Get Your Gun* (1950) and *Kiss Me, Kate* (1953). He introduced Steve McQueen and Lee Marvin to the power of Triumph motorcycles on a hill climb.

Index

Page numbers of illustrations are in italic. Those followed by an asterisk* indicate glossary entries.